The

MONOPOLY
Guide to
REAL
ESTATE

RULES AND STRATEGIES FOR
PROFITABLE INVESTING

CAROLYN JANIK

STERLING

New York / London
www.sterlingpublishing.com

Library of Congress Cataloging-in-Publication Data
Janik, Carolyn.
The Monopoly guide to real estate: rules and strategies for profitable investing /
Carolyn Janik.
      p. cm.
    Includes index.
    ISBN 978-1-4027-5254-4
    1. Real estate investment. 2. Real estate investment--United States. I. Title.
    HD1382.5.J352 2008
    332.63'240973--dc22

                                                                    2008014314

    10 9 8 7 6 5 4 3 2 1

Published by Sterling Publishing Co., Inc.
387 Park Avenue South, New York, NY 10016
© 2009 by Carolyn Janik
Distributed in Canada by Sterling Publishing
C/o Canadian Manda Group, 165 Dufferin Street
Toronto, Ontario, Canada M6K 3H6
Distributed in the United Kingdom by GMC Distribution Services
Castle Place, 166 High Street, Lewes, East Sussex, England BN7 1XU
Distributed in Australia by Capricorn Link (Australia) Pty. Ltd.
P.O. Box 704, Windsor, NSW 2756, Australia

Book design and layout: *tabula rasa* graphic design

Sterling 978-1-4027-5254-4

For information about custom editions, special sales, premium and
corporate purchases, please contact Sterling Special Sales
Department at 800-805-5489 or specialsales@sterlingpublishing.com.

For my son
David,
who provided me with a
quiet place to work in the country.

CONTENTS

INTRODUCTION

It's a Big-Money Game

D id you know that MONOPOLY is the best-selling board game in the world? Over *five hundred million* people have played it. Have you ever wondered *why*? Is it the money or the strategy? What is it about a game invented in 1934 that continues to entertain and entice us today?

I think I know. People enjoy the competition and the strategic maneuverings for money and power. They are captured by the fickle power of Lady Luck and the awesome results of bargaining (also known as *negotiation*). And it's all built upon the oldest and most nearly universal symbol of wealth known to mankind.

"What?" you say. "Is this a finance textbook? Or maybe psychology? Or, worse yet, philosophy?"

None of the above. It's as simple as *Connecticut Ave.* or *St. James Place.* The oldest and most widespread symbol of wealth is *land:* the ownership and possession of a piece of the Earth and the structures built upon that piece. In our language, we call it *real estate.* And everyone is interested in it, in one way or another. Go to any neighborhood barbeque and you're likely to hear the guests talking about some aspect of real estate.

Of course, that's not surprising because both shelter and investments are concerns of our lives. These concerns are mimicked in the board game. When playing the MONOPOLY game, participants buy and sell property, pay or collect rent, borrow or lend money, pay or collect interest, build wealth or sometimes go broke. They must deal with rules and roadblocks, bad luck and good, seized opportunities and missed chances. The MONOPOLY game is like a lakeside reflection of what's *real* in our day-to-day living, but the experience and all its risks are played out in a safe spot and everything is tempered by laughter. That's what keeps us coming back to MONOPOLY for another roll of the dice and another trip square by square, step by step around the board.

I can guess what you're thinking: *buying and selling in the real estate marketplace is hardly a leisure-time activity for most of us.*

You got that right! But when each of us is dealing in the marketplace, we often feel competitive pressure to make the right moves. On the board game or in the marketplace, buyers and sellers each have opposing goals; Lady Luck is an ever-present influence; risks create tension; and the apparent success or failure of certain moves can cause disappointment or elation, satisfaction or frustration. Silently, we cheer; invisibly we hold our breaths. MONOPOLY and real estate are both big-money games. No wonder Americans commonly use the term *the real estate game.*

Perhaps you've dreamed some version of the game that made Donald Trump a recognizable household name. Your dream might be the gathering of a great mass of property resulting in ongoing, six-figure *monthly* income and, of course, secure and very comfortable financial independence. Or you may be more like the majority of Americans who dream of owning a home, watching the equity grow, and knowing that the property's market value is keeping them ahead of inflation. In either case, you're reading this book because you want to get going and you want to be successful.

You *can* do it! At the beginning of the twentieth century, Andrew Carnegie, the founder of U.S. Steel, said, **"More money has been made in real estate than in all industrial investments combined."** At the beginning of the twenty-first century, real estate is still a part of virtually every American's investment list. And you can *still* get into the marketplace. But to do so safely, you need to spend some serious prep time.

I know, nobody likes work. And besides, you've seen those TV spots about becoming an overnight millionaire with nothing down.

OK, I've seen them too. Do you really believe them? Or do you think the stories are "grabbers" to get your attention and persuade you to buy seminars on CDs or DVDs? Before you sign up and get out your credit card, think about how many athletes make million-dollar salaries in the National Football League or in Major League Baseball without having had previous experience and notable success. That's just about the same number of players who become *overnight* millionaires in the real estate marketplace.

Because you are reading this introduction, you probably intend to put some care and concern into this big-money investment. That's good! But be aware that *The MONOPOLY Guide to Real Estate* is not a ten-step program that says *do this* and *do that* and then *do this and that*. That kind of program usually fails because it is based on standardized procedures and the real estate marketplace is full of unique situations. To succeed consistently, you must have an *understanding* of real estate. You must learn the *concepts* that will give you the freedom and power to make decisions profitably.

That's what this book is all about. It is organized into three parts: *Getting In, Getting Around,* and *Getting Out.* Within each part, the chapters are focused on strategies for winning in the particular aspects of buying, investing, and selling. In addition, you'll notice that five different types of boxed material recur throughout the entire book. The material within these boxes has been separated from the main flow of the text to make it easier for you to find and review certain kinds of information. Watch for the following headings.

COMMUNITY CHEST

This is the "good advice" box where you'll find bits of advice on succeeding in the game from some famous and some not-so-famous people. In some boxes, you'll find tips on where to go for more information. And some *Community Chest* boxes will present insights that might alter or expand your perceptions in a tough situation.

CHANCE

Chance boxes are chancy. Most contain warnings about thin ice or otherwise risky situations. Some, however, highlight a risky path that, if navigated properly, could lead to greater rewards.

DON'T GO TO JAIL!

Just as in the MONOPOLY game, you can't play in the real estate marketplace unless you know the rules. If you try to ignore the rules, your fellow players will protest and you may be fined or penalized. Don't *Go To Jail!* boxes contain information that will give you a "heads up" to the laws and procedures you must abide by. Where I can, I also include a sample of the customary and usual penalties for breaking the rules.

WORDS TO *GO!*

A savvy buyer or seller in this game is often tipped off to the inexperience of an opponent when the novice uses a real estate marketplace word inappropriately. *The Words to* GO! boxes contain definitions and examples of idiomatic or customary usage in the marketplace. When you see a word printed in red ink in the text, look for the definition in a nearby box. You won't collect $200 every time you learn a new meaning, but you could lose many, many times $200 if you misunderstand or misuse a word in a negotiation or contract.

RULES AND STRATEGIES

These boxes have been placed at the end of each chapter to jog your memory. Each will restate the most important points in the chapter. Reviewing this material is a great way to do a quick warm-up before heading into the next concept. If anything in the *Rules and Strategies* box sounds unfamiliar to you, go back into the chapter.

And finally, a bit about me. I grew up in a real estate family where property buying and selling, management of rental property, negotiating, and financing were topics of conversation at almost every dinner table. Despite all this vicarious experience, I got into the business because I made a serious real estate mistake. My husband and I bought a tract of undeveloped land from a "kindly" seller who offered us "creative" financing. Like many "kids" in their twenties, we didn't ask for parental advice (we knew everything, of course).

Well, we didn't have the money when the first major payment was about to come due. Oops! I went to work as a real estate agent and listed and sold a house within two weeks.

Yes, I was hooked! Heritage and financial need pushed me on to success. I guess I was just doing what came naturally to me.

But how about you? As you stand right now at the edge of the real estate playing field, you may not feel much like "a natural." In fact, you may feel as though you're about to land on Park Place and have to come up with rent at the hotel or (worse) negotiate a trade of property with the neighborhood MONOPOLY game pro.

Let me wave my wand and say some magic words to help you. Success on the real estate playing field (and in the game of MONOPOLY) is often built on familiarity. *The MONOPOLY Guide to Real Estate* can be your old friend who shows you around and makes introductions. It will make you feel at home. (Yes, the pun was intended.) The book will point out what you need to know to buy a home, to get started in an investment, and to sell a property profitably. It will suggest the questions you should ask. It will advise you where you can best get answers.

Whether you are entering the marketplace for the beginning of a long investment career or for a one-time exercise in buying or selling a home, read this book carefully and always think before you act. Before you know it, you too could become a not-so-overnight millionaire.

Let's roll the dice and start your moves.

BOARDWALK

PRICE $400

COLLECT
$200.00 SALARY
AS YOU PASS

GO

PART I

GETTING IN

CHAPTER 1
What's on the Playing Field?

Throughout the life of our nation, nothing has been more important as a building block . . . than homeownership.
—President Bill Clinton, January 30, 1995

The MONOPOLY board is a fantasy-perfect real estate marketplace. Neighborhoods are not only grouped together by market price but are also color coded. And all the houses look alike. It's a playing field clarified and simplified.

In the real world, it's not quite so neat. City or suburb, it's sometimes hard to tell exactly where one neighborhood ends and another begins. Property values change and selling prices are determined by what a ready, willing, and able buyer will offer and a ready, willing, and able seller will accept. Housing styles have almost as much diversity as *Animal Kingdom*. And questions of ownership and possession keep tens of thousands of lawyers busy.

I'll talk more about the importance of neighborhood and location and the techniques of negotiating in Chapters 3 and 4. We'll work through legal contract and closing questions in Chapter 6. Here at the outset, let's do an overview of what you might realistically buy as an entry vehicle into the Real Estate Owners' Club.

SINGLE-FAMILY HOMES

The majority of Americans want to own their own homes. Most dream about a detached dwelling with a little grass, a few trees, and **fee-simple ownership**. During the past fifty-plus years, this dream has stimulated housing development in ever-widening circles around our cities.

From the air today we can readily discern the housing developments that form the patchwork quilts of suburbia. The patterns of each patch are not only different from those around it but also mark the patterns of population growth. What type of dwelling was being built and what one could choose to buy has changed almost with each decade. As a buyer today, you can often estimate the age of a home by its proximity to the city and by the predominant architectural styles in the neighborhood.

Cape Cods

In the second half of the 1940s, American GIs returned home from World War II. They married, started up the Baby Boom, and looked for housing. American industry responded. Just as Henry Ford introduced the assembly line in the early 1900s and forever changed automobile manufacturing, housing developers introduced large-scale tract construction in the late 1940s and changed the landscape of America.

WORDS TO *GO!*

Fee-simple ownership, sometimes called *absolute fee simple,* is the largest bundle of ownership rights recognized by law. Don't be overwhelmed by the strange phrase; it is the most common form of property ownership. When you own property fee simple, you can sell it or will it to your heirs.

Many Cape Cod owners in the 1950s expanded to a second floor by adding dormers.

The archetype community of look-alike houses began on Long Island, New York. It became the first Levittown. The business plan of Levitt & Sons was to produce a lot of houses, quickly and inexpensively. The idea spread to other developers. Levitt and its competitors chose designs for a small house with a square footprint and steeply slanted roof (sometimes with dormers). Stairs on the main floor led to attic space for "future expansion." Evidently, the style reminded some influential person of the cottages on Cape Cod, and the name stuck.

The design was replicated thousands of times, and the *Cape Cod* quickly became the most popular housing choice of young Americans in the late 1940s and early 1950s. The architectural style, with modifications, is still being built, but if you see a large neighborhood of look-alike capes, you can be pretty sure the houses are fifty-plus years old.

Most postwar capes had one bathroom, two bedrooms, a living room, and a kitchen, but very few exist today as originally built. Dormers have been added and attic space has become bedroom and bathroom space; additions have been built for family rooms, dining rooms, and garages.

Twenty-first century ranches don't belong on the ranch anymore. Many are being built in 55+ condominium communities.

The split-level was widely built in the 1950s, '60s, and '70s. Less so today.

Ranch-Style Houses

As housing communities grew, so did new ideas. If a house with a square footprint and two bedrooms was popular, why not compete in the marketplace by building a rectangular house with three bedrooms all on one floor? And if you named the first housing style after an East Coast spot, why not go to the West for the new name?

The ranch-style house soon overtook the Cape in popularity. In fact it became so popular that "ranch" in American English refers not only to a farm located in the western part of the nation but also to any house with bedroom, kitchen, and living area on one level.

Ranch-style houses were built continuously through the latter half of the twentieth century and are still a popular style. They come in all sizes, shapes, and price ranges and are particularly popular with young families and retirees.

Split Levels

By the late 1950s and early 1960s, the new young homebuyers in the real estate marketplace wanted a place for the family to gather around the television set. Many also wanted a sheltered place to park the car. To answer these demands, the split level came into the marketplace. Like Capes and ranches, it was built in huge look-alike developments.

Early splits have a small kitchen, dining area, and living room on the main level. A half-flight of stairs leads up to three bedrooms; another half-flight leads down to a family room and garage. Most have 1½ baths; newer ones, however, usually have 2½ baths. Some splits have another half-flight of stairs off the garage level to a basement below the kitchen and living area. Laundry and storage space is often on this level.

The big complaint about splits is the stairs. Owners say they don't need to buy a step exercise machine because they spend the majority of at-home hours going up and down the stairs from one level to another.

CHANCE

The upward and/or outward expansion of a house sometimes creates problems. Before you buy an altered Cape Cod or ranch-style home, look carefully at a drawing of the floor plan. What is the traffic pattern like? Is it necessary to walk through one room to get into another? (Typically, the dining room stands between the kitchen and the new family room. Most inconvenient is the need to pass through one bedroom to get to another.)

Imagine yourself through a day living in the house. Do you feel the location of the rooms fits your lifestyle?

Externally, check the roof and foundation at the contact points of the addition. These are often trouble spots. Inside, look for cracks or watermarks.

Raised Ranches

Also advertised as "bi-levels" and "split-foyer homes," the raised ranch was a 1970s favorite. The fad died, however, almost as quickly as it spread. Although some are still being built in the twenty-first century, the style has not been particularly popular. In fact there was a time in the 1990s when Realtors complained that the raised ranch was the slowest-moving housing style.

How did it come to be? Essentially, architects and developers took ordinary ranch-style floor plans, set them on foundations almost entirely above ground, built exterior stairs to the entry, and split the foyer with a half-flight of stairs going up and a half-flight going down. What had been basement space was used for the family recreation room, sometimes an extra bedroom, laundry and storage, and garage space. Most buyers liked the extra living area but *not* the separation of family activities between the kitchen upstairs and the casual living room downstairs. Getting from one space to the other required traveling two half-flights of stairs facing in different directions and located at the front entrance of the house.

Many raised ranches now have additions built to create larger kitchens and main-floor family rooms. Many buyers are still put off, however, by the small landing that is the entrance foyer. It allows virtually no space to greet guests or bid them farewell. Also, there is no entryway coat closet.

This housing style was created in an attempt to give the owner more useable space in a smaller footprint.

A spacious colonial from the 1970s with an unadorned façade that was closer to the authentic architectural style than many later twentieth-century communities.

By the late 1980s, the "colonial" offered many comfort and convenience extras and often a three-car garage.

Colonials

Colonial-style houses, as the name implies, have been around since the New England saltbox and the southern plantation house. In the housing market of the last third of the twentieth century, the word has come to mean a two-story house, usually with a center entrance hall. This building style came into peak popularity in the late 1970s and early 1980s as the first American boomers began to approach middle age and clamored for more luxury, more space, more privacy.

Typically, houses built in the "colonial" plan have four bedrooms and two full baths on the second level, which of course is not *colonial* at all. They feature eat-in kitchens, another half-bath on the main floor, a formal dining room, and both a family room and a large formal living room. Most have at least a two-car attached garage, although some designs on sloping lots place the garage under the house.

Two-story houses, both with and without the colonial facade, have been and still are immensely popular. All other factors being equal, this style of housing is often easier to sell and brings more money than the same square footage in another style.

McMansions

Huge luxury houses on postage-stamp lots became fashionable in the booming housing market of the 1990s. Their facades look Tudor, or Georgian, or Victorian, or Contemporary, or just plain awesome. They usually have four or more bedrooms, three or more baths, and often garages with three or more bays. And they are lined up on curving streets that end in cul-de-sacs, just like the Cape Cods of the 1940s.

They have all these similarities with one major difference: McMansions are not houses for the young or the many. They're not for the old and wealthy either, because most property-rich retirees

In the early 1990s, *modest* McMansions were often built on small lots. Architectural "gingerbread" is a common feature.

In the booming late 1990s, whole communities of minicastles on two- to five-acre lots sprang up in suburbia.

CHANCE

It's unlikely that you will enter the real estate marketplace at the McMansion level. But just in case you recently won big bucks in the lottery, keep in mind that real estate value is based on supply and demand. If demand for gigantic luxury houses goes down, so will their value. On the other hand, a very slow market or a foreclosure on a McMansion can mean luxury and space at a bargain price for you.

don't want to handle that much space. These large and impressive houses appeal to wealthy and status-conscious professional couples in mid-career, usually with children and often with live-in help. McMansion prices now start at about a million dollars and go up.

Antiques, Local Architecture, Etcetera

Many houses that were built before the Second World War are still in the real estate marketplace, and many of them are offered at the lower end of the price spectrum. Some are "cottages," like the Sears kit houses of the 1920s; some are remnants of a time when people designed and built their own houses (when few municipal building codes were in effect); and some are examples of local popular architectural style like the southern porch houses and the western adobes. It is difficult to generalize about these "antiques" because so many factors influence their value as an entry vehicle.

But if you find one that seems appealing, here are a few questions to ask yourself and your Realtor:

• Has the neighborhood deteriorated or held its value?
• What is the condition of the building?
• Is there any evidence of termites or other pests?
• Will a purchase require extensive working-systems (heat, hot water, air conditioning) renovation?

Houses from the early twentieth century are often called "painted ladies" because of the ornate trim work.

• Can you afford the renovations? New plumbing and new wiring?
• Are the facilities, floor plan, and location consistent with your lifestyle?

Generally, old houses in need of renovation, unique houses in unconventional locations (lighthouses, for example), houses converted from other uses (barns, churches, railroad stations, or country schoolhouses, for example) and most other "unusual" properties are *not* good entry vehicles into real estate ownership. Of course there are exceptions, but as a rule of thumb the more unconventional the property the greater the financial and comfort-level risks.

Sometimes a person with foresight does buy what "everyone else" thinks is a white elephant and then proves the majority perception wrong. These entrepreneurs make a lot of money and/or are very happy with their purchases. But for most of us, the risk and requirements of "creative" property investments are usually too great, especially when you are just starting your membership in the Real Estate Owners' Club.

Even when you expect that your "career" in the real estate marketplace will be limited to the purchase and sale of one or maybe two single-family houses that you intend to call *home,* try to think through your plays in the real estate game as an investor would think. Home buying is more than comfort, convenience, security, and growing a nest-egg. Every real estate purchase is both an investment and a complex, high-stakes game. Getting started is easier and safer if you stay in well-traveled lanes and if you stay within the parameters of your skills and knowledge. (There's more about what makes a property a good investment, how to find one, and how to finance one in Chapters 3, 4, and 5.)

MULTIFAMILY HOUSES

For a buyer who has little or no down payment and/or spare cash, buying a multifamily house can be the easiest way into the real estate marketplace. Financing programs are available for those with very little cash in hand, and some even include extra money beyond the purchase price for refurbishing (discussed in Chapter 5). *Plus* the projected rent from the units that are *not* owner occupied will count in qualification calculations for a mortgage.

"Sounds great!" you say. "If that works for both homebuying and investing, the next time I land in an appropriate neighborhood, I think I'll buy one."

Not so fast! As in all of life's games, there are a few challenges in buying multifamily houses. Probably the largest is finding a property that is an appropriate investment. When developers jumped on the single-family homebuilding bandwagon in the late 1940s, they all but abandoned building two-, three-, and four-unit buildings. Most of the

COMMUNITY CHEST

Next to the right of liberty, the right of property is the most important individual right guaranteed by the Constitution and the one which, united with that of personal liberty, has contributed more to the growth of civilization than any other institution established by the human race . . .

—President William Howard Taft (1857–1930),
  American statesman

multifamily houses on the market today date from the first half of the twentieth century.

The U.S. Department of Housing and Urban Development (HUD) considers buildings that have four or more living units as apartment buildings, but there is a gray area at four. They also consider buildings with two to four units as multifamily houses and that's the standard we'll use here. Most vintage multifamilies have one or two units on each of several levels. More recently built multifamilies and some converted older buildings have two units side by side on a single level. These are often called duplexes. Multifamily houses in the United States are usually found in cities and sometimes near the central business districts of suburban towns.

Even though the available financing is often excellent and the rental income can help you make the mortgage payments, pay the municipal taxes, and maintain the building, you must always be aware of the risk areas in this investment vehicle. **Zoning** is one of them.

Buildings that were originally built to be used as multifamily housing seldom have trouble with zoning. Either they were built before the zoning laws were enacted and are therefore **grandfathered**, or the builder agreed to comply with zoning regulations when the property was proposed. Problems with zoning usually come up in pre-World War II, large, single-family houses that have been converted to multifamily use.

Since the great exodus to the suburbs that began in the late 1940s, many large old city houses have been converted into multifamily units, some legally, many without municipal permission or formal recognition. Some do not have adequate bathroom and kitchen space for the number of people housed there.

Be very careful to check the zoning and use status of a multifamily property before you buy. You can do this by going to the town clerk's office and simply asking. They will direct you to the information. Also be sure to make your purchase contingent on a professional home inspection. (More about buyer protection in a purchase contract in Chapter 6.) Ask the home inspector to document what repairs or changes will be needed to meet the current

WORDS TO *GO!*

Properties that were built and in use before certain building codes and zoning ordinances were enacted are said to be *grandfathered.* The law allows that they can continue in use even though they do not meet current standards.

Zoning laws allow a municipality to divide its land into areas and establish guidelines for the type of real estate development and its usage. Residential zones can specify the size of the lots and the number of units in a dwelling. If a property owner within a particular zone wishes to change the size or use of a building (convert a single-family house to a two- or three-unit house, for example, or build an addition and convert a lower floor to office space) he or she must apply to the *zoning board of appeals* for a *variance* or a *nonconforming use permit.* The restrictions for that particular property can then be changed without changing the laws for the entire neighborhood.

building code. This documentation is not only a safeguard against unexpected out-of-pocket expenditures after closing but also a great negotiating tool. (More about negotiating in Chapter 4.)

And what can happen if you don't follow this advice? Your real estate investment can

• demand a lot of cash out of your personal savings after the amount of the mortgage has been set;

• demand a great deal of your time and money in legal proceedings;

• become unprofitable and virtually unsalable.

"How?" you ask.

It's all about municipal law. Even though most of the houses on a given street are currently being used as multifamily dwellings, the area may still be zoned single family on the books. Theoretically, you can be forced to reconvert your purchased multifamily to a single-family dwelling. Of course you can take the matter to court while screaming

DON'T GO TO JAIL

If you see a lovely city house just begging to be converted into a home for you and a rental apartment for income, don't do it on the sly. You can make your purchase contract subject to zoning board approval for the conversion. If you don't get approval, you don't have to buy. Getting that approval (becoming a "legal multifamily") will also increase the value and salability when you decide to cash in your investment.

On the other hand, if you were to buy without approval and make the conversion afterward, someone on the zoning board with an axe to grind might scream *"Foul!"* You could be heavily fined and required to return the building to single-family status or to make extensive renovations and improvements.

"But everyone else is doing it!" But the law moves slowly. Proving yourself right will cost you both time and money.

And what about meeting the building code requirements? A building badly in need of refurbishing can cost you a great deal of money. In many municipalities today, a rental building that changes ownership is subject to inspection and must be brought up to the current building codes. So make inquiries of the seller. Ask about what repairs and improvements have been made and what problems are still pending. Often your best investments in multifamily houses will be found among properties where the owner is also a resident.

Sometimes you can even find multifamily homes in areas where you least expect them. When a homeowner wants to convert basement or attic space or build an addition to accommodate elder parents or other family members, most zoning boards grant the necessary variances. Once the variance is granted and the ancillary apartment created, it can legally remain in use as such. So you buy such a house and the owners (mom, dad, the kids, and grandma) move out. You can now move into the main part of the house and rent grandma's apartment to anyone you choose.

SHARED-SPACE OWNERSHIP

Because not everyone could (or wanted to) own a single-family house, the multifamily houses of the early twentieth century filled an important housing need. So what happened to the kinds of people who lived in them, and their kids, and their grandkids? You'll find a lot of them today in condos and co-ops. This is an area of the marketplace called *shared-space housing*. It is a corner of the playing field where you can find entry vehicles for both homeownership and investment property.

Let's start by clarifying what the words *condo* and *co-op* mean and how the two ownership styles differ. Then we'll consider why you might want to spend some time exploring the possibilities.

Condominiums

The concept of condominium ownership dates back to ancient Rome, but it didn't really catch on in the United States until the 1980s. Today, condos come in every size and shape, from detached single-family houses to attached townhouses; to mid-rise clusters around swimming pools, golf courses, and tennis courts; and to high-rise towers in central city areas. People buy condos as primary residences or first homes, as vacation homes, as investment property, and as retirement destinations.

When you own a condo, you own a designated space established by a master deed (the condo community) and an **undivided interest** in the common areas (or shared space) of the community. Your deeded space may be an entire house and the land it sits upon or it may be the air space between certain designated walls within a building. It might even include a boat slip, a portion of a garage, or an outdoor parking space. Generally, the "shared space" includes roads, landscaping, security, and recreational facilities. In multi-unit buildings, it also includes exterior walls, hallways, basements, stairways, roofs, windows, plumbing, heating and air conditioning facilities, electrical work, elevators, and other jointly used space.

Rules for governance and management of a condo community are established in the master deed. An elected board of directors oversees day-to-day functioning, collects and disburses funds, and considers

WORDS TO *GO!*

An *undivided interest* is an ownership share that cannot be severed or separated from the whole. For example, let's say that your condominium community includes a golf course. You would then own an undivided interest in the golf course. But you could not sell, separately from the unit, your right to use the golf course and you could not legally take home a handful of pebbles from out of a sand trap.

Condominium town houses are usually two stories, but sometimes three. They offer street-level access and a garage.

Mid-rise condos with two or three apartments on each of two to four floors offer single-level living (no stairs). All but the oldest have elevators to service the building.

High-rise condos and co-ops look alike. Top-floor units always sell at a premium.

future options. Each unit owner pays a monthly fee for maintenance of the community. A condominium owner can mortgage his or her unit but the condominium community cannot mortgage the shared space that it owns.

Co-ops

When people say "I'm buying a co-op" they usually mean an apartment in or near a major city. The majority of co-op buildings are located in and around Chicago, Miami, New York City, and Washington, D.C., and most were built before 1940.

Co-op residents usually say "my apartment," implying ownership, but in fact a co-op apartment owner does not own real estate. He or she owns stock in the corporation that owns the building. With purchase of stock shares that are assigned to a particular apartment, the buyer gets a **proprietary lease**. Single-apartment purchases within a co-op building can be financed, but the loans are secured by the stock certificates, not by mortgages.

As with condominiums, a co-op building is run by an elected board of directors. The significant difference in governance is that a co-op board has the power to refuse to sell a unit to anyone for any reason, including no reason. This veto power has been upheld in courts over the past several decades because the existence of a co-op community depends upon the regular payment of established monthly fees by all of

WORDS TO GO!

A *proprietary lease,* sometimes called an *occupancy agreement,* assigns a co-op shareholder the right to occupy a specific unit as long as she holds the shares in the co-op corporation. With share ownership comes an obligation to pay monthly co-op maintenance fees. If a unit holder doesn't pay the fees, she can be evicted from the apartment and the shares repossessed by the lender or the co-op corporation.

its shareholders. Failure of unit owners to pay their fees could mean the collapse of the corporation and the forfeiture of all proprietary leases.

"How could that be?" you ask.

Co-ops are more vulnerable to financial loss than condos because the building(s) and the land are usually heavily mortgaged. These mortgage loans are secured by the real estates; they are separate from the co-op loans made on each apartment. Each unit's share of the mortgage, tax, and maintenance fees on the building is factored into the monthly maintenance fee. So a co-op apartment owner might be paying a monthly maintenance fee for the building *and* a monthly payment on the loan secured by his or her unit. If several unit owners don't pay maintenance fees, the cash shortfall must be made up by the remaining unit owners. If this goes on for any length of time, maintenance fees can go up significantly and more residents may not be able to make their payments. It's a domino effect. Co-op buildings can be foreclosed by mortgage holders or by municipalities for nonpayment of taxes.

Why Buy Shared-Space Housing?

With so many strings attached, why would anyone buy a condo or co-op? Consider these reasons:

• Because it's very difficult to find a one- or two-bedroom home today except in the shared-space marketplace.

- Because maintenance work is supervised by the board of directors and requires neither time nor effort on the part of the unit owner.
- Because condo or co-op investment property does not require landlord supervision tasks beyond rent collection.
- Because many condo and co-op communities provide recreational opportunities that would otherwise be unavailable to a homeowner.

MIXED-USE BUILDINGS

When discussing zoning, the term "mixed use" means that an area has both residential and commercial properties within its boundaries. A *mixed-use building* refers to a single property that contains both residential and commercial space. Typically a commercial establishment occupies the street level and offices or residential apartments the upper levels.

CHANCE

Beware overbuilding! By the late 1980s, condos were so overbuilt that many owners could not sell their units. Others sold the units at such low prices that they had to bring cash to the closing in order to pay off their mortgages. Today, "active-adult" (over age 55) shared-space communities are being built at an astounding rate. This almost frantic development is being stimulated by anticipation of the Boomers coming of retirement age.

In the near future, will there be more such units than there will be willing occupants? What would that do to the values of these properties? You know the answer already. Consider carefully before buying new properties in age-restricted condominium communities. Will property values hold up to the competition from the still newer units to be built? Resales in areas of overbuilt active-adult communities, however, may be excellent bargains.

If you are an independent spirit who does not feel the need to conform to conventional standards of social success, you may gain access to the Real Estate Owners' Club by buying and living in a mixed-use building. (It used to be called *living above the store*.) Like multifamily houses, this investment vehicle provides rental income to help pay the bills while you are getting started in your career. If you have plans for starting a business, it may also provide a very short commute to work.

The two most important factors in choosing a mixed-use building are location and condition.

"Isn't that the same for all real estate?" you ask.

Yes, it is, but the two factors take on double power because you are crossing into two different markets with the same property. What appeals to a residential tenant is often very different from what appeals to a commercial tenant. Value goes up if you can satisfy both.

Even if you plan to occupy the building entirely yourself, you must remember that you will want to sell it someday. Carefully check out the neighborhood for current and probable future appeal. Are there other mixed-use buildings in the area? Who are the commercial tenants? Visit at night. Do the streets appear to be safe? What are the going rents in the area? What is the vacancy rate? What are the taxes on the property? How much will necessary renovations cost initially? How much are maintenance costs on an ongoing basis?

With mixed-use property probably more than with any other type of entry vehicle, you will need to get out paper and pencil for notes and calculations. Crunch the numbers carefully. This vehicle may be easy to get into but difficult to get out of because most mixed-use properties have a much longer on-the-market time than strictly residential properties.

THE FIXER-UPPER

There is run-down real estate in every sector of the marketplace. Many would-be investors believe (and many Buy-My-CDs gurus would like more people to believe) that buying it and fixing it up is a short and sure road to wealth. Anyone who can swing a hammer and swish a paint brush can do it. Right?

Not so! Location is more important in determining value than condition. And some things cannot be fixed without exorbitant expenditure. Should you buy a fixer-upper if the foundation is buckling? If the roof is sagging? What if a house has only one bathroom on the second floor? What if the area where the septic tank is located is soggy and massed with gnats? What if the electrical wiring is so old and poor that an electric tea kettle blows the main fuse? What if the water from the well is not drinkable?

On the other hand, some homebuyers with sharp eyes and well-honed skills have indeed made millions in the fixer-upper marketplace. In Chapter 3 we'll go over what makes a good deal. In the meantime, just remember that it's not only the purchase price that creates a bargain. Before making an offer you must factor in the cost of renovations, the time involved, and the probable value when the work is completed.

LAND AND CUSTOM BUILDING

I probably should not have included raw land in an opening chapter focused on the real estate vehicles that might get you into the marketplace. Why not? Because it almost never works as such.

Land is the most nonliquid of all real estate vehicles. That doesn't mean it's not a solid investment. On the contrary, it means that it is the most difficult to convert to ready cash. Land sells slowly. Its value is difficult to estimate and is dependent on nearby development and municipal zoning restrictions. It usually can't be mortgaged unless you are planning to build on it immediately. It rarely generates any income while you own it. For federal income tax purposes, there is no depreciation allowed on land.

So why am I wasting perfectly good ink and paper? Because, under some circumstances, land is an excellent investment. As Scarlett O'Hara's father said in *Gone With the Wind*, "they aren't making any more of it."

Back in the 1950s and 1960s when the idea of developing homogeneous communities was still rather new and when new housing was still rather affordable, some buyers bought two adjacent lots, built on one and kept the other. (Perhaps they wanted extra privacy or perhaps a place for their kids to play baseball.) Some builders even sold "double lots" that were perhaps just a bit shy of the square footage required by zoning ordinances to qualify as two lots. Some of these properties are still around.

If you can buy a house on land that can be subdivided into two or more lots, or already is recorded as two separate lots, you may have the starter vehicle for a long and very profitable game of MONOPOLY!

The other major reason for buying a piece of land is to have your dream home built on it. Custom building is rarely an entry vehicle to the marketplace (unless you've won the lottery *and* know an architect and a builder you can trust). Some people familiar with the building trades, however, *do* do their own subcontracting. Some come out ahead financially by purchasing land, building, and then subdividing the remaining acreage. Be warned, however, that this is a risk-filled venture.

NEW CONSTRUCTION

You've most likely driven around in developments where you've seen the wooden skeletons of houses that are being built. There's probably been a real estate trailer or office on the property where you can pick a building lot and a housing style to be built on it. These "spec houses" are rarely an entry-level purchase.

Buying a to-be-built or in-process house in a new development is an investment in location and community. It is very rarely a bargain. Developers generally price new houses at the top of the market price for the given square footage. Actually, that's not so bad because you are making an investment in desirability. But be aware that every change from the builder's plan and every extra you add is likely to be priced near top dollar also.

THE RIGHT PROPERTY

Choosing the piece of property that is best for you depends on much more than a roll of the dice, or falling in love with it, or getting a hot deal. Each housing style and location has plus and minus factors. Success in this game depends on knowing your needs and wants, both for the present and for the future, and then factoring those desires with your available money and with the potential of the property to make money for you.

Whether a purchase is your first in the real estate marketplace or your tenth, you'll find questions to consider and many possible answers in the remaining chapters of Part I. This is the section about getting into the game, but even if you are starting out right now as a seller, read through it carefully. It's always helpful to know what problems the opposing players face and what strategies they are likely to use.

RULES AND STRATEGIES

- The *real* real estate marketplace is not a fantasy-perfect world.

- The ancient law of supply and demand still prevails in the real estate marketplace.

- Developers plan and work in response to consumer demands. Therefore, the popularity and availability of different housing styles changes over time.

- The more unconventional a property, the greater the financial risk for investors and the comfort-level risk for homebuyers.

- Zoning laws affect the value of real estate.

- Not every piece of real estate is a good investment.

CHAPTER 2
Who Else Is Playing?

The world is governed by self-interest only.

—Friedrich Von Schiller (1759–1805),
German playwright and poet

You can't play MONOPOLY alone. And if you are playing to win, you can't play effectively without acknowledging the goals, skills, and strategies of the other people in the game. It's exactly the same in the *real* real estate marketplace.

"That's not a problem," you say. "There's only *us,* the buyers, and *them,* the sellers."

Not quite! The marketplace is full of people who don't seem to be playing but who are, in fact, very much involved in your game. In this chapter, I'll identify them for you and tell you how each will or can affect your property purchase.

But first, some important advice, advice with a warning: *play fair, expect others to play fair, but don't trust too much.*

One of the most common reasons novice buyers pay too much for their first property is their attitude of openness and trust. When house hunting, they forget that they are in a competitive marketplace. They reveal their emotions and their motivations. That is a lot like telling everyone at the table how many trump cards you are holding when playing bridge.

Many of the people you'll encounter in the course of making a deal will appear to be doing you a service. And indeed, they may be performing a service and doing it very well, but keep in mind that they are at your service to make a living. Few activities in this world are motivated purely by a desire to serve. I'll discuss some specific real estate examples later in this chapter.

IT'S HARDER TO PLAY WITHOUT AN AGENT

A long time ago when I first started out as a real estate agent, a potential buyer could rarely find and inspect a property without the help of an agent. And most agents held their playing cards (the listings of property for sale) close to the vest.

Once a week the new listings came into our office on 5-by-7 cards, each with one black-and-white picture of the property along with property specifications. Everyone in the office hustled to get out and see what was new. Then we called our customers, made appointments, and drove them to selected properties.

The Internet changed all that. Today, everything is on the Web. Virtually every real estate agency has a site where anyone with a computer

COMMUNITY CHEST

If you find an advertisement for a local property interesting, you can go to *mapquest.com,* key in an address, get directions, and drive by to take a look at the exterior.

If you prefer to drive by "virtually" using your computer, you can go to *Google Maps* and choose *Street View* to get a virtual walking tour of the neighborhood. The danger here is that a neighborhood might *sound, smell,* and *feel* different in person or at different times of the day.

CHANCE

Real estate agents are well-trained professionals, usually outgoing, friendly, and reliable. But when you are in the real estate marketplace, do not consider them as friends (even if your agent is your best friend's spouse). Most agents do not make any money unless they sell property. Selling is therefore the motivation behind everything else. Don't share your opinions of a property's value with your agent, and don't reveal your potential top-dollar bid unless you really *want* to pay that much.

can view its listings. Some agency Websites allow you to view all the local listings, and some allow you to browse nationally. At *Realtor.com* you can also bring up listings anywhere in the nation. Some listings even take you on virtual tours, moving through the property from room to room.

If, through your own resources, you can drive by the outside of a building and get a virtual tour of the inside, what *do* agents really do now? Anything? Some discount and Internet brokers would like you to think *not much*. The fact is: *that's not true.*

Especially in a red-hot market, an agent who knows the local marketplace can find you the right property and then get you the best deal by negotiating effectively. That's where the agent really earns a commission. Negotiating price and terms without an intermediary is difficult because it's so easy for either or both parties to become emotional and blow a perfectly feasible purchase.

In addition, real estate agents generally act as project managers. They follow the deal through until closing (translation: tie up the myriad loose ends). Sometimes, when things don't go exactly as planned, they must also be peace keepers.

Realtors and Others

Many people (including the press sometimes) use the word *realtor* to mean someone who is licensed as and acts as a real estate agent. In fact, the word should always be spelled with a capital letter, *Realtor,* because it is a registered trademark of the National Association of Realtors (NAR). Most, but not all, real estate agents are Realtors.

To be a Realtor, one must be a member of the trade group, subscribe to its Code of Ethics (available at *Realtor.com* or any Realtor Board office) and be governed by its rules and standards. Not many years ago, a broker had to join the NAR in order to share listings on the Multiple Listing Service (MLS). Those listings were usually limited to a single county or Realtor Board.

Today, with listing information readily available to everyone on the Internet, many licensed independent, discount, and Web-based agents are not Realtors. Court rulings have upheld the rights of non-member licensed agents to show and negotiate over Realtor listings.

Should you work only with a Realtor? Membership in the NAR gives you an assurance that your agent will adhere to its ethical standards, but that is no guarantee that he or she will be the best of all possible agents. It is definitely possible to find good, professional real estate agents who are not Realtors.

Brokers

Every real estate broker and every real estate salesperson who works in a broker's office must be licensed in the state where he or she works. State requirements differ somewhat but all states require that an applicant pass a standardized test. Most brokers who pass join the National Association of Realtors and therefore become Realtors. But a broker does not necessarily need to be a Realtor in order to do business in a given state.

Only a licensed *broker* can enter into an agency agreement with a buyer or seller. In other words, it is technically the broker who represents you even though you may never meet him or her while you are working with a salesperson in a given agency. And the broker of record may not be the person whose name is on the sign but rather the office manager for the branch of a multi-office firm.

Except for signing listing agreements, holding **escrow** funds in special accounts, and managing the office, brokers and salespersons

WORDS TO *GO!*

Escrow money is a good-faith deposit made by the buyer and held by a third party (usually the real estate agent or an attorney) until the conditions and contingencies of the purchase contract have been met. It can be returned to the buyer if the conditions and contingences are not met. It will not be returned if the buyer walks away from the deal without justifiable reason.

look and act exactly alike. You could even be working with a licensed broker who is working as a salesperson within a large office.

Real Estate Salespersons

Like brokers, real estate salespersons must pass a test and be licensed in the states where they work. A licensed salesperson must work under the sponsorship and supervision of a broker. In other words, the salesperson cannot enter into an agency contract with a buyer or seller except as an employee of a broker.

Does that make a difference in choosing an agent? Not usually. Many salespersons are very competent and sometimes know their markets better than their brokers. And there is one small advantage to working with a salesperson: if you and your salesperson need some extra advice or perhaps another party to help in a tough negotiating situation, the sponsoring broker is almost always glad to help. The need to consult such an outside party can often be a stalling factor in negotiations, allowing a buyer to review and rethink before moving forward.

A Question of Agency

In whose interest does a real estate agent work? Not too long ago, the correct answer was *the seller*. Brokers signed contracts to represent the

DON'T GO TO JAIL

Some *look-how-smart-I-am* buyers are shown a house by an agent and soon afterward make a phone call to the sellers to ask if those sellers would like to make a deal *after* the *listing expires.*

Don't do it! Not only will you not pass GO! and not collect $200, that cute trick could cost you legal fees in excess of your down payment. Most real estate listing contracts today include a clause specifying a length of time after the expiration date (usually ninety days, but it could be six months or even a year) during which the listing agreement and agreed-upon commission still apply if the purchasing party was shown the property by a licensed agent while the listing was in effect. In other words, if Tom Buyer inspects the house with Jane Agent and, after the listing expires, buys it directly from Joe Seller, there is a commission due on the sale. Technically, Joe Seller is responsible for its payment, but the issue is likely to go to court and cost everyone a bundle.

On the other hand, if you drive by an agency FOR SALE sign, make a note of the address, and two weeks later drive back and notice a FOR SALE BY OWNER sign on the property, you can approach the owner and make a deal. No commission will be due on your purchase if the listing had indeed expired and if you did not set foot on the property while accompanied by an agent. The same goes for listings you see on the Web that later expire.

seller in the sale of property. Sellers were their *clients;* buyers were their *customers. Let the buyer beware* prevailed in the real estate marketplace.

Today a broker can represent a seller or a buyer. Or the broker can act as a *transactional broker,* representing neither party but working to put the deal together fairly and honestly. A great deal of legal mumbo-jumbo has been written about what agency representation means, much too much to fit here. The bottom line is: *the broker and his or her salespersons must act honestly and competently.* The most important messages for you are: *Don't be too free with information. Don't hand over to an agent your heirloom recipes or any other information you don't want the seller to know.*

HOME INSPECTION SERVICES

The professional home inspector is a relatively new person on the real estate playing field. Twenty-five years ago, purchase contracts contingent upon a home inspector's report were few and far between; today a contract without an inspection contingency is the rarity.

Watch the wording, however. Some preprinted contract forms have inspection contingencies stating that if faults are found, the seller will fix them. But, what if you are not satisfied with the fixing? You certainly don't want a house held together with Band-Aids!

Don't fret. You can altar the inspection contingency clause (or any other clause) in a preprinted contract. (More on this in Chapter 6.) It's much to your advantage to word the inspection contingency so that you can get out of the deal if you don't like what you read in the inspector's report.

A professional inspector will test the working systems of the property, evaluate all visible elements of the structure, and then present the buyer with a room-by-room written report. Most inspectors, however, will not take responsibility for reporting on anything that is not accessible to visual inspection such as the condition of

CHANCE

The best inspection contingency states that the purchase is subject to inspectors' reports *that in the sole judgment of the purchaser are deemed satisfactory.* This clause will allow you to walk away from the contract obligations for almost any reason and still have your escrow deposit returned. Or, if you prefer, it will allow you to renegotiate the price or arrange for repairs to your satisfaction.

wiring, plumbing, or heating ducts within the walls. Sometimes the comments of an inspector and the suspicions they generate prompt the need for more specialized inspections such as for termites, radon, or lead paint. Visual clues might also prompt an inspector to suggest further specialized inspections by plumbers, electricians, heating and air-conditioning contractors, roofers, basement waterproofers, and others in the building and maintenance trades. Such inspections, however, can be costly. If any walls or other building surfaces must be opened, permission of the owner is required. You should get a signed agreement (including a clause stipulating who pays for what, if damage occurs) before any inspection goes beyond visual and working systems inspection.

"That's a lot of responsibility on the home inspector," you say. "How do I find and choose a good one?"

That is sometimes a problem because questions of loyalty come up. If a home inspector gets 60 percent of his referrals from a particular real estate agency, one wonders if he will thoroughly report the significance of all flaws. In other words, will the inspector strongly point out something that could "blow the deal" if he has gotten the job through the recommendation of the agent?

On the other hand, it's usually a good idea to choose an inspector who works locally and is aware of common area conditions such as mold and drainage problems in given neighborhoods. If you have a friend or acquaintance who has recently bought property and who was satisfied with the inspector, you might ask for the inspector's name and company affiliation. If you ask your real estate agent to recommend home inspectors, get at least three names and you make the choice. Or check with the national trade associations for members working in your area. The largest is: ASHI, The American Society of Home Inspectors, Inc., 932 Lee St., Suite 101, Des Plaines, IL 60016 (847-954-3185; www.ASHI.com).

The cost of a professional inspection varies from one area of the country to another and according to the size, complexity, and condition of the property. The average inspection takes two to three hours. Houses in need of extensive repair may take considerably longer.

If possible you should accompany the inspector throughout the inspection. And don't be afraid to ask questions. No, you *won't* look foolish for your lack of knowledge or experience and you may just learn a thing or two that will apply not only to this deal but to future purchase-and-sale situations as well.

SURVEYORS

If you are buying a house on a deeded lot (as opposed to a condo or co-op), you may need to hire a surveyor in order to satisfy the mortgage lender regarding exactly what you own. The survey will show not only the boundaries of the property but also the location of all buildings and other improvements. It will also indicate **easements** and/or **encroachments** if there are any.

Often the lender will choose the surveyor and you'll find the charge for the survey listed in your closing statement. Sometimes you can choose and pay the surveyor yourself. And often if a house is changing ownership within a short period (usually two to five years), the lender will allow you to use the survey done for your sellers when they bought the property. This will, of course, save you money. The lender will require that the sellers sign a document stating that there

WORDS TO *GO!*

An *easement* is an interest in a piece of land that does not include possession of the land. For example, a right of way that allows a neighbor the right to pass over your land in order to get to his or her land is an easement.

An *encroachment* is a structure or a part of a structure that intrudes on the land of another. If your neighbor's child's tree-house extends over your property, it is an encroachment.

WORDS TO GO!

Like a Realtor, a *mortgage broker* finds perspective borrowers and lenders and brings them together to make a deal. Brokers do not actually make the loans; they process them. You can get more information from the National Association of Mortgage Brokers at: *www.namb.org.*

Mortgage bankers also process applications but most members of this trade group can and will actually lend the money. In most cases, however, the loans they write are soon sold into the secondary mortgage market. (More about that in Chapter 5.) Your mortgage banker may continue to service your loan (collect your payments) and you may never know who actually holds your mortgage. You can get more information from the Mortgage Bankers Association of America at: *www.mbaa.org.*

have been no changes to the information on the survey during their ownership period.

MONEY LENDERS

Almost no one pays cash for real property in the twenty-first century. Why? It's usually a better financial investment to borrow at least some of the purchase money. I'll explain leveraging in Chapter 5; for now let me introduce you to the people you may or may not meet while trying to borrow the money needed to make your purchase.

Mortgage Brokers and Mortgage Bankers

Real estate financing is a magical and sometimes scary world today. You can inquire about or apply for a mortgage loan for hundreds of thousands of dollars on the Internet. Lending institutions, **mortgage brokers,** and **mortgage bankers** will send you rates and terms within minutes. Or you can apply to a lender by phone and give your information to a mortgage rep who may be sitting at a desk in India. The time-worn scene of a gray-haired banker in a business suit sitting behind a mahogany desk while a dressed-in-their-Sunday-best couple fill out a sheaf of papers (in duplicate) is so rare now that people might stare if they actually saw it.

On the other hand, some mortgage brokers will indeed send representatives to your home to discuss the many different types of mortgages with you. They will make some suggestions as to which is the best loan type for your particular investment situation and point out which lenders offer the best terms. Most real estate agents can recommend mortgage brokers, mortgage bankers, and local lenders with whom they have worked.

Computers today have made the mortgage application process faster and easier. But as in most competitive endeavors, *greed* (both corporate and individual) has also pushed its way into the lending marketplace. There have been federal-level investigations into appraisal practices that came up with higher-than-fair-market value appraisals so that higher loans could be written. Lenders approved borrowers who were only marginally qualified to carry the amount of the loan. And borrowers willingly borrowed more money than they could afford to repay. In a hot housing marketplace, some mortgage brokers and bankers added hidden (very small print) fees to their agreements.

Mortgages lending practices have made more headlines recently than war or weather. The best advice is: *Pay attention to details.* Even if you need to use a magnifying glass, read every word before you sign a lending agreement. If you don't understand something, ask questions until you do.

And use your head! That's a funny phrase for this century, isn't it? Sounds like it came out of the 1950s. But the fact is that many people are relying completely on computer-printed guidelines. In almost every mortgage application, there are extenuating circumstances— sometimes good and sometimes bad. Use the mortgage banker or broker for information and loan availability, but be your own supervisor. Ask yourself if you can really afford what you are promising to do. The decision is yours.

Mortgage Underwriters

You may never meet a mortgage underwriter unless you happen to belong to the same country club as one. But the underwriter who is responsible for evaluating your loan will get to know a lot about *you*. He or she will review your application, check your credit report, predict the likelihood of your repaying the principal, and either approve or decline the loan.

You can make things smoother for the underwriter and thereby perhaps improve your chances of being accepted by supplying all requested information, fully and accurately. Don't, however, volunteer extra information that you have not been asked for: the likelihood, for example, of your soon inheriting your Aunt Tillie's extensive rare stamp collection.

Bank Appraisers

Because your mortgage loan will be a **lien** on your home, lenders want to be sure there is such a property and that it is worth about what you are willing to pay for it. An appraiser chosen and hired by the perspective lender will be sent to inspect the property and report on probable value based upon the condition of the building and the local marketplace sales of similar properties.

The fees for some bank appraisers are included in the mortgage application fee. In other cases, you will find a bank appraisal fee added to the money you owe at closing.

CLOSING AGENTS

The transfer of title to real estate is handled by different **fiduciary** agents in different parts of the nation: sometimes by a real estate lawyer; sometimes by a real estate broker; sometimes by a "settlement agent" who holds escrow funds; sometimes by a title insurance company; sometimes by the lending institution itself. No matter who is in charge of closing your deal, however, be absolutely certain to check through all the numbers and read all the small print yourself. Remember: no one will have your interests as close to heart as you will. (More about closing procedures in Chapter 6.)

WORDS TO *GO!*

A *lien* (rhymes with bean) is the legal right of a creditor to have a debt satisfied out of the property of the debtor. A mortgage is a lien but it is not the only kind of lien. For example, unpaid contractors can file a *mechanic's lien;* if taxes are unpaid, the municipality can file a *tax lien.*

A *fiduciary* relationship is one that requires trust and good will. A fiduciary agent can hold your money in escrow or close title on your property. Real estate brokers and attorneys often act as fiduciary agents.

No matter who actually closes your title, your lender will require you to obtain title insurance. Title insurance, however, does not guarantee good title. Rather it is a guarantee against loss because of a dispute over ownership. The buyer usually pays a one-time fee for title insurance.

UNSEEN POWERS

Whenever you enter the real estate marketplace, your chances for success will be influenced by powers you cannot see. It's important that you know they exist and that you know how their existence can influence your property value. Most of the unseen power lies in the hands of the municipal government. Differences in municipal character and management can mean differences of tens of thousands of dollars in the value of similar properties.

The Tax Assessor and Collector

Every buyer asks, "What are the taxes on this property?" The answer can make a difference in both salability and value.

Real estate in the United States is taxed *ad valorem.* The phrase is Latin and it means *according to value.* The job of the tax assessor in a municipality is to determine the fair market value of each property.

COMMUNITY CHEST

If I am not for myself, who is for me?

—Hillel, the elder (30 BC–10 AD) from Talmud,
The Wisdom of the Father

Reassessment is generally done at five- or even ten-year intervals. Recently, however, some cities and towns are doing a new tax assessment based wholly upon purchase price *every time* a piece of property changes hands.

At some given interval (sometimes yearly), the town management sets a mill rate that will determine how much tax a property owner will pay upon the assessed valuation. A *mill* is one-tenth of one cent. If a town has a mill rate of 5.9, the property owner must pay .0059 cents on a dollar of assessed valuation. That's 59 cents on $100 and $5.90 on $1,000. So a property assessed at $300,000 would have an annual tax of $1,770. That amount is paid to the tax collector. Usually it can be paid annually, semi-annually, or quarterly. Some homeowners prefer to include a monthly payment for a tax escrow with their mortgage payment to the lender; then the lender pays the municipal taxes.

The Buildings Inspector

Most small towns have a *buildings inspector*. Mid-to-large cities have a buildings department within which buildings inspectors work. These municipal employees must be very familiar with the local building codes, because one of their primary jobs is to inspect new construction. They inspect to assure compliance with codes and ultimately the safety of the inhabitants. If your projected experiences in the real estate marketplace include new construction, you will get to know local buildings inspectors.

Buildings inspectors also inspect multifamily units and apartment houses. Sometimes they work on a repetitive schedule (every six months, for example) and sometimes they inspect after each change of tenancy. In many towns, multifamily properties are inspected whenever ownership changes hands.

Buildings inspectors can require that working systems be brought up to code and that a building is structurally sound before habitation is allowed. If you are about to invest in a multi-unit building be sure to hire your own professional property inspector (one who knows the local building codes) before you get permanently locked into a purchase contract. Calculate carefully what changes and improvements are likely to be required and how much they will cost.

Environmental Inspectors

In the early 1990s, the U.S. Environmental Protection Agency (EPA) began requiring environmental inspections in some real estate transactions. Many municipalities throughout the country followed suit. Before you buy, ask your agent to get you information on local environmental protection laws.

The environmental inspector looks at property for contaminated soil, air, or water and for the presence of hazardous substances used in construction (asbestos, for example). You will most likely meet this municipal employee if you are developing land. But even single-family houses can come under scrutiny if, for example, septic tank seepage and well-water contamination is suspected.

Planning and Zoning Boards

We've already discussed the power of zoning in the last chapter. Changes in zoning that are made by local planning boards can immensely affect the value of property. That's one of the reasons it is so important that you are really familiar with the area in which you intend to buy. Get and read back issues of local newspapers from the library reference room. Ask yourself or others who are knowledgeable:
• What is the past record of the planning board?
• Where do they seem to be headed?

CHANCE

Real estate is a tangible, permanent, and solid investment. Nothing will change unless you change it, right?

Not exactly. It's more like: the land is forever but nothing is written in stone. Planning and zoning boards have been known to change their minds, even to redo a town's master plan. With a few flicks of the pen, the value of your property can go way up or way down. Stay in touch with local politics. Planning and zoning board meetings are generally open to the public. Minutes of the meetings are on record in the town hall.

- Is there political infighting within the town?
- What are the forces *for* and *opposed* to change in the town? How strong is each?
- Are there any plans for major highways through or near your town?

Be aware that no nationwide or statewide zoning ordinances exist. For the most part, the responsible use of the land has been left in the hands of local officials. These powers are conferred by state enabling acts.

SELLERS

Now we're playing one on one, Top Hat versus Thimble. Just as in a game of MONOPOLY, what you know and don't know about your opponent can make a difference.

"Opponent?" you say. "Isn't that a bit strong? I know several people who bought houses from really nice sellers. In one case, the seller even gave my friends a short-term second mortgage to help them get started."

Sounds nice, but in the MONOPOLY game, as in the real estate marketplace and in fact in *any* marketplace-the buyer/seller situation is adversarial. Each party is motivated by the attempt to get the best price and best terms for *him- or herself.* Those kind sellers who gave your friends that nice second mortgage probably didn't have an immediate need for all the **equity** they had in the property. They might have considered the second mortgage as cement for the deal, not to mention the distinct probability of a high-enough interest rate to chalk up a good return on the money loaned.

Just as you should consider your own needs and goals when you enter the real estate game, you should consider the needs and goals of the seller before you make your first offer. Try to get answers to the following questions. Your real estate agent can help.

Why Are They Selling?

The answer you get may not be the whole truth and nothing but the truth, but it will give you an angle of view. If the sellers have already purchased another house, there is usually some pressure to sell and therefore, it follows, some pressure to lower the price. If they are moving on a company transfer, they will often have financial support and a need to move quickly; both factors can affect their willingness to lower the price. On the other hand, even with company assistance, they may need all or most of their calculated equity for the down payment on their next home.

WORDS TO *GO!*

Equity is the amount of cash value an owner has in a property beyond the remaining balance on the mortgage and all other liens against it.

Sweat equity is a commonly used term meaning the value added to a home or investment property because of improvement work done by the owner.

Close or *close title* means convey the property from seller to buyer by deed and complete all other necessary paperwork (for example, mortgage agreements and prorated taxes). At the *closing table* the keys to the property are usually turned over to the buyer.

How Long Have They Owned the Property?

Usually the greater the ownership time, the greater the equity. Sellers with a great deal of equity often can afford to be a little more flexible in their absolute bottom-dollar figure. Some, however, are counting on every penny that the listing agent promised them.

What Did They Pay for It?

Purchase price and date is public information and available in the town records office. Ask your real estate agent to get this information for you.

How Long Has the Property Been on the Market?

Time on the market is instant information for the real estate agent. But ask also if the property was listed with any other agent or agents prior to the current listing. Time on the market is usually an indicator of negotiability on price: the longer the time, the more negotiable. Extensive time on the market may be an indicator of overpricing or of some feature or factor that most potential buyers find detrimental to value.

How Soon Do the Sellers Want to Close Title?

Closing date can be a negotiating point in your deal (see Chapter 4). For example, you can offer to pay several thousand less for the property but offer to close sooner if a quick closing is what the seller wants.

YOU, YOU BOTH, OR YOUR TEAM

And finally we come to the most important player(s) in your game. Before you even set foot in the real estate marketplace, it is essential that you know your goals, your financial resources, and your skills, strengths, and weak points.

If you are buying as a single party, evaluate yourself; if you are a couple, evaluate each person and then meld the two profiles into one, because you can support each other in decision-making and play off each other when negotiating. If you are buying as a group of investors, profile each member and make a composite profile, because the whole may well be greater than the sum of its parts.

Following are some important factors in your profile.

Why Are You In the Marketplace Anyway?

Unlike MONOPOLY, few people play the *real* real estate game just for fun. If you are buying property (even a cottage with a white picket fence) purely to make money, you are investing. Your moves and your choices should be based on facts and figures. Your head should rule; there is no place for the heart in the investment game.

If you are homebuying, your heart—how you *feel* about a property—must be a factor. Homebuying is often more of a challenge than pure investing. You are buying a shelter, a comfort zone, a reflection of your taste, and a status symbol in our society as well as a financial hedge against inflation and an investment for the future. With your head in control, test the property against all the standards for a good investment and then let your heart contribute to the *to-buy-or-not-to-buy* decision.

How Much Can You Afford?

Your financial status will set the parameters of your playing field. But the lines are not as rigid as you may think. *Risk taking* is a very important factor in this game and the amount of financial risk you are willing to take will influence the property choices available to you. (More details on risk taking in Chapter 5.)

How Much Free Time Do You Have?

Real estate ownership demands not only money but also time. If you have very little free time, you may find the condominium marketplace appealing. Moderate amounts of free time may encourage your desire to buy and maintain a single-family house. More free time could facilitate landlording in multifamily or mixed-use properties, or buying a fixer-upper and renovating while you live in it.

What Are Your Skills?

If you're "handy" and unafraid, you may be attracted to the fixer-upper, quick-turnover marketplace. If you're good at recordkeeping and people management, investment property may be right for you.

In homeownership, many people have moved up in the marketplace with **sweat equity**. Counting on sweat equity and discovering that you can't really do the work, however, can be hazardous to your financial health, not to mention back pain and headaches. Those property owners who must pay market price for all repairs and improvements have large out-of-pocket expenses.

RULES AND STRATEGIES

- It's easier to get around in the real estate marketplace when you use an agent.

- Keep your opinions of a property's value and your financial commitment plans to yourself. In other words, don't trust too much.

- Use the professional home inspector's report to predict probable cash outlays.

- Renegotiate price with the report in hand or use it to walk away from the contract.

- Recognize that the character of the municipality in which your property is located can affect its value.

- Learn as much as you can about the sellers.

- Use the knowledge of mortgage bankers and brokers, but compare offerings and make your own decisions.

- Know yourself, your goals, your strengths, and your weaknesses in the marketplace.

CHAPTER 3
First Moves

*Order and simplification are the first steps toward the mastery
of a subject—the actual enemy is the unknown.*
—Thomas Mann (1875–1955),
German author of *The Magic Mountain*

You pick up the dice, roll them around in your hand a few times, and toss. You count the squares and, if you're lucky, you land on Vermont Avenue or even St. Charles Place. You buy. So starts the game of MONOPOLY.

A surprisingly large number of people enter the *real* real estate marketplace in a similar way. They see a property advertised in the newspaper or on the Internet; they call the real estate office that holds the listing; and they ask to go out and see the place. The person who answered the phone (the one who, by chance, had "floor time" in the office) shows the property and then takes them around and shows them other properties. Eventually they buy something that they just happen to fall in love with.

That process is about as careful and selective as a roll of the dice and it is definitely not the best way to get into the Real Estate Owners Club. Membership there (as we all know) can be a contributing factor to securing your financial future, so isn't *getting in* worth a little extra thought, time, and effort? Each step in the process of buying a property should be made with knowledge, understanding, and as much control as possible. This chapter will help you set some standards to go by.

CHOOSING A REAL ESTATE AGENT

Of course you can do your property hunting, selecting, inspecting, and negotiating yourself, but using a competent agent will certainly save you time and probably save you money. Most for-sale-by-owner properties (FSBOs, pronounced *fizbos*) are overpriced. Usually, the owners' inaccurate estimate of market value is influenced by two important factors: (1) a genuine love of *home* that interferes with realistic perception, and (2) the irrepressible human need to get as much money as possible. Bragging rights go along for the ride.

A good real estate agent will have been inside many of the properties currently on the market, even some of the FSBOs. He or she will therefore be able to discuss **comparables** with you not only using the listing statistics available to everyone but also adding firsthand inspection information and familiarity with the location. Knowing and understanding the **comps** can keep you from paying too much for a property.

Yes, you can get neighborhood selling prices on the Internet. I recently keyed *home sale prices* into Google and got 308 *million* matches. Most sites are free; try some. The most comprehensive is *www.MLSonline.com* but the available information is also accurate on most of the larger sites. The figures that you get will help you to estimate the market value of your prospective purchase by informing you of the actual selling prices of other houses like it. The sale prices on comps, however, do *not* tell you all the details.

Here are just a few possibilities to start you thinking about what's *not* on the listing sheet:
- The spots of mold in the basement—getting rid of mold can be costly and difficult.
- The appearance and condition of the interior—no listing sheet is going to print out that the kitchen floor hasn't been washed in three years or that a three-year-old's indelible-marker art decorates the upstairs hallway.

WORDS TO *GO!*

The terms *comparables* and *comps* in the real estate marketplace mean properties similar to one that is being considered. Comparison is made based upon location, size, age, condition, and style. *Sold comps* are those properties that have changed hands within the past year or so. The agent can tell you what the original asking price was, how long it was on the market, and the final sale price. *On the market comps* are those properties currently listed and competing with the one being considered. The agent can tell you of any price reductions and how long the property has been for sale. You can also gather your own comps on the Web. Try *www.MLSonline.com; www.domania.com; www.homepricerecords.com;* or any number of other sites. Print those listings you think appropriate and discuss them with your agent.

- The effects of local weather conditions—what printed sheet is going to mention that the unpaved turnaround area near the garage changes into a duck pond with every major rain storm, and into a Canada Goose pond after spring snow melt?
- The unseen realities of the location—for example, the fact that the street is a rush-hour shortcut between two major commuter roads.

OK! OK! You're pretty much convinced that working with an agent is a good idea, especially on your first venture into the marketplace. So how do you find a good one?

First of all try to avoid working with family or close friends. (This may be difficult if your favorite aunt works for the biggest agency in town.) Keep in mind: the real estate marketplace is a place for doing *business,* even when you are buying a *home.*

Work with the agent as you would work with a business associate. Before you make a commitment to any one agent, check his or her qualifications against the following list.

Working Hours

You will want to choose a full-time agent, one who makes his or her living from real estate. Part-timers and weekenders simply cannot keep up with today's fast-paced marketplace where virtually everything is done in "real time."

Knowledge of the Local Area

Choose an agent who lives in or near the area in which you are house hunting. You will get better answers to your questions when your agent is involved in the community you are considering (for example, if he or she has children in the schools or membership in civic organizations). And the longer he or she has lived there, the better. You will be entering the real estate marketplace at a distinct disadvantage if you house hunt with someone whose residence and office are twenty miles away.

Specialization

If you are homebuying, you will want a *residential* agent, not your friend's brother who does mostly commercial work but will gladly take some time away just to help you out. If you are buying a multifamily home, you will need to work with an agent whose office is located in an area where there are many such buildings, including conversions. Your best bet for help in your search for mixed-use property is an agent who does a significant amount of commercial work. If you're purchasing land, you need an agent who has handled the sale of raw land more than occasionally. But that's getting into the PhD realm and you haven't even gotten your real estate BS degree yet!

Experience

Don't fall for a line like "I'd like you to meet Miranda. She's just starting out and can spend a lot of time with you." It takes a lot of time to learn the real estate trade. In fact, about 50 percent of new agents drop out of the business in their first year or two. For optimum results, choose someone who has been working full time for at least three years.

Personality

By definition, *homebuying* is an intimate activity. You will want to choose an agent whom you feel comfortable being with. Of course you want an ethical person, but you also want someone who respects your privacy and doesn't pry unnecessarily beyond the information needed to evaluate your purchase goals. You will also want someone who doesn't push you but allows you the time you need to negotiate or to make a decision. At the same time, however, you want an agent who informs you of customary and usual procedures and of all new developments in the marketplace in general and in your prospective property in particular.

Results

Medals and trophies are mostly good for collecting dust. *But* in the real estate marketplace awards for high sales and/or listing achievements, company recognition awards, and recommendations from satisfied customers all count in helping to choose an agent. Top producers are likely to produce well for you also.

"Those are great criteria," you say. "But exactly where and how do I find such a person?"

Start by watching the real estate section of your local newspaper. You may see articles or advertisements announcing that a certain agent has received company recognition or performed some outstanding community service. Watch the listing-agent names on advertised properties;

COMMUNITY CHEST

When you reach for the stars, you may not quite get them, but you won't come up with a handful of mud either.

—Leo Burnett (1891–1971), American advertising executive and creator of the Jolly Green Giant and the Marlboro Man

someone whose name appears regularly with the type of property you want is most likely to be a competent guide.

Go to open houses. But be aware that not all agents who act as hosts or hostesses for those events meet the above criteria. One of the most common tasks assigned to rookie agents is sitting (as in babysitting) open houses.

When you meet an agent at an open house, ask questions and engage in conversation. The agent will be trying to find out about *you* but you can counter each question with another question about her. In other words, interview a prospective real estate agent just as you would a lawyer or a doctor. You don't have to stay with any one agent just because of a meeting, a one-time showing, or even several showings.

If possible, try to arrange a meeting at the agent's office *before* you make any appointments to go property hunting. You'll get a feeling for personality and an opportunity to ask questions about the market in general and the agent in particular. Once you choose an agent, you can respond to calls from other agents by saying, "Thank you for calling

DON'T GO TO JAIL

A *seller* who signs a contract with a real estate broker to act as his agent in the sale of property agrees to pay a commission to that broker upon a sale. In the real estate marketplace, that broker is usually referred to as the *listing* broker, even though the agency may actually sell the house at a later date. (More about listing contracts in Chapter 13.)

A *buyer* can sign a buyer-broker agreement with any licensed broker. The agreement usually promises that the agent will work in the best interests of the buyer and will be paid a commission by the buyer. In the trade, this agent is usually referred to as a *buyers' broker.* When a contract to purchase is signed, he or she is also referred to as the *selling* broker.

Don't be concerned about the need to pay a buyers' broker commission, however. Payment of commission to the buyers' broker is usually taken out of the amount to be paid to the listing agent by the *seller,* as agreed to in the listing contract. This arrangement has long been referred to as co-broking. Upon listing the property on the market, the listing broker agrees to pay a certain portion of the commission to the selling broker (usually 50 percent).

So you can sign up with a buyers' broker and it doesn't cost you anything, right?

Yes. Well, *usually.* Watch what you sign! Some buyer-broker contracts specify a minimum amount to be paid even if you don't buy a house during the contract term.

And, what if, during the contract term, I change my mind and decide to move to, let's say, San Francisco rather than Los Angeles?

You go house hunting with another agent. And you buy a place in San Francisco. According to the contract you signed, you could owe your buyer-broker in Los Angeles 3 percent (more or less) of the price of your purchase in San Francisco. That's in *addition* to what will be paid to the listing agent and the selling agent in the San Francisco area. In other words, the buyer-broker you signed up with can take money out of your pocket if you jump ship.

The court costs of suing you to get that money are so high that many brokers don't pursue the terms of a broken buyer-broker agreement. But they *could* (especially the larger firms who have their own lawyers).

To protect yourself, *read* the entire buyer-broker contract before you sign. It should allow for cancellation of the contract by mutual agreement. If you cancel, you will still be under contract for all the properties you have already inspected with that agent, but you will be released from obligation to work with that agent in any new endeavors. If you are working with a large firm with many offices or a nationally franchised firm, you may be able to transfer your buyer-broker agreement to another office without cost or penalty.

Be aware: As a buyer, you are *not* obliged to sign any agreement with a real estate agent. Agents have been selling property under the terms of listing contracts for many times longer than even the idea of buyers' brokers has been in popular recognition.

but I have decided to work with [name] who is with [agency name]."
When you see an interesting property on the Internet, you can also
call *your* agent to gather more information or arrange a showing.

WHAT DO YOU WANT?

Getting started in the real estate marketplace means making choices.
Are you planning to enter by the homeownership gate? Or does the
investment gate appeal more? Or perhaps the best way in seems to be
a mixture of the two, in multifamily houses or mixed-use property.
Chapter 1 took you on an all-around tour of the marketplace for
beginners; now you've got to decide what you want.

If you choose single-family houses, be careful not to make your style
choice too rigid. Real estate agents often swap war stories of customers
who came into the office saying that they wanted a ranch-style house
and *only* a ranch and then bought the two-story colonial-style that
another agent showed them just because "it was right around the corner."

CHANCE

Beware of falling in love. It's very easy to allow emotions to rule when
you are buying a home. Especially when you see a beautifully decorated
and furnished builder's model or a newly remodeled used-to-be-a-fixer-
upper. If your reaction to a house is love at first sight, go home, sleep on
it (you probably won't get much sleep), and then in the morning, try to
draw, from memory, a floor plan of the house you love.

Lots of questions will come up. You'll be surprised what you
don't remember. Then try to imagine a day moving from room to
room, *using* the house as it were. Then compare the asking price with
similar properties nearby.

It's good to love your home, at least a little, but the decision to
buy should always be made with your head in control.

Use your price range and the number of bedrooms and bathrooms that you want as the search criteria for the computer. Then consider every style. Location and condition often turn out to be much more important than any particular floor plan or appearance.

Try also to hold back on judgments made from Web views or drive-bys. A property often looks very different once you are inside the front door. I'll give you a personal example. My youngest son was recently looking to buy his first home. He showed me a Realtor's photo, and my reaction was negative. The house was too narrow, too small, no garage. But he and his wife insisted we go to see it. Inside, we realized that there was a large sunny addition on the back of the house, not visible from the road. The "kids" purchased it and it has already appreciated over $100,000. And that's before the planned addition of the garage.

WHERE?

The oldest joke in the real estate marketplace is

> *Q: What are the three most important factors in a real estate purchase?*
> *A: Location! Location! Location!*

The joke has stayed around so long because it's true. Absolutely true. Theoretically you can change any aspect of a piece of property except *where* it is located. And location has an immense effect on value. Exactly the *same* split-level house will have very different market value in Bangor, Maine, and Bergen County, New Jersey, and Houston, Texas, and Tacoma, Washington. On a smaller scale of reference, the same townhouse condominium can have a very different value between Tampa, Florida, and St. Petersburg, Florida, or even within the city of St. Petersburg itself, if one of the locations is near water access.

After you have decided *what* you want to buy, *where* you would like to buy should be the next decision you make, even before you pick an agent. The choice you make can be an area of the country; it can be a list of several contiguous towns; it can be a list of several neighborhoods within one town. The important thing is that you are aware of the importance of location and keep it in mind at all times while you are in the marketplace.

To give you some guidelines, let's divide location into four categories: town, neighborhood, lot, and ownership space within a shared-space community. All the information that follows will not be applicable to every single property you encounter, but the overview will give you a checklist that will stimulate both thought and questions.

The Town

No, I'm not referring to the village center around the colonial green. By *town* I mean *hometown*. That could be Manhattan or North Bend, Oregon. It's the municipality in which your property is or will be located.

The most common inquiries made about a town are tax rate and assessment; the quality of the schools and healthcare facilities; crime rate; services such as police and fire; recreation facilities; shopping; accessibility to the workplace (distance and time commuting); and accessibility to airports, highways, and other means of transportation.

These factors affect everyone, but every property buyer will prioritize them differently. My best advice is to make a checklist for yourself using the blank form shown in the following table. In the left-hand column, list the common inquiry factors noted above. Horizontally across the top, list the towns you are considering. In each square evaluate the factor in that town from 1 to 5 (5 being best).

For example, Smithville, which has a town lake and a senior center, gets a 3 in recreation; Townsville, which doesn't even have a Little League field, gets a 1; and Quarryville, with three parks, a municipal golf course, a multimedia library, a fairgrounds, and a community theater company, gets a 5. For tax rates and assessment, you can enter actual numbers.

If you make and keep such a chart, you can readily evaluate what each town has to offer when you finally get down to comparing the location of one property to another. Be aware that choosing your town is more important than choosing to live at a particular address; the municipality will be a prominent factor in your happiness while you live in the property and/or in your financial return on an investment property.

COMPARING THE TOWNS

	Town 1	Town 2	Town 3
Commuting (distance and time)			
Crime rate			
Healthcare facilities			
Recreation facilities			
Schools			
Services (police, fire dept., etc.)			
Shopping			
Tax rate and assessment			
Transportation (accessibility to airports, highways, etc.)			
Other			

COMMUNITY CHEST

There are many ways to get information that will help you to evaluate a town. Here are some suggestions:

- The Web is a huge source. Type in the town name and state on a major search engine. Your inquiry will usually bring up many Websites including the Chamber of Commerce, department of recreation, and organizations within the town such as the Elks or the League of Women Voters.

- Your real estate agent or the local Board of Realtors office will usually have maps and flyers and perhaps even magazines about where everything is and what's going on.

- The local library is a good place to get historical information on the town and its development. The reference librarians can usually help you to get reports from town government meetings that are on record.

- By all means, subscribe to local newspapers for several months before you start your property hunt. You'll get a perspective on what is of local concern in each of the categories on your town-evaluation chart. The classified ads will also give you a feel for the real estate marketplace.

- A visit to the town hall will allow you to examine the master plan, look at all current zoning districts, and get a glimpse of what the future holds. Take note if there are large areas of undeveloped land; what will be there in ten years and how will it affect taxes? Schools? Recreation? Are there any plans for highway development?

The Neighborhood

We humans like to live in communities with others like ourselves. That is why Levittown became a prototype in the late 1940s and early 1950s and why the Active Adult 55+ communities have become the fastest-growing segment of the new housing marketplace. I'm not talking here about racial or ethnic grouping, but rather about socioeconomic similarity. We tend to live near others who have similar incomes and who share our interests and attitudes. All of that is not surprising when you consider that neighborhood is a major factor in determining the price/value of the properties within it.

A good place to start on your hunt for a good investment property is usually right in the middle of a neighborhood's price range. Such a house ordinarily "fits"; it is protected by the existence of others on both the up and down sides of the price range; and it will move along appreciating (or depreciating) with the whole neighborhood.

Buying the smallest house in a neighborhood often works to increase value somewhat beyond the equivalent property located in a neighborhood of same-size houses. Sometimes, however, it's difficult to attract potential buyers when you try to sell the smallest house in a neighborhood precisely *because* it is the smallest. (The prospective buyers think they may not fit in or be able to "keep up.") Buying the largest house in a neighborhood, especially if there are no other houses like it, usually decreases the equivalent square foot value if it were in a neighborhood of similar houses.

Always remember that federal and state Fair Housing Laws prohibit discrimination in housing because of race, color, religion, gender, sexual orientation, national origin, disability, or children in the family. You can get help from your state attorney general's office. Your local Board of Realtors may also step in.

In addition to homogeneity, there are several other factors that should influence your choice of neighborhood. Consider the following.

- **Security:** Everyone wants a safe neighborhood. Low crime rate, little traffic with a low speed limit, good street lighting, and responsible neighbors will always help maintain value in a property.
- **Convenience:** No one really wants the railroad tracks or a high-speed Interstate in his or her backyard. But convenience to transportation, shopping, schools, and community activities will usually add value.
- **Noise:** Unfamiliar sounds are bothersome to many people. Houses in a neighborhood near an airport, for example, will often be more difficult to sell. The same goes for the house next door to a fire station, the driveway to the local emergency room, or a boarding kennel, just to name a few of the most unpopular locations.

- **Odors:** Response to smell is subliminal; it originates in the non-verbal centers of the brain and can be very powerful. Just a whiff from the waste-treatment plant can nix a deal. The same goes for landfills, factories, and sulfur springs.
- **Animals:** Most municipalities have leash laws but few enforce them strictly. Some buyers are put off by neighbors' dogs that are barking or running loose. Let's not even mention the reaction to homeowners who raise chickens, goats, llamas, or rabbits in their backyards.
- **Trash and Tumbledown:** One house, just one, can decrease value in a whole neighborhood. It's the house with junk cars in the driveway, rusting toys on the front lawn, a screen door hanging by one hinge, paint peeling from the eaves, broken windows at the basement level. Need I say more?

Your Lot

Real estate is the land and everything permanently attached to it. The piece of the Earth that you choose will affect your comfort, the demands upon your time, and the future resale value of the house. If you fall in love with a house but dislike the location or the terrain, try to keep looking. While a house can be duplicated or remodeled, the land cannot be significantly changed.

In the best of all possible worlds, everyone will evaluate each lot and house together as one unit in the course of a house hunt. But in fact many people fall in love with a house, and then evaluate the lot as an afterthought. In either case, let's look at some criteria for your prospective piece of the Earth.

Size

The size of a lot does not affect value nearly as much as its location. Of course, bigger is usually better, but a tiny lot in the Georgetown section of Washington, D.C., is worth many times the value of an acre in Green Valley, Arizona. And even within a single community, a small lot amid similar properties in the middle of a community is worth more than a large corner lot at the edge of the community, on a state highway across the road from Bowl-o-Rama.

CHANCE

Theoretically, ownership of land is not limited to the surface of the Earth. Your ownership rights and responsibilities extend downward to the center of the Earth and upward to the limits of the atmosphere. That's great if you discover oil or gold beneath your lot, but it's not so great if toxic waste is buried there.

A recent TV spot on ABC showed a KB Homes development in Texas that was built on a World War II practice bombing range. And yes, people began digging up bombs. The Army Corps of Engineers came in to inspect the land and dig up the remaining bombs, some of which were still armed. They found hundreds, not counting those under the houses, sidewalks, and roads, that were left where they lay. Houses in the community became virtually unsalable.

Stories of houses built near or upon residential and commercial dump sites are common; do you remember Love Canal? And who could forget Julia Roberts in *Erin Brockovich*? The movie was based on a true story.

If you want to be sure your land is clear of toxic waste or other hazards, you will need to know who has owned it before you and how it was being used. You can have your title insurance company do a title search that will detail all the owners of the property for at least the past century. You can do your own search in the town hall records office. You can also go to the U.S. Environmental Protection Agency (EPA on the Web at *www.epa.gov*). There you will find an abundance of information and articles on hazardous waste, human health protection, and links to state EPAs where you can get local regulations and news.

Terrain

Most buyers prefer level. A level lot is easier to maintain and lends itself better to backyard recreation. Steep slopes with steep driveways are often hard to sell, especially in climates that have a long, snowy winter. Houses built below **grade** level are unattractive to many buyers because cars passing on the road look in at the second-story windows, not to mention the rain and road water that can come cascading right at the house. Water in the basement is a common problem in such properties. In some areas of the country, mudslides are also a problem.

Shape

Given a choice, most buyers prefer to avoid lots with unusual shapes. Rectangular is most common and most preferred, followed by square. Such lots are easier to fence, easier to landscape, and easier to maintain as one's own. Pie-shaped lots are often used in developments where the roads curve upon each other. Be aware that the angles that create the point of the pie mean less land either in front of your house or behind it, depending upon whether your house faces the point or the "crust." Most pie-shaped lots have more front yard than backyard.

Good depth of property (an intangible, measured by good feeling rather than running feet) usually refers to the land behind the house. Privacy and recreational space behind the house are usually preferred to a wide side yard or large front yard.

The View

Some views, such as waterfront or mountaintop, can increase the value of a piece of property, both financially and personally. But most of us aren't that lucky; we look out on another house in our neighborhood or perhaps some woods or a field. If the view is pleasant and non-threatening, it will help to maintain value. If, however, the view includes unpleasant or undesirable elements such as power lines, railroad tracks, commercial or industrial buildings, or dilapidated and abandoned houses, it is likely to decrease both salability and value.

Drainage

A lot situated at the lowest point in a development of houses or **below grade** is likely to collect runoff water. Often the basement of the house on that lot will flood. Many builders install **sump pumps** as a protective device in houses likely to collect water in the basement. Be aware that if there is a power failure during a heavy rainstorm, the sump pump will not work and the basement is likely to take on water.

When discussing land development, *gradient* and *grade* usually refer to the degree of slope of the land. The terms *above grade* and *below grade* usually refer to the relationship of a building to the grade of the road surface on which it fronts.

A *sump pump* is a basement pump that removes accumulated water from a sump hole. The sump hole, or pit, is usually dug by the builder in a corner of the foundation. Water accumulates from under the foundation into the pit and the pump sends it through piping to a location farther from the house.

A *septic system* is a private waste disposal system used in areas where municipal sewers are not available. There are a number of designs from old-fashioned cesspools to stepped structures to which the waste and water is actually pumped uphill. Old systems may be grandfathered, but all new systems must meet strict environmental standards. In many rural and suburban areas, the location of septic systems is on file in the town records department.

Leaching lines, leaching fields, and *leach trenches* are all methods of removing liquid waste material from sewage by filtration through sand, gravel, tiles, stones, or other means. You can often spot where they are located because the grass will be greener.

A *perc test* (*percolation test*) is used to determine the ability of the soil to absorb liquid. A test hole is dug, usually with a backhoe, water is poured in, and its drainage is timed. Some fees for a perc test include a soil analysis.

Often wet basements are also a problem in areas where the soil is dense and claylike and in areas where the water table is high.

Poor drainage on the land can also cause serious health problems. In areas where **septic systems** are used for waste disposal, water that should be draining through the **leach lines** seeps to the surface. This standing water can become a breeding area for bacteria, mosquitoes, and other undesirables. In long periods of wet weather, septic tanks can stop working and toilets may back up. If you are suspicious about drainage, ask your home inspector or real estate agent about getting a **perc test** (percolation).

If a lot is located in a "flood hazard area" the seller is obliged to inform you. Flood hazard areas throughout the country have been designated by the Army Corps of Engineers. Buying such a property will require federal flood insurance before you can get a mortgage. Don't assume that you're safe if your prospective property is nowhere near the Mississippi or any other major river. Flood plains and flood hazard areas can include coastal property, land surrounding seemingly minor streams and waterways, and even, under some conditions such as the likelihood of hurricanes, land abutting scenic drainage ponds and canals.

Vegetation and Landscaping

Appropriately planted trees and shrubs can enhance privacy. Generally the best landscaping uses plants that occur naturally in the area. If you choose to bring in other plants or if you see them on a lot you are considering, you may be committing time and money to maintenance.

Many buyers are attracted to properties that back up to open-spaces land, woods, or even a golf course. No one living behind you makes your land ownership seem greater. Be careful to check out the zoning of that land, however; you probably wouldn't be happy if those pretty little woods were changed into a small strip mall for a convenience store, gas station, and Laundromat.

Fences

Poet Robert Frost picked up on a local adage when he wrote the line "good fences make good neighbors." For the most part they do, and attractive fencing usually increases value. Beware the high stockade fence, however. Is there a problem with the neighbors? Ask around, if you can do so tactfully.

Your Deeded Space

If you plan to buy a condo, you may or may not own any land. In some communities, you will own only the space between certain walls, floors,

COMMUNITY CHEST

We abuse land because we regard it as a commodity belonging to us. When we see land as a community to which we belong, we may begin to use it with love and respect.

　　—Aldo Leopold (1886–1948), U.S. forester

We shape our buildings: thereafter they shape us.

　　—Winston Churchill (1874–1965), British statesman and author

and ceilings and an undivided interest in the land. If that's the case, you can still evaluate the land upon which the entire condominium community stands against the standards for "town, neighborhood, and lot" as described above. Then you should consider your *deeded space*.

In a high-rise community, consider where the unit is located within the building. Generally top-floor units, corner units on upper floors, and units with maximum privacy or a good view bring the most money. Lower-floor units and units contiguous to community gathering areas usually bring less money. Location near an elevator or trash chute is usually considered a negative. It may lower selling price a bit but it only rarely breaks the deal.

In a garden-style condo community, end units are a plus and center units with no side windows a negative. A site near the main entrance gate or near a main access road is usually less valuable than a site farther into the community and nearer to recreation facilities. Units that back up to ponds sell more quickly because most buyers like the privacy and separation that the water provides. The same is true of units that back up to golf courses, walking trails, and bridle paths. Increased value is not usually true of units that are contiguous to a community swimming pool or tennis courts because many residents are bothered by the noise of these activities.

Ownership of a boat slip associated with your unit is a definite plus. It will appreciate in value right in step with your unit. In some condo communities, you are allowed to sell the boat slip separately if you sell to someone else within the community. In others, the boat slip is tied to the unit.

Structure and Condition

Taking into account location and square footage, new houses usually sell for top prices, but close behind on the price curve are meticulously clean, perfectly maintained, and beautifully decorated resales. Most buyers want to move in without facing the need for immediate and extensive refurbishing. And usually they will pay for that privilege.

Some buyers, however, have a keen eye for bargains and will recognize that a house overcrowded with shabby furniture, decorated with dirty fingerprints, and surrounded by weeds and overgrown shrubs can in fact be structurally sound. Let's look at some points to *check out* before you make an offer and call in a home inspector. All of them apply whether the property is bright and shiny or rather frayed.

The Foundation

In the real estate marketplace, the word *foundation* refers to any construction that is below or partly below ground level and upon which the house is built. It can be a full basement which is usually seven or eight feet high, a crawl space that puts anywhere from a foot and a half to four feet between the ground and the floor joists, or a slab (usually concrete).

A slab should lift the wooden floor joists at least six inches above ground level. If you see crumbling at the corners or wide cracks anywhere, suspect trouble.

Fewer houses are now being built using a crawl space, but many still exist in the marketplace. If you can see into the crawl space, check for adequate ventilation and look out for standing water in corners and low spots. Be sure your inspector checks and reports on this hard-to-get-to space.

Water is the most frequently encountered problem in the basement. Be aware that foundation materials (usually concrete and/or concrete block) are not waterproof. A basement that regularly floods is virtually unusable for storage or as a children's rainy-day play area. If you see a yellowish-brown or white line at an even level around the basement walls, it is probably a high-water mark either of a flood or of a risen water table during a period of high rain. If moisture is gathering outside the walls of a basement, you may see a white fuzz inside. It is called *efflorescence*.

Serious cracks in a foundation can indicate instability or deterioration. Be particularly mindful of cracks that start as hairline and get wider or cracks that extend from top to bottom. All long, horizontal cracks should be inspected by a professional.

The Framing

The horizontal and vertical boards that create the skeleton of the house are called the *framing*. Often in a finished house, you can detect the use of improperly seasoned lumber in the framing or uneven settling of the foundation by cracks on the interior walls at the door jambs or at the corners of windows. Other indications of poor construction are floors that slope and separation between the baseboard moldings and the floors.

CHANCE

Just because they appear level, don't assume that countertops and floors are level. Carry a small ball or even an old-fashioned marble in your pocket when you go house hunting. Place it on a surface and see if it will roll, and in which direction. A rolling ball could indicate uneven settling. Ask your professional home inspector to check for structural soundness.

The Roof

The framing underlying the roof in today's new houses is usually pre-fabricated and structurally sound. The attics of older houses, however, have been assembled in many ways. Look at the roof line. It should be straight. If you see sagging (I've seen them as bad as a sway-backed horse), call in a roofer in addition to the home inspector. That is, if you *must* have that particular property.

You can sometimes detect a leaking roof from inside the house. The incoming water leaves an irregular brown stain on ceilings and walls. This marking is very difficult to cover over with paint and cannot be washed out. If you can get into the attic, shine a flashlight beam at the rafters. Water stains will be dark with an irregular edge. Remember, no roof will last forever.

Most asphalt shingles have a life expectancy of fifteen to twenty-five years. More recent fiberglass shingles have a somewhat longer lifespan. Tile roofs depend upon both the quality of the tile and the quality of the installation.

Exterior Walls

Studies show that exterior painting has the greatest return to the seller in dollars spent for spruce-up. Market value of the property is increased by up to ten times the cost of painting. So why am I talking about return to the seller in this chapter for buyers? Because flaking, peeling paint turns many buyers away from an otherwise sound house. Try to judge the structure, not the appearance. If the house is sound and you like it, get an estimate for a new paint job and use the cost as a negotiating tool. (More about negotiating in the next chapter.)

Appearance does matter, however, when you look at decks and the walls of any additions to the original structure. Any evidence of separation should be taken very seriously both for financial and safety risks.

Systems, Pests, and Problems

By now I'm sure you understand why I think hiring a professional inspection service is money well spent. There are so very many

DON'T GO TO JAIL

This box should actually be titled *Don't Send Your Seller To Jail!* In today's marketplace most states require a seller disclosure statement in writing. The wording of the forms differs locally but essentially the state requires that the seller make known to real estate agents and prospective buyers all material defects in a property that would not be apparent during a routine inspection. There are questions on the form for the seller such as "Has there ever been a flood in your basement? How deep?"

But don't take anything on the disclosure form as gospel. In the first place, few sellers really have the technical knowledge and impartial perspective necessary to evaluate the structure and working systems of their homes. Secondly, they want to make the sale and might conveniently "forget" a defect.

Taking a seller to court for false disclosure is very expensive. Spend a little extra time and money, if necessary, on careful inspection and testing, *before* your contract becomes binding.

---

aspects to a home purchase, all financially risky, that no one should go through without all the help he or she can get. The following are items the home inspector will check, but you should know about them too.

- **Electrical, Plumbing, Heating, and Cooling Systems:** Your inspector will run virtually every appliance and system to check for "good working order."
- **Water:** If your prospective property is in a rural area, you will be required to have the water from the well professionally tested. No lender will make a mortgage loan without evidence of potable water.
- **Waste Disposal:** It is difficult to judge the efficiency of a septic system in dry weather. You can ask to see the last report from the septic tank cleaning company or you can include having the tank pumped and cleaned at the seller's expense as a contingency of the

sale. If the property has municipal sewers, ask if there is a separate sewer service tax. Have the inspector verify that the sewer pipes are up to municipal code.

- **Chimney Construction:** Have your inspector check the interior of the fireplace for chemical buildup and the outside to be sure the fireplace chimney is not pulling away from the house. (This does not happen often, but it is a huge expense and dangerous when it does.) Also be sure the inspector checks all the flashings between the chimneys used for heat and venting and the roof.
- **Termites:** Some home inspection companies include inspection for termites in their contracts; others leave termite inspection to an extermination company. Termites are more common in the south, but they exist everywhere, even in parts of Alaska.
- **Radon:** An odorless, colorless gas, radon levels can be detected through the use of meters or air sampling kits. Many inspection companies include the testing. If yours does not, get it done by a radon testing company. At high levels and constant exposure, the gas is a carcinogen.
- **Lead Paint, Asbestos, and Urea-Formaldehyde Foam Insulation (UFFI):** Your inspector will be familiar with these and other hazards in buying an older dwelling. If you have questions about these items in the inspection report, your real estate agent can put you in touch with local public health agencies.

JUMPING IN

Are you ready to go into the marketplace now? Ready to buy? There's a lot more to learn about negotiating, home financing, and getting the deal down in writing. But still, you are now ready to *start* your househunt process.

You should know what type of property you want even if you don't know yet what you can afford (see Chapter 5). You should know where you want to buy and you should be able to evaluate neighborhoods and lots. You should know what to look at and look for regarding structure and condition. And you should have a pretty good idea of what you want from a real estate agent.

Start reading listings on the Internet. Start driving around in neighborhoods that interest you and watch for FOR SALE signs. (I'll tell you how to work through a for-sale-by-owner in the next chapter.) Watch the ads in your local newspaper. And go inside at open houses.

But *don't* take out a pen and your checkbook; not yet! For your comfort and financial safety, you still have more to learn.

RULES AND STRATEGIES

- You can now sign a contract with a real estate agent to represent *you* in your property hunt and in your negotiating. But read the contract (every word) before you sign it.

- Beware of love at first sight. Your head should make the significant decisions in the real estate marketplace.

- Choose the *location* of your prospective property carefully. Evaluate the town, neighborhood, lot, and, when applicable, condo space.

- The *condition* of a building can usually be remedied; faults in *structure* may not be correctable, or if so, only at heavy cost.

- Carefully read the sellers' disclosure statements. Then examine everything and judge for yourself, with the help of professionals where needed. Not everything written on paper tells the whole truth.

CHAPTER 4
Offer and Counteroffer

Keep strong, if possible. In any case, keep cool. Have
unlimited patience. Never corner an opponent,
and always assist him to save his face. Put yourself
in his shoes—so as to see things through his eyes.

—Sir Basil Liddell Hart (1895–1970),
British author and military historian

Grace under pressure. Ernest Hemingway used the theme again and again in his stories of men at war and/or in love. Like love and war, negotiating for a house (especially your first real estate purchase) is a pressure situation. And like the Hemingway heroes, you will do better if you can maintain a cool and graceful attitude.

To do that you'll need no brawn, just brain food.

What's brain food? Actually in the MONOPOLY game and in the real estate marketplace, the essential ingredients for success are not food at all. The best negotiating enhancers are an understanding of the negotiating process and confidence in your strategy. Let's see how we can enhance those brain waves.

BEFORE YOU MAKE AN OFFER

Once you have focused in on a prospective property, the negotiating process does not start with your first offer. It starts with self-assessment; then a property and market evaluation; then seller assessment; and *then* a written offer.

Know Thyself!

In Chapter 2 we talked a bit about evaluating your own real estate game strengths and weaknesses. Now let's get to what makes the game go round: money. To win on the MONOPOLY board and in real estate, it is essential that you carefully examine your financial resources. Ideally you would do this every time you passed *GO!* and started on your way around the board again.

In the *real* real estate marketplace, there's an alternative to before-you-roll-the-dice financial scrutiny that works well whether you are a first-timer or an experienced player returning to the game after three or more years. The strategy is: *look!*

Before you commit to buying *anything,* it's a good idea to spend some time *just looking at property.* You will want to become familiar with the local marketplace and with your particular response to different kinds of property. This is an essential setup activity and it will help to keep you from making an impulsive decision, one propelled by "Oh, we just love it!" Go out looking *without* your checkbook.

Meanwhile, create your financial profile. Here are the questions for which you must get answers. Read Chapter 5 to find out how.
• How much cash or equity do you have?
• How much are you willing to use for the down payment on your next property?
• How much mortgage can you carry?
• How much are you able or willing to pay monthly for mortgage, taxes, and insurance?

The answers to those questions will determine the properties from which you can choose. A well-trained real estate agent will try to get the answers "for" you; it's called *qualifying the buyer.* But it's really better to get them for yourself.

You don't want an agent, even a buyers' agent, who knows your absolute top-dollar limit. No agent will negotiate for you hard and sincerely if she knows you can go to a higher price.

"But then how can I accurately determine what I can afford?" you ask.

For help in qualifying yourself, you can go to any local lender. It will only take a short time with a mortgage rep, and you will often get a conditional commitment for a given amount. The commitment is conditional upon the value of the property you choose.

Property and Market Evaluation

Before you make your first offer on a property, it is essential that you have an estimate of its **fair market value**. *Estimate* is, of course, the key word, because no one knows the actual number until the sale closes. The estimate, however, should be based on the facts available in a **comparative market analysis** or **CMA** and should include data regarding the pace of the local marketplace. (More about pace in just a bit.)

WORDS TO *GO!*

Fair market value is defined in the real estate marketplace as the highest price a ready, willing, and able buyer will pay and the lowest price a ready, willing, and able seller will accept. In other words, it's a *meeting of the minds* between buyer and seller. An estimate of fair market value cannot be verified until a property is actually sold.

A *comparative market analysis* (CMA in marketplace lingo) estimates fair market value by comparing the subject property to similar properties that have been sold or are currently on the market. It factors in all the data available on *comps* (see page 53) and adds in the pace of the local marketplace and the professional opinion of the agent doing the analysis.

CHANCE

Never calculate your first offer as a percentage of the asking price.
(For example, "Houses are selling at 98 percent of asking price in this
town so I'll make my first offer at 95 percent of asking price.") Every
seller of real estate can set his or her own asking price, with or without
professional advice. There are no controls except supply and demand.
Especially in for-sale-by-owner situations, the asking price may be too
high for the local market.

Ideally, you'd like to pay less for the property than the CMA estimate. And you'd like to get some extras thrown in, the assurance of
good condition, and a closing date to your liking. That's what negotiating is all about. Just remember, however, that the seller has goals too.

Except in an extremely hot and fast-paced marketplace, the estimate of fair market value is not your starting point. It is a negotiating
number to keep in mind at all times. It will influence many of your
strategies and in the final rounds of negotiating, it may actually be
mentioned and used as a lever.

Seller Motivation

Why are they selling? We talked about seller profiles in Chapter 2. Now
that you have selected a property and are ready to make an offer, you
should gather as much information as you can about the seller's position.

But be aware that you may not always get the whole truth. Sellers
do not want prospective buyers to know that they may be making
mortgage payments both on the house they are selling and a house
they have just bought. They certainly don't want buyers to know that
they are financially strapped for any reason, especially looming foreclosure. And sellers do *not* want buyers to know that something the
sellers want is dependent upon the sale of their property, for example

getting their dream location on the eighteenth hole in a retirement community where lots are selling at a fast pace.

So how do you get accurate information about the sellers? Read the information available on the listing, listen to everything the listing agent or the agent showing you the property tells you, ask more questions, and then put the pieces together. Questions like *How long has the property been on the market? How many showings in an average week?* and *Have there been any offers?* can provide additional insights into seller motivation and anxiety.

If you can get to talk informally with the sellers themselves, you will often be flooded with information, sometimes conflicting information. Everyone likes to talk about his or her *unique* problems. (They are rarely unique.) Sometimes sellers will actually brag about a feature that many buyers would find objectionable. For example, "there's a beautiful stream running through the neighboring property just behind that stand of trees." Many buyers with children will be put off for safety reasons; buyers who have witnessed the power of rushing water will walk out in back to examine the topography.

Be friendly, concerned, sympathetic, and listen well. Ask questions. Always start conversations with the *good* things like the cul-de-sac down the road; once talking, the sellers may complain about the not-so-good things such as how they are *always* the last street plowed in the winter or how your kids will probably like the kids next door who sometimes pick flowers from right against the house.

COMMUNITY CHEST

The real art of conversation is not only to say the right thing in the right place but to leave unsaid the wrong thing at the tempting moment.
—Lady Dorothy Nevill (1826–1913), British writer and hostess

Let the conversation become comfortable and friendly, but be careful not to reveal too much about yourself, your motivations, goals, needs, and preferences. Everything you say can and will be used against you.

Set Your Parameters

The next-to-last step before you make your first offer is to set the end points for your money. Now that you know the probable market value of the property, what would you consider a *steal-it* price? Are there circumstances in this deal that might lead you to believe in the possibility of a real bargain? Or is the pace of the local real estate marketplace so fast that a low-ball offer would simply allow someone else to get the deal?

The opposite of *steal it* is top dollar. *Top dollar,* however, has two facets: (1) the absolute top dollar that you can afford to pay, and (2) the absolute top dollar that you think the house is worth.

When calculating affordability, real estate professionals will tell you that it's not just the price that counts. You must factor in the

CHANCE

You shouldn't go beyond your personal evaluation of top dollar in affordability and/or property worth even if, or especially if, you get into a bidding war. Let's say you were to scrape together or borrow more down payment money (enough to bid higher). Should you bid higher? It's a huge risk. Buying a house beyond your affordability numbers could markedly increase the stress in your life and thereby your health and comfort.

If you lose out to another bidder on the house of your choice, let it go emotionally. You may have much the same feeling as you did after the breakup with your first love, but there will be another house. Perhaps even a better one.

amount of mortgage loan, the interest rate, the municipal taxes on that particular property, the cost of the homeowner's insurance that the lender will require (usually, at minimum, the amount of the mortgage loan), flood insurance if you are in a flood zone, and condominium fees if you are buying in a shared-space community. The calculation takes a little paperwork because a lower mortgage interest rate can mean more borrowing power and therefore a higher top-dollar price. On the other hand, high municipal taxes can put one house out of your reach when a house at the same price in another town with lower taxes is affordable. Real estate brokers do have computer programs that can help you determine mortgage qualification requirements for given properties.

Your evaluation of the second factor (the worth to you of the property) may be more or less than the real estate agent's CMA. A great deal depends on the pace of the local market and your particular need and desire for that particular house. In a fast market, houses sell near, at, or above the CMA. In a slow market, they can often sell below the CMA.

On a personal evaluation level, ask yourself which is more important to you and your family: *probable appreciation* or *comfort?* If you are buying a house with the ideas of breaking into the Real Estate Owners' Club and then of making a killing so you can go on to bigger and better things, you will want to stay at or below the CMA figure. If you are buying a house because you love the location, the view, the great schools for your kids, and the commute, then you may want to evaluate top-dollar worth to you at a bit more than the CMA figure, if necessary.

Gauge the Local Marketplace

And finally, you *must* take the pulse of the marketplace *before* you make your first offer. A fast market or slow market nationally or regionally will determine many of your negotiating strategies. But the pulse you want to feel is the pulse of the *local* marketplace.

Despite the fact that huge national and international mortgage lenders and real estate brokerage franchises have moved into the twenty-first century marketplace, homebuying and individual property investment still take place in a local milieu. The national economy, in general, and real estate, in particular, can be bubbling like an active volcano while at the same time a particular geographical area, an individual state, or even a particular town can be in a metaphorical dry gulch. The opposite can be true also. The national economy can be depressed while a particular area may be spiraling up in value.

You, the buyer, therefore must gather information on the pace of the marketplace for the state, county, and the particular town where your property is located. You want to know if a **sellers' market** or a **buyers' market** prevails now, in real time; not what's coming or what recently has been. Any real estate agent can help you to get this information or you can go to the office of the local Board of Realtors. You will want to know the average time on the market for property of the type you are considering and you will want to compare that figure with the national average. You will also want to know at what percentage of original asking price most properties are being sold, both locally and nationally.

MAKING A FIRST OFFER

OK, you're ready. You know what you can afford and you've picked the property, estimated market value, set your steal-it and top-dollar

WORDS TO *GO!*

In a *sellers' market* or *fast market,* there are more interested buyers than there are properties for sale. Usually properties sell quickly and near their asking prices. Sellers have the negotiating advantage.

In a *buyers' market* or *slow market,* there are more properties on the market than there are interested buyers. Usually properties take longer to sell and often sell well below their asking prices. Buyers have the negotiating advantage.

CHANCE

Beware the unusual! When you find a property that has been long on the market in a *sellers' market,* ask *why?* Is it far overpriced? What do other buyers know about the location or structure that is keeping them from making an offer? Is there something about the topography of the lot or the floor plan of the house that most people find objectionable? (Even if you don't see it, it will probably affect your selling at some point.) If the asking price is low and the real estate agent is telling you it's really worth a lot more, why hasn't someone already bought it?

When you are considering an unusual property or one that seems too good to be true, it's a good time to ask for another showing. Bring your family or some good friends along on the inspection, if possible. They may have a different perspective and see things that may surprise you.

prices, and evaluated the seller's position. *Now* what do you do? You make an offer.

If you are using a real estate agent, the procedure for making a first offer is pretty much standardized across the country. If you are working on a for-sale-by-owner deal, there are a lot of variables and you will more or less have to gauge the situation and respond accordingly. I'll get to FSBOs in just a bit.

How It's Done (with an Agent)

The spread and predominance of national real estate franchises (Century 21, REMAX, Prudential, just to name a few) has done a lot to standardize property-buying procedures and to improve agent training. There was a time when some agents made first offers and negotiated price by phone, without a single signature from the buyer. Some other agents used a short form or *binder* for the first offer. Neither of these options are commonly used today.

"Why?" you ask. "Why not find out if you can make a deal without a lot of needless, fussy paperwork?"

First, verbal negotiation is always weak. Sam Goldwyn of Hollywood fame said it best: "a verbal contract isn't worth the paper it is written on." Both buyers and sellers often have second thoughts after their verbal agreements.

Second, a binder can be more binding than either party intends. The data on that scrap of paper (sometimes a half sheet in red, pink, or yellow) is usually all about the price, nothing but the price. It usually does not allow for what-ifs and if-possibles (contract contingencies). Furthermore, a binder signed by both parties could be waved about by an irate real estate broker demanding payment of his commission even though the deal fell through.

So much for what *not* to do. Let's move on to the best way to make a written offer. When you are ready, have your agent help you to fill out a real estate purchase contract and sign it. Virtually every

COMMUNITY CHEST

In many areas of the United States, attorneys do not close title on real estate purchases. (Title insurance companies, lenders, or closing agents do the job.) But that fact does not mean that you cannot rely on advice from an attorney and buy yourself some thinking time in a real estate deal. You can write an *attorney review clause* into your purchase contract above all signatures. It should read:

This agreement is subject to review and approval as to form and content by an attorney of the buyer's choice. The attorney may rescind the contract for any reason before midnight on [date].

Three to five working days is a common review period. Attorneys for both parties may agree to extend this period if there are problems that need to be worked out.

DON'T GO TO JAIL

Avoid *binders* used in lieu of written contracts. Think about these possibilities: On a signed pink slip, you make a low offer. Your intention is to open negotiations. Surprise! Surprise! The seller accepts and countersigns the binder. *Voilà!* A meeting of the minds! Signatures from both parties! Under some circumstances, buyer and seller could have just put themselves under contractual obligation.

Problems can easily grow out of the fact that most binders do *not* include any contingencies. What if you can't get a mortgage? What if there is a major structural flaw? What if you need to sell your house before you can close but the seller wants to close next week? Without contract contingencies, you must "live with it" or "work it out." Either could prove painful and you could find yourself in court.

If you *must* negotiate price *only* with a signed short form, be sure to print the following statement above your signature:

This agreement is contingent upon a mutually agreeable purchase contract to be drawn and fully executed by all concerned parties on or before [date]. (Allow five business days.)

broker has on file "standardized" printed contracts with all the appropriate blanks to be filled in by the buyer. I'm going to spend almost a whole chapter (Chapter 6) talking about how to protect yourself in the purchase contract. Be sure to read it before you sign one. But right now register in your personal computer (that's your head) that the purchase contract to present your offer should say what you want it to say. Nothing on the pages of preprinted contract forms is carved in stone. Wording can be changed. Clauses can be struck out or added in.

Read everything carefully (every word) *before* you sign. Then send the agent off to the seller with your offer, the contract, and your **earnest money** check.

WORDS TO GO!

Earnest money (sometimes called *hand money* or *good-faith money*) is an amount of money (almost always a check) given by the buyer to the agent upon the signing of an offer to purchase. It can be any amount, but a token $1,000 is common practice. It is usually deposited in the broker's escrow account. If a meeting of the minds is reached and contracts fully executed, the earnest money along with additional escrow deposits is held by a **fiduciary** until all contract contingencies are met or until closing. If a buyer and seller cannot agree upon the terms of a sale, the earnest money is returned to the buyer.

In the dictionary, *fiduciary* means of, *relating to,* or *involving a confidence or trust.* In the real estate marketplace, a fiduciary is usually a neutral third party (broker, banker, closing agent) who holds earnest money and escrow money.

How It's Done (without an Agent)

If you are purchasing property in a for-sale-by-owner situation, you should choose and meet with an attorney before you make your offer. If your offer is accepted, you will need someone who is trustworthy and competent and who knows real estate law in your state. Your attorney can help you draw the contract, review any changes that the seller requests, and hold all escrow monies. That's the easy part.

Negotiating is the hard part. Real estate is big, big money for most of us. The cliché repeated often in the media is "the biggest investment most people ever make."

To the effects of that bundle of the money, now add all the emotions called up by the word *home.* Often you'll get more than 2 + 2 = 4; you'll get irrational fireworks.

Despite the potential for igniting explosions in response to a low dollar figure, the first offer should be made in person. It's much too easy to slam down an old-fashioned receiver or shut down a cell phone. Once an angry *No!* is followed by a click, it's much *more* difficult to start a second round of negotiations. On the other hand, it's *not* a good strategy to present a low offer in the seller's living room. You might literally be shoved out the door, and *that* is really hard to recover from while saving face (for both parties).

So how do you negotiate in person? First choose a neutral place. Most common is a restaurant at off-hours, but libraries, municipal recreation facilities, and condominium communities often have rooms where people can meet. Then begin your meeting by saying some positive things about the property. Move on to presenting *your* comparative market analysis of the subject property with other properties in the area that have been sold or are on the market. (Data is available on the Web, just use a search engine for *home sale prices.*) Ask the seller to acknowledge that the information is accurate. Then name any factors that may decrease the value of the subject property.

Finally, present all the information in printed form. (Print out some comps on the computer.) And present a printed sheet with your offer price, your name, your phone number, and your e-mail address.

Stay cool no matter what. Every raised voice shakes the negotiating table. Don't allow yourself to become angry just because the seller is angry, or insulted, or incredulous, or disparaging. Don't expect or accept an immediate answer. (Unless, of course, the seller just says *yes!*) In fact, tell the seller to think about it and get back to you. Assuming both parties have Internet access, suggest that the response be made via e-mail. The print medium filters out angry looks. Responses can be

COMMUNITY CHEST

What I've learned about being angry with people is that it generally hurts you more than it hurts them.

—Oprah Winfrey, American talk-show host

COMMUNITY CHEST

What if a buyers' agent has been working very hard for you for some time when you notice a FOR SALE BY OWNER sign on a lawn in one of your favorite neighborhoods? You don't feel comfortable negotiating solo. What should you do?

Contact your agent immediately before some other agent persuades the sellers to list with him or her. Your agent needs the permission of the sellers to show the house and negotiate on your behalf. That can be done with a one-day/one-client Open Listing. The seller agrees to pay a certain commission (it does *not* have to be the usual 6 percent) if you buy the house but reserves the right to sell the house to anyone else without paying a commission. The house does not go up on the Multiple Listing Service with this arrangement.

The other alternative is that you, the buyer, agree to pay your agent. Again this fee does not need to be 6 percent or any percentage of the sale price. It can be a flat fee agreed to between you and the agent. Many agents maintain that they save the buyers more money through savvy negotiating than the fees they are paid.

thought through and revised before sending. When you reach an impasse, suggest another meeting. Be as flexible as you can.

If the seller should accept your first offer without further negotiation or *whenever* the seller accepts your offer, do *not* exchange any money. All deposit monies in a real estate transaction should be held by a fiduciary. Instead, shake hands and give the seller your attorney's card. Then, at the first possible moment, get on your phone and call your attorney. Have a contract drawn *ASAP!* If you've made prior contact with the attorney and established yourself as a client, it's really a matter of filling in the blanks. As soon as the contract is prepared, hand carry it to the seller for signatures. *Do not rely on the mail.*

Especially in a fast market, you, the buyer, must do many of the jobs of the real estate agent, and that includes messenger service.

Remember that there is nothing reserving that property for you until the purchase contract has been signed. We all like to think that every person will honor a goodwill handshake agreement, but it doesn't always happen. I've known several people who have lost a property because they waited too long between the handshake and the contract.

COUNTEROFFERS AND MORE NEGOTIATING

If you choose to open negotiations with a low-ball offer in a buyers' market or in any market on a house that has been for sale for a long time, don't let an agent brush you off with comments like, "That's ridiculous! They'll never accept that! I can't go to those people with an offer like that!"

The agent not only *can* go to the sellers with your offer, he or she *must* make the offer. Real estate laws require that every written offer be presented to the seller. In some cases where a listing agent and another agent representing the buyer are involved, the buyers' agent must go to the listing agent before presenting the offer. Sometimes the two agents present it together.

In any case, insist that the offer be presented in person, not by phone. A good agent will always do that if it is possible. Do *not* tell the agent that this offer is only an opener and you intend to go higher. (If you do that, you throw away half of your trump cards.)

There are many ways a seller can respond. Each type of response sends a different message. Let's go over some of the most common.

Absolutely Not!

Your seller is, in fact, insulted by your low offer. Or perhaps the *insulted* attitude is the little scene acted out by the seller in front of the real estate agent. In truth, he may be quite happy to see that someone has expressed interest but he doesn't want the buyer or the agent to know that.

I once presented a really low offer to a single woman in a somewhat run-down Cape Cod. She picked up a mop that was standing in the corner of the kitchen and literally chased me out of the house by repeatedly swinging it at me. I was *done,* but my buyers still wanted the house. They raised their offer by $15,000 and I went back (wearing jeans and running shoes).

I think the seller was a bit embarrassed. She not only let me in, she served me coffee and made a counteroffer $20,000 above the buyers' second offer. We made the deal by splitting the difference and allowing the seller to remain in the house for two months after the closing (paying rent of course).

I'm telling you this story because it illustrates a major premise of negotiations: *don't say* "absolutely not!" *and don't take* "absolutely not!" *for an answer.* If a seller responds with a negative and does not counteroffer, it does not mean the deal is dead. If you want the house, you can make another offer.

A Minute Reduction

What if the seller responds to your initial low offer by reducing the asking price by one or two thousand dollars? In today's real estate marketplace, a couple of thousand dollars is a handful of pennies! But don't be put off.

A minute reduction in asking price sends the message that the seller wants to sell and is willing to negotiate but feels that the initial offer is too low. (The mid-point between the two prices is much lower than the seller's rock-bottom figure.) You can keep negotiations going by raising your offer. At this point, you might well go a bit above your *steal-it* figure, but not much, unless you are working in a fast market.

A Significant Reduction

A seller who makes a significant reduction in response to a low first offer wants or needs to sell and is willing to go lower. Don't pay much attention to words like "that's my lowest price, I won't go any lower." It's a very rare seller who will stick to the number without any flexibility. Halfway between the numbers is a good second offer.

If your second offer prompts another counteroffer from the seller, but you are still thousands apart, it's time to call for reinforcements.
• You can make yet another offer just slightly higher and ask for extras such as appliances, a lawn mower, window treatments and blinds,

CHANCE

If you are house hunting in a very fast sellers' market, you may not have the luxury of starting your negotiating with a low offer. Ask your agent to do a CMA on the house and come up with a realistic selling price. When you have that figure (it will only take a few minutes), make your offer just a bit lower.

Why not make your offer at the CMA figure? You can, in a fast market. But even in a hot sellers' market, it's usually a good idea to let your seller feel that the final purchase price was negotiated. If you initially offer full price, sellers sometimes think they could have gotten more if they had set a higher listing price. That feeling can make for a rocky road to the closing table.

lighting fixtures that have been listed as not being included, and even furniture. These extras are significant savings for you because they represent out-of-pocket costs after closing.

- You can also negotiate for seller payment of a structure-and-working-systems warranty offered by the inspection company. Again, this represents a possible significant out-of-pocket savings.
- You can negotiate for seller payment of closing costs. Who pays what (title transfer taxes, title search, title insurance, closing agent's fee) at closing is usually determined by common practice locally, but everything is negotiable.
- You can negotiate for a seller buy-down of the mortgage rate. (More about buy-downs in the next chapter.) A buy-down would allow you to pay a bit more for the property because your mortgage payments would be lower in the initial years.
- The seller can renegotiate the real estate commission. Commissions based upon a percentage of the sale price have become quite large in the spiraling real estate market of the 1990s and first few years of the twenty-first century. The big numbers have encouraged the growth

of discount brokering. (More on discount brokering in Chapter 13.) That competition has also put some flexibility into the fees that full-service brokers are willing to accept.

• You can negotiate with the closing date. This is where your knowledge of seller motivation comes into play. If the seller wants to close quickly because he is carrying mortgages on two houses, you make your first offer with a suggested later closing date (three or four months from contract signing) and then move up to a quick close as an incentive for the seller to lower the price. If you know that the seller has not yet found another place to live, you can start your negotiating with a request for a quick closing and then lengthen that closing time as you ask the seller to reduce the asking price.

IT'S A WRAP!

The conventional wisdom in the real estate marketplace goes something like this: *it's a good deal when all parties are happy or when all parties are screaming "Ouch!"* Negotiating is the process of coming to a meeting of the minds. Be prepared to give up some things (like money) as well as to get some things (like time or extras). Respect your opponent, keep your cards close to your chest, and think before you speak.

In the course of negotiations, changes in price or terms can be made on the original contract form, but each change must be initialed by all concerned parties. Sometimes, when there have been several rounds of negotiations and lots of revisions and cross-outs, a conscientious agent will reprint the contract putting all the current data onto a clean form. If this is done, just check to be sure there are no typos before you sign again.

Once everyone has agreed to the terms of the contract and signed and initialed where necessary, a signed original of the contract should be delivered to each party. In fact, technically, it's not a binding contract until every party holds a copy. Fax and e-mail transmissions are valid and binding, however.

Once you have settled on all the terms and everyone has signed everything, you may be tempted to let out a sigh and relax. *"Finally!"*

But hold on. You still have to arrange financing, work through inspections and contingencies, and go to the closing. That's why there are two more chapters in Part 1 of this book.

RULES AND STRATEGIES

- Do the necessary preparation work *before* you make an offer.

- To negotiate effectively, you *must* know the pace of the local marketplace.

- An agent is required by law to present every written offer to the seller.

- Make your offer on a contract that says what *you* want to say. Preprinted contract forms can be altered to your liking.

- Be aware that negotiating requires patience and step-by-step pacing. Being in a hurry, trying to skip steps, and getting angry all will cost you money.

- Use a contingency clause in the purchase contract to allow for review by an attorney of your choice.

- Negotiating without an agent requires printed-out data and lots of tact.

- Always negotiate with more than money. Extras like appliances and window treatments, closing costs, closing date, and occupancy are all powerful tools.

CHAPTER 5
You and the Money

I don't like money actually, but it quiets my nerves.
—Joe Louis (1914–1981),
U.S. boxer, world heavyweight champion

The word *mortgage* comes from the old French language, meaning *dead pledge.* "Wait a minute! That's a bit of an oxymoron," you counter. "If a person is dead, how can he make a pledge?" Hmm . . . On the other hand, maybe it's a pledge so big that if you don't fulfill it, you're *dead!*

Pretty funny! But in the joke there's a kernel of truth. Financing a real estate purchase calls for a big-money loan. If you don't pay and the lender forecloses, you may be facing financial ruin or, at the least, a major setback. That's the dark side of the mortgaging coin. The bright side is the likelihood of building wealth.

Today, only a very small number of people pay cash for a house in the United States. That may seem strange to you considering the wealth in this country and the current number of retirees who have amassed tremendous equity and are moving down in house size. Not to mention investors swinging their profits from one property into two others.

What's the motivation? Why do most people take out mortgage loans? Investors call it **leveraging** and the strategy works in exactly the same way for homebuyers.

USING OTHER PEOPLE'S MONEY

It's important to understand the concept of using other people's money. Legally, that is. Leveraging is a primary principle in real estate finance and without it most of us could not be homeowners. Let's consider an example because it's probably the best way to explain how successfully leveraged purchasing works.

In 2001, Sally and Tim Buyer bought their first home for $200,000. They had saved $20,000 and used it as their down payment, taking out a mortgage loan of $180,000. In 2006, they sold their home for $350,000. The selling price was $150,000 above their purchase price. So they made $150,000 in five years, right?

Not quite. To get closer to their actual profit, you must deduct some costs from that $150,000: the real estate commission they paid on the sale, the cost of the improvements they made to the property (if any), and the cost of borrowing money (the interest paid during those five years).

WORDS TO *GO!*

In the real estate marketplace, to *leverage* means to use a proportionally small amount of money (your down payment) to secure a large loan for the purchase of a property.

Appreciation is an increase in the relative value of a property. It can be brought about by economic factors such as diminished supply and increased demand for the type of property, geographic factors that increase demand such as the new location of a major employer nearby, and improvements by the owner that enhance desirability.

CHANCE

Oh, boy! Leveraging is great! Let's put $1,000 down and make a million!

Sounds like you're practicing for a TV infomercial. Cut! It doesn't work that way. First of all, lenders set limits on how much you can borrow. They call it *qualifying*. They use the probable value of the property to be mortgaged, the amount of the mortgage loan, and your income and outstanding debts to calculate guidelines for your maximum loan amounts. We'll discuss more about loan qualifications in a bit.

And secondly, leveraging is not *always* as profitable as it has been in hot sellers' markets. If you were to borrow heavily at a high interest rate and the real estate market were to turn sluggish, as it did in 2006–2008, you could end up paying out more in interest than the property increased in value over a given period of time. If the property decreases in value before you sell it, you could actually be required to bring additional cash to the closing table in order to pay off the mortgage. This rarely transpires, but theoretically it could happen.

For the sake of illustration, let's say the real estate commission was $21,000, major improvement costs were the $4,000 they paid for new flooring for the family room, and the mortgage interest paid over five years was $50,000. That's a total of $75,000.

OK, you say. That still leaves $75,000. A profit of $75,000 in five years isn't too bad considering that you've been living in the house and not paying anyone any rent.

That's right! But the *real* investment picture is even better. To make that $75,000 in five years, Sally and Tim did *not* invest $200,000 (the original price of the house). They invested (put at risk) only $20,000 (their down payment). So $20,000 turned into $75,000 in five years. That's a 375 percent increase. You can chalk some of that dollar growth off to inflation, but not all of it. There was real **appreciation** in the property.

You may be asking yourself, *what about mortgage principal and taxes? Where do they fit in?* During those five years, Sally and Tim did pay their lender over $50,000 in interest, but they did *not* pay rent. If you consider the mortgage payments and the municipal taxes paid as a part of your living expenses (the rent), homeownership looks even better. In a sellers' market, sellers can often count on having lived virtually free in their homes and still take away the down payment for another home. Even in a buyers' market, where the takeaway dollars are less, house value appreciation often allows owners to have had shelter at virtually no cost.

THE RISK OF BORROWING

Virtually every time the economy slows down significantly, radio and TV talk shows and the real estate sections of newspapers feature stories on **foreclosure** and its effects on homeowners. But in fact, unless we have experienced it, very few of us understand the foreclosure process. Knowing what actually happens when losing the house looms is somewhat complicated by the existence of two types of home-purchase loans in the United States (the mortgage and the trust deed) and by the role of each state in determining how foreclosed property will be treated.

Mortgage Loans

A mortgage is a document used to create a lien against property for money owed. Foreclosure proceedings can be started when debt

WORDS TO *GO!*

Either in or out of court, *foreclosure* is the procedure that will extinguish all ownership rights of the *mortgagor* (buyer/owner) and turn title over to the *mortgagee* (lender). The lender will then be able to sell the property to satisfy the lien (mortgage loan) against it.

Most lenders do not want to foreclose on property; it is both expensive and time consuming. If you know you are in financial trouble, approach your lender *before* you get a notice of foreclosure. Many lenders will rearrange terms and payment schedules to accommodate borrowers with short-term money problems.

payment is not made as scheduled. Each mortgage agreement (including yours) specifies how many missed payments will put the loan into default. Default allows the foreclosure process to begin. Even if you think foreclosure could *never* happen to you, find, read, and understand the default clauses in your mortgage loan documents.

In addition, each state in the United States has laws regarding foreclosures. These laws govern procedure (warnings and notices, for example); time delay between declaration of default and foreclosure (in some places two years); and in many states *statuary redemption periods* during which the original owner can pay off all the debt and reclaim the property, even after it has been sold at auction. You can get information on the foreclosure procedures in your state from your state's attorney general's office.

Trust Deeds

Sometimes called a *deed of trust,* a trust deed looks, smells, and feels like a mortgage and it is often talked about as a mortgage. But for the borrower, it is really a much riskier loan agreement than a mortgage. This type of home financing is prevalent in the western part of the United States where foreclosure can be as swift as roping a calf at the rodeo.

When a borrower agrees to a trust deed to secure a loan, title to the property does not pass to the buyer (called the *trustor*) at closing.

Instead the deed is held in trust by a third party (called the *trustee*) for the lender (called the *beneficiary*). Title is not transferred to the buyer/owner until the loan is paid in full. Property in default can be sold at auction or "on the courthouse steps" with very little waiting time and without legal entanglements.

You'll find more information on foreclosure proceedings in Chapter 7.

LENDERS' ALPHABET SOUP

Have you ever wondered where lenders get all the *other people's money* that is used in the real estate marketplace? Certainly it's not printed on demand like the brightly colored denominations of the MONOPOLY game. The U.S. Treasury Department is always watchful, and the *real* green stuff actually has to *come* from somewhere real.

Years ago (the mid-1980s and before), most home mortgage loan money came from the savings & loan (S&L) industry—the hometown banks where ordinary Americans kept their savings. But most S&Ls went belly-up in the late 1980s. After the Federal Deposit Insurance Corporation (FDIC) bailed them out, savings banks and savings & loan associations virtually disappeared from the American Main Street.

So where does the money come from now? The loans are written by the big multi-office commercial banks and by mortgage specialty companies, but the actual money to make the loans comes from investors. Most home-mortgage loans today are sold into the secondary mortgage market. Because large companies in this market buy mortgage loans, the mortgage lenders have an ongoing source of money to lend to the next applicant. Lenders can act (lend more money) without waiting out the **term** of the loan (often thirty years, at least on paper).

Holding the purse strings for the source of more mortgage money gives the secondary mortgage market tremendous power. The major players in this financial arena set the qualification guidelines for most loans, which is a bit intimidating if you think about it. What if you don't meet their qualification guidelines? All is not lost. You can still get a **portfolio loan**, but you will pay more for it.

WORDS TO *GO!*

You'll come across these words when talking with loan officers, reading loan offerings, or in your own mortgage-loan agreement.

Amortization: the paying off of a mortgage loan over a given term with scheduled equal monthly payments of principal and interest. At the beginning of the term, the payments are mostly interest; at the end of the term, they are mostly principal.

Application fee: the amount charged to apply for the loan, usually nonrefundable.

Appraisal fee: the amount charged for the bank appraisal of the property. Note that even though the buyer pays the fee, the appraisal belongs to the lender.

Annual percentage rate (APR): the actual rate of interest including fees and other factors that is being charged for a loan. Federal truth-in-lending laws require that lenders disclose the APR of every loan offering.

Balance of the loan: the unpaid principal at any given point in time.

Buy-down: a cash payment to the lender from the seller, buyer, or a third party to persuade the lender to lower the interest rate to be charged in the early years of a loan. Buy-downs facilitate qualification and are commonly used by large developers to entice young buyers who have incomes that are likely to increase.

Call: the right of the lender to demand payment of the entire balance of the loan if the repayment terms of a mortgage are not being met.

Cap: limitation on the amount of interest-rate change allowed in a variable-rate loan.

Certitude of performance: a lender's evaluation of how much risk is involved in making a loan.

Collateral: property pledged as security for a loan.

Due on sale (also called an *alienation clause*): a provision in the mortgage-loan agreement stating that the entire principal balance is due and payable if ownership is transferred to another party. This clause prevents assumption of a mortgage.

Equity: the amount of cash value an owner has in a property beyond the remaining balance on the mortgage and all other liens against it.

Interest: money paid for the use of the lender's money.

Interest rate: the cost of borrowing money, usually expressed as an annual percentage of the principal.

Loan-to-value ratio (LTV): the relationship between the amount to be borrowed and the appraised value of the collateral real estate. It is expressed as a percentage. If you put $20,000 down on a $100,000 property, your loan-to-value ratio is 80 percent.

Lock-in: a clause in a loan agreement that prevents the borrower from repaying the loan prior to a specified date. When pertaining to a mortgage-loan application, *lock-in* refers to a guaranteed interest rate for a specified period of time.

Origination fee: a charge to make the loan more profitable to the lender, just like points. Unlike points, it is usually stated as a flat amount rather than a percentage of the loan.

Points: an up-front fee charged by the lender. One point equals one percent of the principal. Ironically, points are sometimes called the **discount.**

Portfolio loan: a mortgage loan that the lender does *not* sell into the secondary mortgage market. Often these loans are secured by good-risk properties when the buyer does not meet the prevailing secondary-mortgage-market qualification or down payment guidelines. Many of these loans are from local banks and the lender usually charges a higher interest rate and higher fees than competing large nationally located lenders.

Principal: the money borrowed; the amount of the debt not including interest.

Teaser rates: low initial interest rates to attract buyers. The mortgage-loan agreement specifies how much the interest rate will rise, when, and how often.

Term: the agreed-upon period of time during which the loan must be paid off.

COMMUNITY CHEST

Following is a list of the major players in the secondary mortgage marketplace. Most have information available for prospective home-buyers on their Websites or by mail.

Fannie Mae (formerly the Federal National Mortgage Association) is a government-sponsored corporation that sells mortgage-backed securities. (These securities are investment opportunities based upon expected return of borrowed money with interest,) For up-to-the-minute information on their lending guidelines, contact them at:

> 3900 Wisconsin Avenue NW
> Washington, DC 20016-2892
> 800-732-6643, www.fanniemae.com

Freddie Mac (formerly the Federal Home Loan Mortgage Corporation) is a stockholder-owned corporation that buys mortgages from lenders and issues mortgage-backed securities. Check with them at:

> 8200 Jones Branch Drive
> McLean, VA 22102-3110
> 800-424-5401, www.freddiemac.com

Ginnie Mae (Government National Mortgage Association) is the mortgage arm of the federal Department of Housing and Urban Development (HUD). Contact them at:

> 451 Seventh Street SW, Room B133
> Washington, DC 20410-9000
> 202-708-1535, www.ginniemae.gov

Neighborhood Housing Services of America (NHSA) works with local Neighbor-works Organizations (NWOs) to provide a secondary market for nonprofit neighborhood revitalization loans. Contact them at:

> 1970 Broadway, Suite 470
> Oakland, CA 94612
> 510-832-5542, www.nhsaonline.org

Am I overwhelming you? Hang on. The best way out is through. Financing your first real estate purchase is not what most people call fun, but you can't just toss the game's rulebook back into the box and decide you'll learn while playing. Mistakes in this game are much too costly.

So you stand there, mesmerized by the crepe paper streamers and neon signs, at what seems to be a gigantic gaming resort. Even the language seems challenging, almost foreign. So many strange words and all those acronyms! Or at least you *think* they're acronyms.

You're not at a gaming resort, believe me! You're in the home finance marketplace. And worry not. I've put all the neon signs and streamer pieces into boxes for you, with translations. In one box, I've listed the major buyers in the secondary marketplace (on page 104) and in the other, I've gathered the most commonly used finance terms (on pages 102 and 103). You can dip into the information whenever you need it. Right now, let's move on to an overview of the types of mortgages available in today's marketplace.

Fixed-Rate Mortgages

When I first ran out onto the field in the real estate marketplace, no one was using the term *fixed-rate mortgage*. That's because it would have been redundant; every mortgage had a fixed rate. In those good ole days, you borrowed the money to buy the house and you promised to repay it over the course of x years (usually thirty) at a specified rate of interest. Quite simple, really.

Today, fixed-rate mortgages are still available but they are not by far the only offerings in the Great American Finance Mall. And things have gotten more complex.

Adjustable-Rate Mortgages

Also called variable-rate loans, adjustable-rate mortgages, or ARMs, are everywhere and they are dressed in the latest fashions. These loan agreements allow the interest rate to be "adjusted" (changed) at specified intervals. The rate adjustments protect the lender from being stuck several years down the road with low-rate loans when interest rates have gone up.

For borrower protection, an ARM loan agreement should contain an interval **cap** that sets the maximum interest rate change (up or down) that can be made on any rate-change date. (Two percentage points is common.) A life-of-the-loan cap sets the maximum amount that the interest rate can increase or decrease from the initial rate. (Six percentage points is common.)

The interval at which the rate can be changed is an important aspect of all ARMs. In some agreements, rates can be changed at six-month intervals; other agreements provide for as much as a *seven*-year interval. The most common intervals are one, two, or three years. If rates are relatively low when you apply for the mortgage, try for the longest interval for your rate protection. You may find, however, that the interest rate being offered by lenders changes with the increases in the interval term. The lowest rate will usually be associated with the shortest interval.

Convertible Loans

A clause in some mortgage-loan agreements allows for the conversion from an adjustable rate mortgage to a fixed-rate mortgage at a named date (or dates) in the future. This opportunity is generally a plus feature for the borrower because things *do* change, and converting your loan is an option open to you but never required. If rates were to be low around the time specified for a conversion opportunity, you could convert and thereby fix a lower rate for the duration of your mortgage. But read the terms in the conversion clauses carefully; sometimes there are fees involved.

Interest-Only Loans, Straight Mortgages, or Term Loans

Would a rose by any other name still be a rose? And still have thorns? We've all become so accustomed to **amortizing** mortgages (mortgages that eventually get paid off) that the recent advertising push for interest-only loans seemed like a new financing option. It isn't and it includes some thorns.

Interest-only loans, straight mortgages, and term loans are all different names for the same package: a nonamortized loan written for a specified period, at the end of which the *entire* amount borrowed (**principal**) is due. The thorns on this rose are the years and the money; many of these mortgages are written for a short term, at the end of which you have to come up with all the money. And even if a straight mortgage is written for thirty years, you still have to pay back the principal at the end of the mortgage term. After thirty years, however, you probably will have built up enough equity through appreciation and inflation to more than cover the amount due.

Unless there is a **lock-in** clause in your mortgage agreement, you can refinance at any time, changing the nature of the loan, the interest rate, the term, and perhaps withdrawing some of the equity. Refinancing, however, usually involves some fees. If you change lenders, you may be required to repurchase title insurance. That can be expensive.

Balloon Mortgages

Balloons are first cousins to interest-only mortgages. Let's say you are making payments on a loan as though it would amortize over thirty

CHANCE

Straight mortgages and balloons can enable financing when there seems to be nothing more conventional available. They might also give you five to ten years with a lower rate and lower payments. BUT the risk is that you are tied to a date in the unknown future. What will the financial marketplace be like when you face refinancing? There have been times during the past century when home mortgages were virtually unavailable at any interest rate. In the 1980s, home mortgage rates were approaching 20 percent!

The risk in nonamortizing mortgages diminishes significantly if you are planning to turn over the property in a short time. Best bets are investment fixer-uppers and home purchases when you are relatively certain that you will be transferred within the next five to seven years.

years. But it has a balloon clause that requires you to pay the *balance of the loan* at ten years. You will still owe most of the principal.

Balloons are usually found in so-called creative financing, especially when a seller is offering to hold the mortgage. Sometimes they turn up in the finance marketplace when interest rates are particularly low and lenders are offering **teaser rates**. The low-interest ARM that you are offered may include a balloon payment due at, let's say, five years. Of course, you may have sold the property by then. But if you don't plan to sell, check to see if there is a refinancing clause right next to the balloon clause. The lender will promise to refinance on the balloon date at the interest rate current at that time. This arrangement effectively eliminates the protective power of the life-of-the-loan cap. The need to refinance may only be a buzzing fly in your mind at the time you take out the mortgage; the new interest rate required five years later may feel more like the sting of a wasp.

Insured Mortgages

If you have a substantial income but are short on ready cash, you may still be able to get a mortgage with as little as 2 or 3 percent down by using mortgage insurance. The mortgage insurance industry promises lenders who write loans with loan-to-value (LTV) ratios above 80 percent that they will get their money back in the event of default by the borrower. The borrower, however, pays for this insurance with an increase in his or her monthly payment.

The FHA (Federal Housing Administration, a part of HUD) insures mortgages for average American houses. (They've insured 34 million since 1934.) The VA (Department of Veterans Affairs) guarantees mortgages for qualified veterans. And there are a handful of private mortgage insurance (PMI) companies currently operating in the United States that will insure mortgages with up to 97 percent LTV ratio. You can get printed information about their offerings in many Realtor and HUD offices.

COMMUNITY CHEST

Let us all be happy and live within our means, even if we have to borrow the money to do it with.

—Artemus Ward (Charles Farrar Browne) (1834–1867), American lecturer and humorist

There is a wealth of information in print and online regarding insured mortgages.

- To get information from the FHA go to www.fha.gov. Or call 800-CALL-FHA (800-225-5342).

- To get information from the VA go to www.va.gov and look for home loan programs. You can also contact local VA offices by phone.

- For private mortgage insurance companies, you can key private home mortgage insurance into a search engine such as Google. My computer came up with 11 and a half million sites. You won't even need the first 100 to get the information you need.

- There is also abundant information available on mortgages and homebuying in general through the government's Consumer Information Center. You can send a postcard to request a catalogue (PO Box 100, Pueblo, CO 81002), or call (719-948-4000) or go on the Website (www.pueblo.gsa.gov).

Purchase Money Mortgages

A purchase money mortgage is a lien given by the buyer to the seller in lieu of cash. In other words, the seller is holding the mortgage and the buyer is making payments. Some purchase money mortgages are for 100 percent of the selling price, which means the seller doesn't get any cash at the closing but will receive monthly payments for the term of the loan. You may hear experienced players in the real estate marketplace saying that the seller sold the house and *took back a mortgage.*

Most seller financing is for a short term. Straight mortgages and balloons are commonly used. This type of financing often shows up on the marketplace when interest rates are high enough to discourage buying. Offering a mortgage is a means of stimulating interest in the sale of a house.

If you decide to use seller financing, short term or long, be certain to have an attorney who is experienced in financial law review the mortgage agreement. Words are very quiet on paper, but they can cause tumult if called up to enforce a point or require compliance.

Land Contract or Contract for Deed

Also called an *agreement for deed,* an *installment sale,* or *articles of agreement,* the land contract is both a purchase contract and a finance instrument. It is most commonly used when mortgage money is tight. It is an agreement between buyer and seller that has all the characteristics of a mortgage or trust deed, but is not one. The buyer is called the *vendee* and the seller-lender is called the *vendor.* Under this agreement, the seller remains the legal fee-simple owner of the property, which makes foreclosure especially easy. But the buyer agrees to occupy the property and to pay the seller a certain installment (looks, smells, and feels like rent), as well as the taxes, special assessments (if any), hazard insurance payments, and maintenance costs (looks, smells, and feels like ownership).

The price of the property is agreed upon in the land contract. Depending on how the contract is written, all or part of the monthly payments can be credited toward the agreed-upon purchase amount. The buyer does not take title to the property until the entire purchase price has been paid. Many buyers make payments until they have accumulated a credit balance that is the equivalent of a down payment. Then they seek conventional financing.

When using a *land contract,* if the buyer defaults on payments or is in breach of contract, retribution is hard and fast. (It could be as little as thirty days to eviction.) All payments that have been made are forfeited to the seller and the seller takes possession of the property again.

There are advantages to the land contract, especially if you are short of down payment money or would like to try living in an area for a short time before you make your more definitive choice. Also a plus is establishing the price on the date the contract is signed. This named figure does not change and it is a safeguard against a rapid price escalation in the area. But there are also risks. A land contract is a purchase contract and a mortgage-loan contract rolled into one. Be certain you have yours drawn and/or reviewed by an attorney of your choice.

GETTING YOUR MORTGAGE LOAN

Now that you're leaving the gym a bit sweaty from your home-finance workout, you might want to take a quick look at your own home-buying situation before you shower and get comfortable. You're going to have to gather some documents and crunch some numbers, but read through this whole section before you do that.

How Much Can You Get?

Banks are in the business of making money. They want to write mortgage loans that are secured by good property (property that is likely to appreciate) and they like to be repaid by good people (people who are unlikely to default). The guidelines of the secondary mortgage market are strict and getting even more strict as are the policies of the mortgage insurance companies.

So what can you get? That depends on the property you want to buy, the amount of your income, the amount of cash you have available for down payment and closing costs, and the amount of your outstanding debt.

It used to be that most people would do this calculation at home and get a ballpark figure. Today everything is computerized and the government will do the qualification for you. For a quick online calculation of how much you can afford, go to the Ginnie Mae Website (*www.ginniemae.gov/2_prequal/intro_questions.asp?Section+YPTH*).

If you'd like to make a stab at qualification with pencil and paper, here's how:

DON'T GO TO JAIL

If you're serious about qualifying for a mortgage and getting that coveted *APPROVED* stamp, *don't tell any lies, not even fibs, on your mortgage application.* (An intentional omission is also a lie, by the way.)

Technology today is like the intricate webs of a million spiders superimposed, connected, and configured into a three-dimensional globe. If you overstate your income, understate your debts, or "forget" about a bankruptcy or a tax lien, it will show up in your credit history. Mortgage underwriters may be happy, cheerful people, but they *don't* like surprises. You will do better if you state problem areas, each with an explanation.

For Conventional Loans

Calculation 1: Take the buyer's gross monthly income (before taxes are taken out and including both spouses) and multiply by 28 percent.

Calculation 2: Take the buyer's gross monthly income (before taxes and including both spouses) and multiply by 36 percent. Then add together all the monthly debt obligations and subtract the total from the 36 percent figure.

The lesser of these two figures is the borrower's maximum allowable house payment. "House payment" includes principle and interest on the mortgage, municipal taxes, condominium association fees, and hazard insurance. In the trade, that is talked about as PITI: principal, interest, taxes, and insurance. Tsk! Tsk! Isn't it a pity we have so much to add up?

For FHA-insured Loans

Calculation 1: Use 29 percent instead of the 28 percent figure stated above.

Calculation 2: Use 41 percent instead of 36 percent. Proceed as under conventional loans.

These qualifications are, of course, not accurate-to-the-dollar figures, but they will give you an idea of what neighborhoods and housing styles you can reasonably explore.

What Documents Do You Need?

It's all about numbers. You'll need records of your salary and your spouse's salary. W-2 or 1099 tax forms or several consecutive paycheck stubs are good. If you are self-employed, you will need copies of your tax returns for the past two consecutive years. You will also need records of any other regular monthly income such as alimony/child support received, rental income, and pensions. Calculate the total figure for monthly income and collect all the paperwork that demonstrates it.

Now turn to your debts. Make a list of amounts owed and monthly payments on car loans, credit card debt, education loans, alimony/child support payments, and other debts. You will need statements for the credit card bills and documentation for the other debts.

You will also be required to verify the amount of cash you have on hand for the down payment and closing costs. Gather statements for your savings account, checking account, individual retirement account (IRA) or other retirement-fund contributions, stocks and bonds, and other savings.

If your parents or some other relatives have promised help with the down payment, you will need a gift letter from them stating the amount. That money will need to be transferred into your account well before the closing.

Where Do You Apply?

There are literally millions of mortgage sites on the Web. You can get virtually instant answers to your questions about offerings and your qualification. I suggest, however, that you talk with some local lenders and perhaps with some mortgage brokers whom your Realtor might recommend. I'm not saying that the Web is a bad financial marketplace, just that it's nice to get some figures and advice from real people.

You can get prequalified for a given amount on the Web (even at the FHA and VA sites) or you can get a letter from your local mortgage broker or banker. These letters can help with negotiation, especially in a hot market, because the seller wants to know that the bidding buyer really can afford the house.

Once you've picked the house and shopped for the money, you are ready to take the big leap: signing a contract to purchase. That's the next chapter.

RULES AND STRATEGIES

- Leverage is a basic strategy in the real estate game. It significantly increases potential profits.

- Leveraging can be a path to losing money if the real estate market goes sour.

- Mortgages and trust deeds function in essentially the same way, but trust-deed loans can be foreclosed faster and with less legal red tape.

- Mortgage loans come in many shapes and sizes; the trick is to pick one that fits you.

- There's a plethora of information and opportunity on the Web, but talk with some local experts in person too when you evaluate the available choices for financing.

CHAPTER 6
Get It in Writing

The first thing we do, let's kill all the lawyers.
—William Shakespeare (1564–1616),
English playwright, from *Henry VI,* Part 2

A German-American friend of mine was hosting a weekend visit not long ago. On Sunday afternoon he cut the last of the pie in half and then asked me to choose which piece I wanted.

"Either one, Chris," I said.

"No, you must choose," he replied. "My father always said that the person who does *not* do the cutting gets to choose first."

I smiled. I thought of Chris as a child in Berlin during World War II and I realized that his father must have understood a lot about human nature. Despite the tremendous generosity of many people, don't most of us like to keep the best for ourselves? Don't we often try to take the bigger piece? Perhaps that's a clue as to why our society has turned handshake agreements into written contracts.

Of course, the MONOPOLY game has been successfully played now for 75 years without written contracts being exchanged between players for the purchase or sale of properties. But closing dates, escrow funds, inspections, liability, maintenance, title insurance, real estate commissions, and *time is of the essence* clauses don't apply in the

WORDS TO *GO!*

Real estate purchase/sale contracts are *bilateral contracts.* That is, they are two-way agreements. Each party agrees to act in response to the action of the other. The seller agrees to sell and the buyer agrees to buy, both according to the terms of the contract. A real estate purchase/sale contract is not valid, therefore, unless both parties agree to every clause.

If the original contract has no additions, deletions, or changes, then signatures at the bottom of the last page are sufficient. Any changes, however, *must* be initialed by all parties in the transaction.

A *consideration* is anything of value (usually money) that one party gives to another in exchange for a promise or action (such as turning over title to a property).

world-famous game. The *real* real estate marketplace, however, *needs* clear, accurate, strong **bilateral contracts**. They are the walls and the gates that secure the playing field.

WHAT DOES A TWENTY-FIRST-CENTURY PURCHASE/SALE CONTRACT NEED?

Technically, a contract doesn't need an attorney review clause. Recall the sample I gave you on page 86: *This agreement is subject to review and approval as to form and content by an attorney of the buyer's choice. The attorney may rescind the contract for any reason before midnight (date).*

Attorney review, however, is right at the top of *my* "need" list. I urge you strongly to include these two sentences in every purchase contract you sign. The clause will enable you to seek professional advice, to review all the terms of the contract carefully (in the privacy of your home without time pressure), and ultimately, to walk away from the purchase without financial loss if you begin to have serious doubts.

The attorney review clause is buyer-protective, but not essential. Now let's go over what's necessary to make a bilateral agreement into a legally binding contract.

- **In writing:** To be enforceable, every real estate contract must be written.
- **The date:** An undated contract is not legally enforceable.
- **The identities of the parties:** The full name of each person who is involved in the buying and selling of the property should be included in the contract and each should be identified as "buyer" or "seller." It's also a good idea to include the address of each party, especially when the seller lives somewhere other than on the subject property and/or when a divorce or an estate sale is involved. To avoid a possible **cloud on the title** in divorce or estate situations, it's also advisable to get a **quitclaim deed** from the party that did not get the house.

DON'T GO TO JAIL

A *cloud on the title* could darken many of your days in the real estate marketplace and cause you legal problems long after you close. A *quitclaim deed* can solve the problem, without shouts, threats, or sleepless nights. And no one will go to jail.

A cloud on the title is an *invalid* encumbrance on a property. If the encumbrance were valid, it would have an effect on the rights of the owner. The lack of validity, however, does *not* prevent a one time owner or potential heir from filing suit for his/her claim. For example, a former owner might file a claim against the property when ownership was, in fact, forfeited in a divorce settlement.

A quitclaim deed is a release that removes a cloud on a title. The person who signs it (*grantor*) gives up any claim or interest in the property in question. Sometimes there is a financial settlement to encourage a claimant to sign. For example, one or more of several heirs may sign a quitclaim to his or her interest in the property in return for a cash settlement.

- **Identification of the property being sold:** The street address is the most conventional way to identify property and it is legally acceptable; in most condominiums, the unit number must also be included. If there is a problem with identification, property can also be identified by municipal tax block-and-lot number. As a last resort, a professional survey can be done and the coordinates included in the contract.
- **A consideration (purchase price):** The full amount of the purchase price should be written into the contract, no matter what "creative" financing you may have agreed to with the sellers. The amount of your earnest money check should be acknowledged.
- **A date and place for closing the title:** The date and place for the closing are often changed by mutual agreement, but some *day* and some *place* must be named in the contract.
- **Signatures:** Each person involved in the purchase and each person who currently holds title to the property must sign the purchase/sale contract. A missing signature can invalidate the whole deal.
- **Everything within the limits of the law:** Everything agreed to in a real estate purchase/sale contract must be legal. A contract with a clause that includes the crop from the back pasture (a marijuana field) may be void, or the specific clause may be void, depending on the laws of the state where the property is located. An owner cannot sell something that he does not own, the river rocks in the middle of the Mississippi River, for example. And all parties entering into a purchase/sale contract must be legally eligible to do so. For example, minor children and the mentally incompetent are generally excluded.

CONTINGENCIES TO PROTECT YOUR INTERESTS

Think about your purchase: what would be a deal breaker? Every "if" you come up with should be listed in your contract as a **contingency.** The contract is not binding on either party until all the contingencies have been met. Following are some of the most common contract contingencies.

WORDS TO *GO!*

A *contingency* in a real estate contract is a clause creating conditions that must be satisfied before the contract is fully enforceable.

The Mortgage Contingency

If you can't borrow the money, you can't buy the house. Realtors try very hard to avoid deals that fall through because of financing. They offer to help with qualification *before* you go house hunting and they will put you in touch with lenders and their mortgage reps after you choose a house. Sometimes they will even help you to find "creative" financing.

In the purchase contract, you will want to account for, on paper, the source of every dollar you are spending to buy the house. You will list your earnest money, the additional escrow that you will deposit if the offer is accepted, the amount of additional cash you have on hand for the down payment, and the amount of the mortgage loan for which you will apply. All factors listed should add up to the purchase price.

It is essential that the mortgage contingency contain an expiration date (usually called the *cut-off date*) by which you must have a commitment letter from a lender. (In times of heavy buying, this date can be extended if you ask in advance and can show that you have made a good and honest effort to procure financing.)

The Inspection Contingency

Inspections have become so commonplace in the homebuying process that inspection contingencies are usually written into preprinted contracts. Negotiations on price are often reopened *after* the professional inspection, but don't take your opportunity to renegotiate for granted. Some printed contracts simply state that the owner will make the necessary repairs. How do you know those repairs will be acceptable to you?

CHANCE

In your contract, you must name the amount of mortgage loan that you will need to purchase the property. (You can put down more than you actually *need,* if you prefer, but be sure that you can qualify for that higher amount.) If you'd prefer not to take any chances, however, your mortgage contingency should not record more than the mortgage amount. On the contract, you can spell out:

- The type of loan you will apply for (conventional fixed-rate, with or without private mortgage insurance, FHA, VA, state supported, adjustable rate, interest only, or whatever it is you want). If you include your preferences in your mortgage contingency and you don't get the type of loan you apply for, you can't be forced to accept a different loan with terms that you do *not* want in order to purchase the property. Of course, you *may* still choose to accept a different type of loan, but you don't have to do so.

- The maximum interest rate you are willing to pay. Many real estate agents like to write "at the prevailing rate" in the contract. If you do this and the mortgage market changes, you could be strong-armed into a higher rate and thus higher monthly payments. Be reasonable, however; name the current going rate as your maximum rate.

- The maximum number of points you are willing to pay. (Sometimes when negotiations are close or the market is very slow, a seller will volunteer to pay a point or more on the buyer's mortgage loan.)

- A cut-off date that allows enough time to make the mortgage application and get a commitment letter. Ask for more time than you think you need.

- A gift letter. If you have been promised a gift of money toward the down payment, make your purchase contingent upon getting a signed and notarized letter stating the intention of making the gift. (The bank will require this letter with your mortgage application, so you might as well put it into the contract.) If someone were to have a change of mind about the gift money, you won't be held to the contract.

Your most powerful tool for getting repairs done to your liking is the ability (threat?) to walk away from the purchase. You don't *have* to walk away of course, but the possibility gives sellers the jitters. (And rightly so. A house that is reported *on deposit* and then comes back on the market carries a black smudge. Everyone asks, *Why?*)

Let your contract state that you (the buyer) can and will judge the impact of the professional inspection. Use the clause mentioned in Chapter 2: *this contract is contingent on an inspection report that* in the sole judgment *of the purchaser is deemed satisfactory.*

And then there are the specialty inspections. Because malfunctions or problems can be threatening to one's quality of life, some structural and working-systems inspections are mentioned as contingencies in addition to the contingency for a professional inspection. Often specialized professionals or companies are hired to check for these problems and evaluate their effects on habitability. The most common specialized inspections are adequacy and good working order of septic or other waste disposal systems; asbestos or other hazardous insulation; lead paint; necessity for flood or earthquake insurance; potable water; radon; and termites or other insect infestation.

Sale of Your Home Contingency

Most real estate agents do not like to include a *sale-of-the-buyer's-home* contingency in a contract, and most sellers like it even less. From the buyer's point of view, it is a safety clause. After all, you can't buy this house without access to the equity in your old house. Sometimes however, a request for this contingency can put the deal in jeopardy.

I'll talk more about sell one/buy one situations in Chapter 14, but for now be aware that your negotiating hand is stronger if you don't include this clause. Sellers don't like it because it creates a domino effect with no controls. For example, let's say you include this clause and you quickly sell your house *but* your buyer includes the same clause on his or her contract. That house is overpriced and doesn't sell. Your deal falls through, and as a result the original deal on the house that you want either falls through or is significantly delayed while you attempt to put your house back on the market. It's a sad and sorry tale, but it *does* happen. Most real estate agents can tell you horror stories about domino deals.

If you have a house that must be sold before you can buy another, you can and should negotiate for a later closing date on the house you want to buy. Or you might negotiate by giving the seller a choice: either a later closing date or the contingency on the sale of your house. Most often you can get the later closing date, but in a fast-moving market, the seller sometimes will refuse outright or give you the sale-of-your-house contingency with a "reasonable" cut-off date (two to six months) that will negate the contract if you do not have a valid purchase contract on your house by then. When you do get the contract for the sale of your house, you can approach the seller of the house you want to buy for a new closing date.

FINE PRINT AND MORE PROTECTION

In every good purchase/sale contract, there are other provisions that ensure the fair and equitable transfer of title from one party to another. Sometimes it's a real chore (or is that *bore?*) to read through all this endless small print.

So what if you don't? Think of some possibilities. What if you just signed your name on the bottom line and later discovered that you had promised in writing to do something you don't want to do? What if you had promised to keep the lawn mowed until closing?

Or what if you forgot to write into the contract that the dining room chandelier was to be included in the purchase price? It had, in fact, been a part of your negotiations, but no one wrote it in. Upon the day of closing, you go through for the pre-inspection and the chandelier is gone, replaced by a $100 Home Depot special-sale item. At the closing table the sellers don't show up and you have no proof that the chandelier was included. The real estate agent who took the listing gets out the listing contract and points out that it says specifically that the chandelier is *not* included. You have no recourse.

So read everything carefully before you sign. And don't feel intimidated just because someone is looking over your shoulder, or rattling papers, or looking repeatedly at her watch. The need to read without time pressure and to understand the fine print is one of the many reasons I recommend using the attorney review clause. You may have no intention of using an attorney, but the clause is there to buy you time.

Liens and Other Encumbrances

The seller should state and promise that **clear title** can be delivered at the closing. If the seller has not made them known, liens on the property (such as first and second mortgages, mechanics' liens, or tax liens) will turn up in the title search. All liens should be paid out either before closing or from the proceeds of the sale and thereby removed. Quitclaim deeds can be used to settle ownership disputes.

In some cases, a buyer can and might agree to assume responsibility for paying out a lien. Local sewer assessments are a good example. Or in a condo or co-op community, an assessment may have been levied over several years to pay for new elevators. A buyer might agree to continue the payments. On the other hand, as a part of the negotiations on price, he or she could insist that the entire balance of the assessment be paid out from the proceeds of the sale.

Assumable mortgages are another type of lien that is often not paid out at the closing. They're hard to find in today's marketplace, but when a mortgage is assumable, the buyer takes on the balance due and all the original payment terms. The assumable mortgage remains a first-mortgage lien. Many buyers will take out a second mortgage or

WORDS TO *GO!*

In the real estate marketplace, *title* is the right of ownership. A *deed* is the document that conveys title.
Clear title is title without clouds or encumbrances.

WORDS TO *GO!*

Specific performance in the real estate marketplace means the requirement to adhere to a legal contract strictly or substantially according to its terms.

Time is of the essence means exactly that: time and specific dates are essential to the agreement.

other type of loan to make up the difference between their down payment and the equity the seller has in the house.

Buyer or Seller Default

Somewhere in the small print of virtually every purchase contract is a description of what remedies are available if, *after* the contract is fully executed and all contingencies have been met, the seller refuses to sell or the buyer refuses to buy. For the buyer, the penalty is usually forfeiture of the escrow deposit. A seller can be forced to sell through a court order called **specific performance**. If a buyer wants and intends to buy the property but continues to delay the closing, or if the seller wants to sell but continues to delay the closing, either party can serve notice that **time is of the essence**.

But think twice before you brandish this sword; *time is of the essence* does not enable an instantaneous closing. Usually notification is required at least two weeks before a time-is-of-the-essence date can be set. And fairly often the dispute is taken to court, where the sands of time drop slowly indeed. If possible, use your real estate agent to negotiate or arrange to talk with the seller in person. Try to work out your dispute. Lawsuits are very expensive.

Maintenance, Damage, or Destruction

A clause in the purchase contract usually states that the seller is responsible for delivering the property in the condition it was on the day that the buyer saw it and/or that the contract was executed. Usually this clause requires that the seller maintain insurance coverage during the period between contract and closing.

So what happens if a hurricane picks up the community raft and slams it into the front porch of the seaside property you have contracted to buy? If the contract was carefully worded, the seller must restore the property to its former condition or better. Be aware that such an occurrence can significantly delay the transfer of title.

Broom-clean Condition

Maybe they should change this to "vacuum clean." Does anyone use a broom through the whole house anymore? But then again, "vacuum" would imply *nothing left*, and there will always be some residue of past occupancy, if only dust.

The words *broom clean* do still appear in most purchase contracts, but don't expect Snow White and the Seven Dwarfs singing "Sweep the Floor." This contract clause means that all refuse and all of the sellers' personal property will be removed from the premises before the closing. If the movers are still there when you go to the closing table, have the closing agent hold some money (a few thousand) in

COMMUNITY CHEST

A piece of paper blown by the wind into a law-court may in the end only be drawn out again by two oxen.

—Chinese proverb

escrow to be sure all unwanted items are removed before the sellers get their money.

Day-of-Closing Inspection

Every contract should give the buyer the right to inspect the property just before taking title to it. Do this inspection! Take along a note pad (or your laptop) and your digital or cell-phone camera. If you find anything missing or objectionable, or if the property has been "let go" and has deteriorated, you can discuss it at the closing table. Show the images.

Most problems discovered on the day of closing need not prevent the closing. You can estimate the cost of bringing everything back to what it was when you signed the contract and have that amount (plus a little) held in escrow. You can take title to the property but establish that the sellers will not get their money until the repairs have been done and their cost has been deducted. Or you can negotiate a flat fee to be deducted from the money you must bring to the closing table. (The sellers get that much less for the house.) Then you can go out to dinner to spend a little of that extra cash.

TO BE ESTABLISHED

Despite the fact that your real estate agent or lawyer will most likely go into the supply closet and pull out a preprinted contract, remember that every purchase/sale contract is unique. There is only one deal that involves you, the seller, and the specific piece of property to be bought or sold. You can change *anything* on the printed page. And you can, and *should,* add items.

"More?" you ask. "What now?"

Some very important words. Read on.

What Stays with the Property?

Don't be shy. Under items that remain with the property, list everything that is not screwed or nailed down and a few things that are. It only takes a few strokes of the pen to write wall-to-wall carpeting, all window treatments and hardware, all installed lighting fixtures, dishwasher, range top, oven, microwave oven, refrigerator, dining room chandelier, central vacuum system, air conditioning units, and clothes washer and dryer.

According to most state laws, everything that is permanently installed remains with the property. But you'd be surprised how sellers interpret "permanently installed" and by what they will try to take along. Some items like the refrigerator and a washer or dryer do not automatically stay with the property but their inclusion is often part of the negotiation.

Even if certain items are named in the listing information you are given by the real estate agent, name them again in your purchase contract. Early in my career, I sold a house with the window treatments included. On the day of the closing, the buyers and I inspected and admired again the floor-to-ceiling draperies, which had been drawn closed. How nice, we thought, we can inspect them in their entirety. No one bothered to open the draw drapes.

The next day, I got a frantic call. The sellers had removed all the sheer draperies between the window and the antique satin draperies we had been admiring. The closing was over, the money and the title had changed hands, the sellers and their moving van were already in another state.

From that day on, contracts that I helped buyers fill out contained a *lot* of detail. Should someone ask you why you are bothering with so much detail when it seems that you and the sellers are in complete agreement and everyone is so nice, just smile and keep writing. You can always say, "Well, if everyone is so agreeable, no one should object to writing down our agreements."

What Doesn't Stay with the Property?

If the seller has a metal garden shed at the back corner of the property and you absolutely do *not* want it, write into the contract that it must be removed. The same goes for children's swing sets, above-ground swimming pools, hot tubs, and anything else that is cumbersome and difficult to transport. Along with all the other problems of moving in, you don't want the necessity of hiring a hauling company.

Who Is Responsible for What Monies?

Just to keep everything clean and happy, write into the contract that you, the buyer, have the right to choose the escrow company (who will hold your deposit monies) and the closing agent. You want someone who is neutral, rather than someone who is looking after the interests of the seller. Should the deal fall through, you will want your deposit returned as soon as possible (or sooner).

Agree, in writing, about who will get the interest on the escrow deposits. Sometimes all interest is paid to the buyer, sometimes it is split between buyer and seller, and sometimes escrow funds are held in non-interest-bearing accounts. Interest on escrow monies often becomes a problem when the escrow amount is large and the time period to closing long (several months).

Agree, in writing, how rents, special assessments, and taxes are to be apportioned. Usually it is according to the number of days of ownership in the year from the date of closing. If occupancy agreements allow the sellers to remain in the house for a period of time after the closing, or if the buyer is allowed to take possession before the closing, these apportionments can be altered.

Write in the amount of the real estate commission and who will pay it. *I know, I know!* These details are set down in the listing contract and commission is not your responsibility. On the other hand, it doesn't take much effort to add the clause. You don't want your

WORDS TO *GO!*

Among the dictionary definitions of *assign* is: to transfer (property) to another, especially in trust or for the benefit of creditors.

In a real estate purchase contract, the right to assign is the right to allow another party to fulfill the terms of the agreement.

DON'T GO TO JAIL

This little antic probably won't put you behind bars but it could cause you considerable financial pain and get a lot of people very angry.

Some people (very few, but some) try to negotiate on two properties at the same time. They sign two different purchase contracts, give earnest money checks to two different real estate agents, on two different houses, in two different neighborhoods. They think they're smart. They're going to get a really good deal, right? They can only afford to buy one house; the other contract will fall through and they will be the winners, happy in their bargain.

Maybe and maybe not. What exactly *is* a good deal? There's more to buying a home than how much it costs. Do such people know what they want? What they need? I believe it's better to make the best deal you can on the house you most want than to let the Dollar make the decision for you.

How could a double-dealing buyer lose money? If two sellers were each to accept the offer made on each property, the buyer will lose the earnest money on at least one deal and face the possibility of a suit for specific performance. If the double-dealing buyer had signed buyer-broker contracts with the real estate agents, he or she or they could owe commission on the deal they intentionally let go. It could get messy. Furthermore, if the real estate agents, the sellers, or the neighbors find out what went on, well, our double-dealing friends could spend many years living near people who won't give them a nod in the grocery store. In a way, they'll be in jail.

closing prolonged by a discussion of which agent should get how much money.

The Right to Assign

Adding the right to **assign** your purchase contract takes just three words after your name as the buyer: Percival and Claudia Buyer, *and/or assigns*.

"Why is that important?" you ask. "Haven't we got enough words already?"

Nope! The right to assign gives you power, the power to give or sell the right to purchase the property (in other words, the purchase contract) or to pass it on to your heirs. This right is extremely important in a hot market where you could conceivably sell the property for a higher price before you even closed on it. Remember things can and do happen that radically alter plans.

YOUR CLOSING

Going to your first closing is a bit like getting accepted to college or reporting for a new job. There are so many papers to sign, so many commitments to make—everything is happening so fast, and everything is so important. If you spend a little time in preparation and take the procedure step by step, however, you'll find that it isn't really bad at all.

COMMUNITY CHEST

If you can afford it, buy title insurance for the full purchase price. Title insurance protects against loss resulting from a claim against the property. It does not guarantee that you will own the property forever, but that you will be reimbursed for your expenses and loss if a claim against the title does come up. The fee for title insurance is calculated as a one-time charge paid at the closing. Some buyers include seller payment of title insurance as a part of their negotiations.

For more information about title insurance, contact:
American Land Title Association (ALTA)
1828 L Street NW, Suite 705
Washington, DC 20036
202-296-3671, www.alta.org

The closing procedure is the transfer of title from the seller to the buyer. It will be handled by a closing agent who is by law required to inform you in advance of the charges and of your financial responsibilities. You will be required to bring cash or a cashier's check to the closing or to have your down payment money direct-wired to the closing agent.

Your mortgage lender will probably require title insurance for at least the amount of the mortgage. You will also need to have your hazard insurance and flood insurance (if necessary) in place. Your closing agent will register the deed, pay the necessary taxes, and otherwise tie up loose ends. And you will get the keys.

RULES AND STRATEGIES

- A purchase contract signed only by the buyer is a written offer. A bilateral contract must be executed by all parties to be binding. Each interested party must initial every change.

- Take every word seriously in a purchase contract and don't assume.

- Protect your interests with an attorney review clause.

- Spell out every element of the contract contingencies.

- Avoid misunderstandings by putting negotiated agreements and expectations in writing.

- Include the right to assign in your contract.

- If there are questions or problems at the closing table, have sufficient funds to cover their resolution held in escrow.

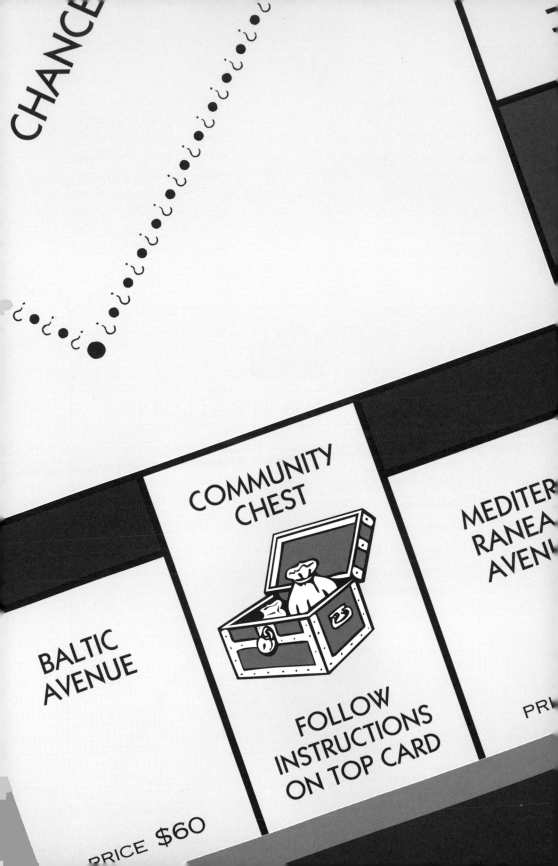

BOARDWALK

PRICE $400

COLLECT $200.00 SALARY AS YOU PASS

GO

,60

PART II

GETTING AROUND

CHAPTER 7
Tax Sales, Foreclosures, and REOs

During the housing boom, subprime mortgages allowed
borrowers with little in the bank to buy homes.
Low initial interest rates on the loans are expiring,
pushing mortgage payments up and sending many
borrowers into default and foreclosure....

—Reuters, San Francisco, November 20, 2007

In the first decade of the twenty-first century, politically correct people don't talk about looming foreclosures, theirs or other people's. But those foreclosures are real and many. From Passamaquoddy, Maine, to Ka Lae, Hawaii, Americans have felt and are feeling financial pressures. Some have been unable to make their scheduled mortgage payments and have lost their homes. This economic stress has created a red-hot foreclosure marketplace for investors with cash and courage.

Foreclosure, bank repossession, and seizure of real estate for unpaid property taxes all begin with default on scheduled payments by men, women, couples, families, and/or small and large businesses in serious financial trouble. Sounds bleak, doesn't it? Could you go willingly into a marketplace where your stairways to success would be built upon other people's financial failure? Could you still feel good about yourself? Sleep at night?

What if you stood to make $100,000 this year in this marketplace? Some people have said they would feel like Piranha waiting for the next body to drop in. And others? Others have said, "That's business. I play by the rules, but I play to win."

How about you? Would you help out a cash-strapped fellow MONOPOLY player by offering to buy Park Place and Boardwalk, each with a hotel, for the price of the land alone?

OK, that might sound like fun. But could you do it if a real family were going to be evicted?

If you can indeed separate real estate business dealings from your emotional responses, if in other words you can keep your head (and the bottom line) in control over your heart, you definitely should read to the end of this chapter. If you're not sure, read it anyway; you'll probably learn something you'll be able to use in another marketplace.

Most young entrepreneurs would likely reply to concern about evicted homeowners by saying, "Get over it, Baby!" And actually, that's good advice. You are now in the investment section of *The MONOPOLY Guide to Real Estate* and to win on this playing field, you must put aside all of your warm and happy thoughts of home. Real estate investment is a business. Purchasing someone else's failure (tax lien properties, foreclosures, and REOs) is always a business venture, a deal that has the potential for tremendous profits, but also, sometimes, for significant losses. There is no room for emotions in the investment sector of this game. Let's look around the foreclosure marketplace and see what we find.

Statistics about abandoned slum housing in our largest cities paint a dark picture, one that has frightened even experienced investors away from big-city investment purchases. But slumlording is only one end of this property spectrum. Today there are financially stressed properties available in virtually every price range.

Small cities, small towns, and even rural areas also have foreclosed and empty buildings that you can buy for the proverbial song. The key property question in this investment marketplace is not *can you afford it* but rather *what can you make of it?* If you think you can answer with an attainable image and a profit figure in mind, your first step is to understand how the building got to the state it's in; your second step is to learn how to acquire it.

TAX LIENS

I keyed *tax* + *lien* + *certificate* into Google yesterday. I got over two million hits. Are you surprised? Especially since you didn't know that the three words together had a special meaning until just now? Tax sales and certificates are big business in the United States. Many people are making money in this marketplace, but only a small percentage of them are really investing in real estate. Let me explain.

WORDS TO *GO!*

A *lien* for unpaid taxes is an encumbrance on the title. Federal, state, or local tax liens take precedence over all other liens including mortgage loans. Properties can be and are seized and sold for unpaid taxes.

Foreclosure proceedings are stimulated by default on a mortgage or trust deed loan. The process will extinguish the ownership rights of the mortgagor (borrower/owner).

In the real estate marketplace, *REO* means *real estate owned.* (In some areas, it is written *ORE: owned real estate.*) These terms are used for properties that the lender (bank) has acquired through default on its loans and foreclosure.

Lis pendens is a phrase we have appropriated from Latin for our law-terms dictionary. It means a pending lawsuit. Lists of *lis pendens* are made public. For prospective investors, these lists are a means of getting information on property that might soon come up for sale.

In rem is Latin also and, literally, means *against a thing (as a right, status, or property).* It is used in the real estate marketplace to signify the stock of buildings and land owned by a city because the buildings have been abandoned. For example, when he took office, Mayor Giuliani was concerned with New York City's vast holdings of in rem housing.

Depending on state law, there are two ways for a property to be sold for unpaid taxes. You can buy a tax-sale deed or a tax-sale certificate. The United States is somewhat evenly divided between deed states and certificate states, and some states allow both. Be aware, however, that such a state law can be changed in any given year by the vote of a legislature. Be sure to check with your state attorney general's office regarding the state's foreclosure laws.

Tax-Sale Deeds

Most tax sales are auctions. Sometimes they take place literally "on the courthouse steps." More often they take place in the town hall or in rented space in a hotel or other public facility.

As in an antiques auction, most tax-sale auctions require that you register with the sheriff or the designated manager of the auction. You are usually given a number placard with which to bid. In theory, your bid must cover the amount of back taxes owed on the property plus the expenses incurred in its seizure and sale. Often your only competition is the mortgage holder. If that is the case in a tax sale, you might as well go home because the bank will win. Mortgage lenders are not about to lose their collateral to unpaid taxes.

In fact, an unpaid tax bill is a valid reason for a lender to start foreclosure proceedings on a mortgage. Most lenders are well into the foreclosure process before a tax sale has even been scheduled. If they are not, it's not from lack of concern about the money involved. There may be some unseen strings attached. Federal laws provide that if there is a government-insured mortgage loan (FHA, HUD, VA, for example) on a property that is to be sold at a tax-forfeit sale, the government agency has one full year to pay the amount due and redeem the property. Don't even *think* about fighting with the government!

If there is no mortgage on a property being sold at a tax-forfeit sale, you may indeed have the chance of picking it up for back taxes and expenses. That could be as little as 10 percent of market value.

BUT! (Isn't there always a "but"?) But the deed you will be given at the tax sale will probably *conditionally* transfer ownership from the delinquent owner to you, the successful bidder. And sometimes a tax-sale deed that does transfer ownership *wholly* to the buyer is held by the municipality *unrecorded* for a period of time. (You don't "own" the property until the deed is recorded.)

Because stress-sale properties are forced sales, they are a high-risk game vehicle. This real estate investment demands patience and perseverance. The **redemption period** is always a factor. And unfortunately, the tax-sale buyer has no control over redemption possibilities. Each state determines its own procedures for transfer of title in a tax-forfeited sale or a foreclosure.

In all but two states, Delaware and New Mexico, there is yet another redemption-period complication. According to law in forty-eight states, all lien holders of record on the tax-delinquent property must be served notice that they have a right-to-redeem priority until the end of the redemption period. ("Lien holders" could include second-mortgage

CHANCE

Don't count on getting occupancy and/or clear title easily or quickly. Most states include *redemption periods* in their tax-sale statutes. These laws allow the delinquent owner to reclaim the property by paying the back taxes and the accumulated expenses and interest over the stated period of time. Redemption periods in the United States run from 180 days to four years.

So if you buy a property at a tax-forfeit sale, you may have the deed in hand, but you may never actually *own* the real estate. Surveys have shown that 90 percent or more of tax deed and certificate sales are redeemed by the delinquent owner or another party of interest.

So what's in it for you, the buyer? Why even go into this jungle with all its vines and thickets? Well, there's money in it. To reclaim the property, the delinquent owner or other eligible party must pay you interest during the redemption period and the interest rate is high. (Fifteen percent or more is not unusual.)

holders, mechanics' liens, condo association unpaid fees, etc.) Even if you win the bid at the auction and the delinquent owner/borrower heads south, these lien holders can claim the property by paying the taxes due, interest, and expenses. The good news, however, is that after the redemption period expires, you will take title and *all prior liens are extinguished.*

In Delaware and New Mexico, liens that are attached to the property prior to the attachment of the tax lien are *not* extinguished. That means that if you do indeed take title to the property, you will owe money to everyone who had attached a lien before the tax-sale business started.

Real estate owners whose property is being sold for back taxes often have many problems. And unfortunately, tax-sale buyers have almost as many problems trying to clear up the results of the former owners' problems. To get clear title, tax-sale buyers might be required to show up in court for an **action to quiet title**.

Taking *possession* of the real estate acquired in a tax-forfeit sale is another problem. Often eviction proceedings against the tax-delinquent former owner are necessary. Sometimes this procedure is slow indeed and subject to still more state and local statutes. (For example, in New Hampshire, a property owner cannot evict a family during the winter.) And not infrequently, the place is a shambles by the time the redemption period has expired and the former owners have moved out.

So at the end of the day, how much did you really pay for this tax-sale bargain property? How much did you pay *after* you have added in all of your expenses? (You can read more about fixer-uppers and how much they cost in the next chapter.) And how much did you pay in personal stress? For some people, tax-forfeit sales are an exciting, challenging, and profitable game. Others choose to play somewhere else.

Tax-Sale Certificates

Believe it or not, buying tax-sale certificates is even more complicated than buying tax-sale deeds. In the states and areas that use certificates, forfeiture of one's property because of tax delinquency does *not* convey ownership to the highest bidder. Instead, a tax-lien certificate is issued.

WORDS TO *GO!*

Action to quiet title is a legal phrase describing a court action to establish rightful ownership of real estate that has been disputed. In every state, all parties with a potential interest in the property are notified that a lawsuit has been filed to determine the validity of the title. The court then hears the case and rules on the matter. The decision establishes *marketable title.* If you and your attorney have done your work carefully, it should go in your favor. Without marketable title, however, the property is unsalable and you will have to work out a settlement with the claimants.

It creates a first priority lien on the property, with a right to foreclose that is subject to the state's statutory right of redemption.

At any time during the redemption period, the delinquent owner can pay the certificate holder the full amount that was paid for the tax certificate, *plus interest,* and sometimes additional expenses and penalty fees. The municipality sets the interest rate. It is usually very high, sometimes as much as 15 or even 20 percent. But still the overwhelming majority of tax-lien certificates are redeemed. Most investors who "buy" tax-delinquent properties make their money on interest and penalty fees.

If by the end of the redemption period, a tax certificate is not redeemed by the tax-delinquent owner or by another eligible person such as an heir or another lien holder, the cost of investing in this property begins to get more expensive, quickly. The tax-lien certificate holder must initiate foreclosure proceedings in order to take title to the property. He or she cannot take possession until the foreclosure process is complete.

After the buyer has clear title, there is yet another trying process: the former owner/occupants must be evicted. If the foreclosure must go to court or if a suit is filed against the property,

COMMUNITY CHEST

A lawsuit is a fruit-tree planted in a lawyer's garden. —*Italian proverb*

your time and money expenditures may run like wild horses who know no fences.

FORECLOSURES

Fear of an unfamiliar process and costs with five or more zeros keep most homebuyers and first-time investors away from the foreclosure marketplace. Just as in tax-forfeit sales, a foreclosure sale can take place "on the courthouse steps." More often, foreclosure auctions take place indoors, at an advertised place.

There will usually be at least one other bidder at a foreclosure auction: the representative of the lender. He or she traditionally opens the bidding with the amount of the balance on the mortgage or with the **upstart price**. If there is no one else bidding, the lender will be given title to the property.

Now doesn't that sound simple? Just like the MONOPOLY game! A mortgage is foreclosed and you hand back the card to the bank. Easy. But it's not quite so easy in the *real* real estate marketplace. First of all there are two rather different financing documents being used in the United States: the mortgage and the deed of trust. The foreclosure procedures are different for each.

The Mortgage Foreclosure

The mortgage foreclosure process starts with a seller in financial trouble. Usually when three months of payments have been missed and the borrower has not responded to inquiries from the lender, a bank attorney initiates foreclosure action. The necessary documents are filed with the clerk of the county where the property is located and a *lis pendens* is filed. If the seller does not respond, the bank attorney submits a report stating the numbers and terms of the mortgage to the court and usually requests that the court appoint a referee. The referee reviews the documents and reports to the court. The judge almost invariably issues a Judgment of Foreclosure and Sale in favor of the foreclosing lender.

The process has then started in public view but state laws govern the amount of time required to settle the action. Most mortgage-loan foreclosures in the United States take from twelve to eighteen months.

The auction to sell foreclosed property must be advertised in accordance with local statutes. At the auction, the referee or other court appointee reads the terms of the sale to the attendees. The auction may be conducted verbally or by sealed written bid. The highest bidder will receive the equivalent of a *purchase contract* and will be required to leave a hefty deposit, usually 10 percent of the purchase price in the form of cash, a money order, bank check, or certified funds. The closing date is usually soon; thirty days is common. And if you can't raise the full purchase price or get financing before the closing date, you will probably lose your deposit money.

WORDS TO *GO!*

The *upstart price* at a mortgage foreclosure auction is the price set by the judge in the Judgment of Foreclosure and Sale. It usually includes the mortgage-loan balance plus unpaid taxes, legal and court costs, and possibly liens and judgments attached to the real estate. It is the floor for the opening bid. If the property sells, the funds are allocated at the closing.

CHANCE

If the property is not purchased at the auction, title is conveyed to the mortgagee (lender). It has then become a REO, also known as a *nonperforming asset.* The lender is free to dispose of (sell) the property in any legal manner.

The Trust Deed Foreclosure

Foreclosing a trust deed generally takes from four to twelve weeks, not months or years. There are no courtroom entanglements because the title is *not* in the borrower's name but rather held by a trustee. (If this sounds confusing, just read about it in Chapter 5 again.) The **power of sale** clause found in all trust deeds is the supercharger that speeds up everything. It literally sidesteps the judicial system.

Here's how it works : When a borrower has not made scheduled payments, the trustee (the party that holds the deed, most often a title insurance company) records a notice of default and sends a copy to the trustor. (Yes, ironically, that's the borrower; the lender is called the *beneficiary*.) After waiting for the period of time required by state statutes, the trustee then posts a notice that the property will be sold at auction. After the posting is first made, there is another period of time during which the borrower (trustor) can make the back payments. If the borrower can't or doesn't make the payment, the property is auctioned. Proceeds go to the lender.

The Challenges, Risks, and Rewards of Stress-Sale Property

Many of you are new to this playing field in the real estate marketplace, so let me take a little time to review the potential rewards and possible risks. Stress-sale property is not a version of the MONOPOLY game for the faint of heart.

- **Money:** Making money is why we play. Once you get to know this marketplace, you'll find many ways to build wealth. Why else would there be literally millions of Websites that come up when you do a search for *foreclosure property* or *tax-lien certificates?* You can subscribe to services that send lists of auctions, lis pendens, even foreclosure notices across the nation. Or you can watch your local newspaper. I suggest you start locally.

- **Money without Work:** With more than 90 percent (some say more than 97 percent) of tax-lien certificate properties being reclaimed during the redemption period, aren't these certificates a low-risk, high-return way to invest money? It certainly looks that way on

WORDS TO *GO!*

The *power of sale* clause is found in all trust deed agreements. It allows the trustee to sell the property at public auction *without* getting permission from the courts.

paper, but what happens if the property is *not* redeemed by anyone with a legal interest in it? Now you have a piece of paper that says you can do the work to get the deed. Do you really want to do a foreclosure and an eviction and then sell the property? Do you really have any choice?

- **No Mortgage Contingency:** As I mentioned in Chapter 6, the mortgage contingency is a major element in the protective paperwork that you sign when making a real estate deal. But there is no mortgage contingency in the auction contract. If you can't get the purchase money in time for the closing, you lose your escrow deposit. You'll not find a lot of friendly helpers in this version of the game.

- **No Inspection Contingency:** Sometimes you just can't get inside of a house that is up for auction; it has been boarded up or the current occupants won't let you in. On the other hand, sometimes there are contact numbers in the foreclosure notices through which you can arrange a showing. In some cases, you may even be able to hire a professional inspector to go through the property and give you a report. But nothing in that report will be a negotiating tool because there is no negotiating. The report might affect the number you choose for your top-dollar bid, however.

- **As-Is Condition:** In stress-sale property transfers, the lender usually promises nothing. You are buying everything that is permanently attached to a certain piece of the Earth. You may not know if the plumbing works, if the heating system heats, if the septic system drains, if the roof leaks, or if the attic has been converted to a resort condominium for squirrels.

- **Quick Closing:** Closings on stress-sale properties are usually scheduled in thirty days, more or less. This can be either good or bad. If you have the money and are anxious to get the process started so that you can flip the property and take your profit, a quick closing is good. If you must go out and find financing for your purchase, a thirty-day closing date may feel awfully tight.

- **State Laws Regarding Redemption Periods:** Take some time to talk with your state attorney general's office or a good real estate lawyer near you. Before entering into the stress-sale property game,

COMMUNITY CHEST

you absolutely *must* know how your state laws will affect your ownership strategy and your chances to make a sizeable profit.

• **Clouds on the Title:** The deed the lender gives you on a foreclosed property will not guarantee clear title. Liens or other encumbrances might surface after the auction or the closing. Sometimes it is very difficult to get title insurance on stress-sale property. Also check with the lender's attorney or the foreclosure referee to ascertain what kind of lien is being foreclosed. If you are bidding on a second-mortgage foreclosure, you will be buying a lien, not a house. You will have an ownership interest in the house but it will be subject to the first mortgage. Some first-mortgage lenders allow the top bidder on the second-mortgage foreclosure to assume the first mortgage. These arrangements might even be made *before* you go to the auction, to be enacted if you are indeed the top bidder. Other auction bidders who plan to live in the house make arrangements for a new mortgage that will cover the outstanding balances on both the first and second mortgage loans. If everything works out, you, the bidder, will take possession of the house (after you get the original owner out, that is).

- **Evicting the Owners:** It could take a long time and you might not recognize the property when you finally do get possession. Talk with your lawyer about eviction procedures in your state and municipality *before* you buy at auction. This is a situation where what you don't know really can hurt you.

- **Evicting Tenants:** Some leases survive a change of ownership. If you buy a multifamily house at auction, you may have to accept the tenants until the termination date of their lease or leases. If a lease does not survive the change of ownership, you can start the eviction process immediately after the closing, but be aware that it may take a while.

REOS OR NONPERFORMING ASSETS

Buying bank-owned property directly from the lender is usually less risky and less troublesome than buying at auction, but also, often, less potentially profitable. Most REOs are listed either with Realtors or with licensed sales agents. Few lenders are in the business of marketing property for sale. They would rather work with money.

The Sources of REOs

So how do lenders get their "nonperforming assets"? We just talked about foreclosures and tax-sale auctions, but that's not the *all* of it. With foreclosure looming, some homeowners try to protect their public image and credit rating by turning the property over to the lender. This happens more frequently when there is a small amount of equity in the property because the borrower has little to lose (as with so-called subprime loans). The lender is not required by law to accept a **deed in lieu of foreclosure** (sometimes called a *friendly foreclosure*) but it is usually less expensive and less time consuming than initiating foreclosure proceedings.

Because lenders incur fewer expenditures and time delays, deed in lieu of foreclosure is also preferable to lenders when market prices have

CHANCE

Federal regulations prohibit lenders from "dumping" foreclosed property into neighborhood real estate listings at prices that are pennies on the dollar of fair market value. So you'll find that most REOs are listed at or near the going price for the neighborhood. But . . .

"Bank-owned" does not mean nonnegotiable. You can make an offer and present your reasons why the property should sell at a lower figure. There will probably be some degree of softness in the price, depending on market conditions. Much more likely, however, you can negotiate for lender concessions on mortgage terms including interest rate and points, closing date, and closing costs. Some buyers of REOs pay no points, no closing costs, and no fee for title insurance, and they get a mortgage loan that is written at an interest rate lower than the best (lowest) going market rate.

Be cool, not too anxious, not too quick. This is a business deal.

fallen and the property is now worth less than the original price. Owners who have considerable equity in a property, however, should think twice before choosing this easy way out. Why? Well, if a lender forecloses and the auction bidding goes higher than the debt-balance-plus-costs, the surplus must be turned over to the mortgagor (borrower).

"Well, that's OK," you say. At least the borrower gets something.

It's not OK, really. If the property sold at a price higher than the mortgage balance in an auction, what might it have sold for in the marketplace? And the borrower/owner gets only what's left after all expenses are deducted. Owners or borrowers should think before they give up their houses without making efforts *and* they should make appointments to talk with their lenders.

The U.S. Department of Housing and Urban Development (HUD) estimates that less than 50 percent of homeowners who are facing foreclosure contact their lenders. Whether because of fear, shame, or simply lack of knowledge, these desperate homeowners are

CHANCE

If you buy one of the few finished or "almost finished" units in a bankrupt development, be aware that you will have to live with unfinished landscaping (dirt and dust) and unfinished construction nearby. This could be an attractive hazard for young children.

Even though your purchase price will probably be well below the market value if the development were complete, there is some financial risk. Until another developer takes over, you won't know for sure what will be built on the undeveloped land. For example, a new developer /buyer and the lender could come up with a plan to re-subdivide the land. If you had bought a single-family house, you could be one of a dozen such houses facing the prospect of high-rise rental apartment buildings to be built on three sides of your little group.

giving up a negotiated chance to save their homes. Once contacted, many lenders will work out new terms and payment schedules for mortgagors in distress.

Another source of nonperforming assets in lenders' portfolios is the failed developer. When a **plat plan** or a master deed is filed with a town's planning board, the subject property is usually raw land. Millions of dollars are needed to create buildings, roads, landscaping, and utilities. Most developers borrow almost all of the money.

A builder/developer can go bankrupt for any number of reasons. Sometimes foreclosure is an unnecessary step for the lender because the loan was structured as a **joint venture**. The builder signs off, but the lender then holds title to a tract of land with buildings in various stages of completion. Because banks are definitely *not* in the business of building houses, most lenders try to find another developer. Often, however, the "almost finished" properties are sold to individual bidders. The prices are usually well below market value, but the property may require the buyer to invest some money in completion costs in order to get a **certificate of occupancy (CofO)** from the town.

UNCLE SAM, FANNIE MAE, AND FRIENDS

The United States government and the secondary mortgage market own a lot of foreclosed properties that they would like to sell. But in this free country, each group has its own selling procedures. The following is a quick list with some contact points where you can get more information if you are interested.

Fannie Mae

Fannie Mae (nee *The Federal National Mortgage Association*) is the largest buyer of mortgages in the American secondary mortgage market. Essentially, the organization hires real estate brokers to sell its REOs. You can

WORDS TO *GO!*

Deed in lieu of foreclosure is a mutual agreement between the borrower and the lender to settle the debt by the owner *offering* and the lender *accepting* title to the property. Second mortgages and all other liens remain in effect.

Plat plan (no, it is not plot plan!) or *plat map* is a surveyor's or architect's drawing showing how a parcel of land is to be divided into lots. It does not show topography.

In the real estate marketplace, a *joint venture* (sometimes called *participation financing*) is an arrangement between an entrepreneur and a lender in which the lender puts up all or part of the required cash in return for a share of the profits.

A *certificate of occupancy* is a written statement by the local buildings inspector that the property in question is approved for occupancy. Regarding new construction, in most areas you cannot close title without it.

get a list of Fannie Mae foreclosed property that includes property specs and the names and contact information for approved real estate brokers on the Web at *www.FannieMae.com.* (Go to the FannieMae-Owned Property Search page.) Favorable mortgage terms are frequently offered.

Freddie Mac

Freddie Mac was once *The Federal Home Loan Mortgage Corporation,* but he changed his name. Like Fannie Mae, this publicly chartered corporation is a major player in the secondary mortgage market and they too get foreclosures. They sell through real estate brokers who also manage the properties in each state. *Home Steps Asset Services* is their division that markets foreclosed homes. They often offer special financing for qualified buyers. Contact them at *www.HomeSteps.com.* By phone you'll have to look up FreddieMac in the directory and ask them for HomeSteps contacts near you.

HUD

HUD—sounds tough, doesn't it? But we all know this huge organization as the United States Department of Housing and Urban Development. The Federal Housing Administration (FHA) is a part of the HUD family and it sells houses through FHA Foreclosures or HUD Sales. A prospective buyer must work with HUD's designated real estate agents in the area.

The FHA acquires property through the foreclosure of loans that it has insured. When the property is foreclosed, the FHA has a year to pay the lender the balance due on the mortgage, expenses incurred by the foreclosure, and all other liens, and then take title. These properties are then auctioned through sealed bids that must include 10 percent of the bid price as earnest money.

To get the names of designated real estate agents and information on upcoming auctions, call the HUD phone number listed in your directory. On the Internet, go to the HUD homepage at *www.HUD.gov* and select Surplus/Excess Properties or HUD Homes. Or try *www.FHA.gov* under Homes for Sale. HUD/FHA auctions are also advertised in local newspapers.

VA

Like the FHA, the Department of Veterans' Affairs acquires property when loans that it has guaranteed are foreclosed. The VA's foreclosed property is handled by the firm of Ocwen Loan Servicing, LLC in West Palm Beach, Florida. You can get listings of VA REOs for sale at *www.ocwen.com*. You do not have to be a veteran or a member of the military to buy a VA foreclosure.

By phone, you can try to get selling information by starting at your local VA office. Or, more effectively, you can search their Website at *www.VA.gov*. Go to the Home Loan Guaranty Services Web page and you will be referred to other sites for more information.

FDIC

We all know FDIC as the Federal Deposit Insurance Corporation, the friendly government entity that insures our money against bank failures. It rarely makes the headlines, except back in the 1980s when Saving Banks failed across the nation. That crisis was the stimulus for the creation of the RTC (Resolution Trust Corporation) that disposed of foreclosures on real estate of all kinds. Today the RTC has quietly evaporated, but you can access FDIC-owned foreclosures at *www.FDIC.gov*. Go to Asset Sales on the horizontal site bar at the top of the page.

THE SAFER SIDE OF STRESS-SALE PROPERTY PURCHASES

"Why bother with REOs?" you ask. "Most of them are listed pretty close to everything else in the neighborhood."

That's true and there may or may not be a huge amount of negotiating room. But if you really want to own and live in the house rather than flip the ownership for profit, you'll find a lot of plus marks in the REO corner of the real estate marketplace.

Most lenders attempt to bring their REOs up to marketable standards before listing them for sale. The former owners and any tenants are usually evicted; most REO sellers work to remove liens and obtain clear title; often REO sellers make cosmetic repairs to the property; and a buyer can usually negotiate for more extensive repairs if structural problems are discovered.

Buying a REO is much like buying from the seller down the block; you can make an offer on a lender-owned property with a contract similar to one you would use in an ordinary seller/buyer purchase. And you can negotiate. And the best part is that you can negotiate over financing, often to get extremely favorable terms.

WHAT'S IN THIS MARKETPLACE?

There is a bell curve of stress-sale real estate purchases available to beginning investors. At one end are the vacant apartment buildings, often abandoned and city owned. They are for the few well-experienced investors with plenty of wherewithall. There are many thousands of them available across the nation, and they can sometimes be bought for a dollar. But unless you are experienced in rehabilitation and reconstruction, neighborhood regentrification, and building management, I suggest that you do not start out by buying an abandoned apartment building, no matter how cheap.

At the other end of the bell curve are seaside estates and large tracts of land. Believe it or not, both come up for auction from time to time. But if you are still learning your way around this marketplace, don't buy them! At least not now. The estates simply require too much on-hand cash, not only in purchase price but also in property taxes and maintenance costs. Raw land is always a high-risk investment.

So what's in the bubble in the middle of the bell curve? You'll find a bit of almost everything else in the marketplace. Foreclosures and tax forfeiture can happen to any kind of person or property. Your job is to choose a property that is suitable to your current financial parameters, your knowledge and skills, and your goals. The biggest part of the bell curve's bulge will be filled with multifamily houses, fixer-uppers, small apartment buildings (six to eight units), mixed-use buildings, condos, and vacations homes. Condos and condo vacation homes are the easiest to manage because the communities are governed and maintained by boards of directors.

RULES AND STRATEGIES

- Few investors who buy tax-lien certificates or tax-sale deeds actually take title to the properties they bid on. Expect to make your money in interest and penalty fees.

- The owner's rights of redemption vary from state to state. Know your state laws.

- Obtaining clear title, evicting occupants, and accepting the property in as-is condition are major concerns in the stress-sale marketplace. Pay attention to details.

- Several government and government-supported companies offer foreclosed property for sale to the general public. Search around on the Web.

- REOs (real estate-owned by the lender through foreclosure) are usually listed in the marketplace at or near fair market value. They are, however, negotiable. Financing terms are also negotiable. Ask for everything you want.

- To enter the stress-sale marketplace, choose an investment vehicle you can manage. You may not be ready to refurbish a run-down house on Baltic Avenue or pay the taxes on that property on Park Place. But you noticed that the player who owns St. James Place is a little short of cash. Hmmmm . . .

CHAPTER 8
The Fixer-Upper

Something made greater by ourselves
and in turn that makes us greater.

—Maya Angelou (1928–), American poet and
author, a definition of work from "The Black
Scholar Interviews Maya Angelou"

Gather ingredients, mix well, cook, flip, douse with sweet syrup, and enjoy! A recipe for pancakes? No, this is a get-rich-quick scheme for rundown properties in a slow market—the sweet syrup being profit, of course. You'll read the phrase in newspapers, magazines, and book titles; hear it on the radio; and see it on TV: *flipping property.* I wish it were so easy.

The motivation is money, of course. Why else would someone want to buy a house that screams out for both work and time commitment, not to mention a significant cash investment? But people do. In fact, a lot of people do. The idea wouldn't be so popular in the real estate marketplace if there weren't some significant success stories being discussed at cocktail parties, presented at expensive seminars, and broadcast on the airways. Yes, it *can* work, if you choose the right property.

TWO ROADS/ONE GOAL

Everyone who seriously considers buying a property in need of repair sees the profit potential in bringing it up to the standards of the surrounding property and/or improving its market appeal. But the highway to this goal splits into two different roads. In some ways the pavement on each road is quite different, in some ways very similar. The directional signs at the fork say HOME and INVESTMENT.

If you buy a fixer-upper to be your home while you do the fixing up, the potential profits increase because you will be able to take advantage of homeowners' tax benefits and because you can choose to spread the cost of improvements over time. (You will be making mortgage payments rather than paying rent, so your investment will provide you with shelter while you do the work to make it better.)

But be aware of the inevitable annoyance factors in living with a work in progress. Consider the increased risks for small children when nails, hammers, saws, paint, and other tools are a part of day-to-day life. Be aware that "the house" will demand a lot of your free time. And

COMMUNITY CHEST

Your *Uncle Sam* encourages homeownership. He even lets you skip paying taxes on the profits you make when selling your homes over your lifetime. To qualify for this tax exemption, the house must be your primary residence and you must have lived in it for at least two years. For a married couple filing jointly, $500,000 of *profit* is exempt from capital gains tax. For a single person, head of household, or married person filing separately, $250,000 of profit is exempt from capital gains tax.

Unlike the tax law prior to 1997, you need *not* buy a more expensive house to qualify for the exemption. Even more important, it is *not* a one-time-only exemption. You can use it again and again, but not more often than once in two years.

DON'T GO TO JAIL

Even among condos, there are opportunities for fixer-upper bargains. The exterior may look like every other condo in the community, but the interior may be begging for some TLC (tender loving care). If there are a number of units for sale in a condo community, the one in need of cosmetic repair will likely sell at below-market value. But don't let your creativity get out of control. You can't make any changes to the exterior (not even change the color of the front door) without approval from the board of directors. Community rules about changes can even affect the interior. For example, the condo is a townhouse style (two stories) and you're sure that an elevator (personal size) would greatly enhance its market value. The board may rightly refuse to let you add the elevator shaft to the exterior. If you start without permission, you'll be in trouble with the law.

money. And be aware that this is the place where you will *live*, the place that you will come home to in the evening. The location of the property you choose to fix up will be extremely important because your investment will be in *your* neighborhood. You won't be able to escape to someplace else when the working day is done. When you buy a fixer-upper to be your home, you should love it, at least a little.

If you buy a fixer-upper purely as an investment and never intend to occupy it, the cost of necessary repairs and the time needed to do them become more significant factors in your potential profit. Remember, you will be making mortgage payments, tax payments, and insurance payments during your ownership period. Unless the property is generating income, those payments must be subtracted from the profit number you seek. The pace of the marketplace (more on this in Chapter 11) will also be a major factor in your investment success, because it will affect not only marketing time but also potential appreciation.

Judge the location of your fixer-upper purchase even more carefully than the condition. You can fix or fix up almost anything, but the value, nature, and appearance of the properties adjacent to yours and within the neighborhood will determine the top limits of your profit. Observe carefully, crunch the numbers, and don't let emotions into your deal.

A QUESTION OF CHARACTER

Are you right for the fixer-upper real estate game? It really isn't everyone's cup of tea. After buying their first home, many people never want to do it again, and if that first home was a fixer-upper, many people swear they *won't* do it again. The fixer-upper is a type of purchase that makes many demands on the buyer/owner. In alphabetical order, let's look at some of the personality traits that increase the odds for success.

Assertiveness

You must be willing to make things happen. Very little will get done if you wait for a flooring salesperson to come to your door and offer you the "best deal you can find anywhere." You've got to go out and look at what products are available at what price.

WORDS TO *GO!*

Setback lines are part of local zoning ordinances. They establish the closest distance from each property boundary line where improvements can be built. Typically the setback from the street is the greatest distance. Generally, other houses in the neighborhood comply with the same setback creating relatively even frontage on the road. Side setback lines are usually closer to the lot line and determine the minimum distance between two buildings.

CHANCE

If you bang your thumb almost as often as you hit the nail on the head, you may want to forget about fixer-uppers and consider some other investment vehicles. Subcontractors are expensive. Every job you can do yourself or with friends and family contributes to your bottom-line profit.

If your neighbor tells you the town won't let you add on a garage because it will come too close to his lot line, you've got to check the zoning laws, get out your plat plan (survey), and measure the **setback lines**. Will your garage be just inside the dotted line or just over it? If the garage will be over the line, even an inch, you must make a plan, petition for a variance (see Chapter 1), and present it to the planning board. If you don't, you will never get that garage, legally.

Attention to Detail

You won't need a Sherlock Holmes-style magnifying glass to succeed in fixer-uppers, but you will need a mind that respects numbers and cares about what's beneath surface appearance. You *must* calculate probable costs in doing the fix-up *before* you make an offer. And you must *not* calculate by the ballpark method. If you are redoing a kitchen, for example, you can't say "Yeah, about $15,000." You should list every element in the kitchen makeover with a documented estimate of cost. You will be amazed at how fast a few dollars here and a few dollars there can add up at the bottom line.

You also must pay attention to the details of your contracts with subcontractors and workers and about the quality of their work. Remember: the quality of the work remains long after the paycheck is cashed. Whether you are doing the work yourself or you are paying to have it done, "that's good enough" will come back to haunt you.

Awareness

Awareness doesn't show up on IQ tests. I've known men and women who were brilliant academically and couldn't tell you that it was likely to rain today. Awareness is paying attention, consciously and subconsciously.

To be aware of whether the real estate marketplace is quickening or slowing down, you have to read newspaper articles, consider the economic statistics, talk with professionals, and then capture the beat. The talent for awareness often lies in putting together what is said and unsaid, what is promised and done or not done. Awareness of where a *neighborhood* is heading on the quality-of-life scale can significantly add to your wealth. If you know New York City, think of the Harlem brownstones.

Creativity

Creativity is mostly the ability to see what isn't there. Think of two adjoining rooms crammed with stuff. The carpeting is patterned with pet stains, three dog crates are under the dining room table, and the cats' litter box is behind the couch. The chandelier has been removed and wires protrude from the ceiling. Baskets of laundry are strategically situated about the room, and you have to walk around the ironing board.

OK, you have the picture. Now, can you picture those rooms with the wall between them taken down? They have become a living room with a dining ell. Bamboo hardwood flooring has been installed and oriental area rugs add an artistic touch. The walls are the color of French vanilla ice cream, the windows are clean, and the sun is streaming in.

If you can do that mental transformation, you are a prime candidate for fixer-upper investment. Just remember to balance your creativity with your accounting skills.

Perseverance

You've got to stay the course in this investment vehicle. Partly finished fixer-uppers sell more slowly than their originals. To prospective buyers, it seems that the renovations that have been completed only highlight what *else* has to be done.

DON'T GO TO JAIL

If your plans include changing the exterior shape of the building or changing the use of the building, don't assume that you can take care of the details after you close. The town may say *"No way!"* and you'll be stuck in your boat without an oar. Put a contingency in your contract that makes the deal subject to planning board approval for the changes you want to make. This will delay the closing a bit, but consider it insurance.

Self-Confidence

If you don't believe that you can and will succeed, you probably won't. But beware of overconfidence. Some jobs really do require professionals. Trying to do the impossible or overly risky can end up costing you more money than you could possibly have saved with the do-it-yourself approach.

Willingness to Take Risks

Fear of the unknown freezes some people. But is there any activity here on Earth without some risk? Real estate is considered a safe investment for most people, but some do lose money on this playing field. When they do, there are often lots of zeros involved.

So what should *you* do? Well, if you want to sail to somewhere, you must first leave port. Don't do anything impulsively. Study the facts. Consider your odds, your options, and your opportunities. Then act. Putting your money under your mattress won't improve the quality of your life.

FINDING THE ONE FOR YOU

Most inexperienced homebuyers stumble on fixer-uppers because the advertised price is lower than similar properties at which they have been looking. Some people are astounded when they walk in the front door and see the proverbial "mess." Those who are better prepared are knowledgeable homebuyers who are seeking a less-costly doorway into the Homeowners' Club, and investors. They come with their digital cameras and notebooks.

Properties with foreclosure looming and post-auction REOs (see Chapter 7) are usually good hunting grounds for the fixer-upper buyer. Many are low or moderately priced or open to extensive negotiation.

Owner-occupied or held properties that have languished on the market because of disrepair also show up regularly, and believe it or not, in every price bracket. I once looked at a house in Sawgrass, a very upscale golf community in northern Florida. The property was vacant, but the owners must have played a lot of golf while they lived in it because nothing had been done to maintain a good appearance, much less enhance it. Grout crumbled from between the bathroom tiles wherever the mold would let it. In the kitchen, the pattern of the glass stovetop could not be seen through the caked grease. A dog had left his artwork in the claw medium on the doors to the outside. The swimming pool was slime green. Need I go on?

If you tell your real estate agent that you are looking for a fixer-upper at an incentive price, he or she will know which properties to show you. But no matter how low the price seems at first inspection, don't make an offer based on asking price. Work the numbers. Get

CHANCE

No, you won't look foolish if you return several times to reinspect fixer-upper properties. Some savvy buyers even schedule (and pay for) a professional inspection before they make their first offer. The inspector will list the problems and can often help to estimate the cost of repairs. The inspection report then becomes a negotiating tool.

accurate estimates for the cost of bringing the property up to your specific standards. Remember, the asking price is set by the seller. (Sometimes I think there is even an *inverse* correlation between good maintenance and price!)

HOW TO SPOT A GOOD DEAL

Investing in fixer-uppers is more than finding a cute house that has been ignored for too long. You've got to consider the location, the market appeal, the costs of buying, and the costs of fixing because, at some point, you will be selling. Following are some clues.

About Location

- Look carefully at fixer-uppers in areas that are close to higher-priced neighborhoods or to new construction.
- Watch for neighborhoods experiencing revitalization, especially where scattered houses have already been **refurbished** or **renovated**. If you look in established historic preservation areas, you will have to comply with state and federal laws for **restoration** but you will have an invisible protective shield around your investment property.
- Look for a property on a low-traffic street.
- Check out areas that are stable and well kept and in which your prospective property is among the smallest and/or the only run-down house.

About Market Appeal

Whenever you buy property, you should always consider it from a seller's point of view. Some things just bring in more prospective buyers and usually generate higher offers:

- At least one bath (or lavatory) per floor.
- An eat-in kitchen.
- A gathering room (also called a family room or media room) on the main floor.
- A garage or carport.
- Lots of sunlight; dark houses sell more slowly.

WORDS TO *GO!*

Fixer-upper words are often tossed about interchangeably on this playing field. Following are some definitions, just for clarity.

Refurbishing: This requires superficial work that most experienced homeowners can do with or without some hired help. For example, scrubbing and cleaning fixtures and surfaces; painting interior surfaces; painting the exterior; removing wallpaper and repapering; replacing broken windows; sanding and refinishing wood floors; spackling holes or cracks in wallboard or plaster; replacing gouged, scratched, or dented moldings; replacing electrical fixtures; trimming and landscaping the lot.

Renovation: The dictionary definition is "restore to life, vigor; revive; renew," and that pretty much says it all. Renovation usually includes everything listed under *refurbishing* above and kitchen and bathroom remodeling including new cabinets, countertops, fixtures, and appliances; new windows, skylights, sliders, etc; new carpeting or flooring; and sometimes new siding.

Rehabilitation: This is another "restore-to-life" word, but with the connotation of *make livable again.* When you say you are "rehabbing" a building, most people get the idea that you are virtually gutting and rebuilding. In addition to the changes listed above, rehabilitation can include a new roof, siding, insulation, stairways, heating, plumbing, waste disposal, electrical systems, and even the foundation.

Restoration: In the real estate marketplace, *restoration* usually means historic restoration; all changes must comply with state and federal statutes.

WHAT THE NUMBERS MEAN

How does a buyer decide on the opening bid for a fixer-upper? It should never be an impulse number: "Ahhh, let's try $200,000." And it should never be a percentage of the asking price: "Ahhh, let's see . . . the agent said houses are selling within 5 percent of asking price. They're asking $265,000. Let's offer $238,500, as that's 10 percent off." Stop! Think again! What if the property is only worth $225,000, on a good day?

Start by estimating the fair market value of the property if it were in good condition or at least comparable to the other similar houses in the neighborhood. Your real estate agent can get you comps, or you can go on the Web and get the selling prices in the neighborhood. Key *home sold prices* into a search engine and you'll get plenty of choices.

Now add up all the estimates for the cost of work, repairs, and replacements that will be necessary to bring the property in line with the neighborhood. Subtract that figure from the market value of the house if it were in good condition. Now you have *probable value as is*. But you want to make money on this deal, not just break even, and you don't even have a breakeven number yet.

Start another line of figures. If you are an investor, add up the cost of carrying the mortgage, taxes, and insurance during the period you intend to own the house. (This step does not apply to the homebuyer who will live in the house.) Estimate the real estate commission on the probable selling price after repairs have been made. Estimate your federal capital gains tax; it will be lower if you hold the property for one year or more. (This does not apply to homeowners.) Estimate your closing costs for both the purchase and the sale. Add up all these figures and subtract the total from the probable value as is. Now you have your breakeven figure.

The next question is, *how much money do you want to make?* Do you want to double your investment? Doing that is easier than you think. For example, let's use the $265,000 house we mentioned above:

A: Asking price: $265,000

B: Probable value today as is: $225,000
   (calculated using the factors above)

C: Probable value with repairs completed: $280,000

D: Probable cost of repairs: $25,000

Subtract D from C to get your
working number for value. ($255,000)

E. Miscellaneous, closing, and carrying costs: $14,000

F. Estimated real estate commission on sale: $15,000

Subtract E and F (total : $29,000) from your working number $255,000; that equals $226,000. At that purchase price you break even selling in a year. (It is possible to change these numbers with a short-term rental.)

Now let's say you are using $10,000 as the down payment for a government-insured mortgage. And assume you want to double your money.

COMMUNITY CHEST

Some state-government agencies are making efforts to renew our cities and are offering financing help to buyers of inner-city properties in need of repairs. You can contact your state or local housing departments for more information. Or you can go on the Web for information regarding the 180+ public agencies that provide mortgaging assistance. Just go to the box that lists state agencies and click on your state. You can get the contact information you need at:

National Council of State Housing Agencies
444 North Capitol Street NW, Suite 438, Washington, DC 20001
202-624-7710, www.ncsha.org

To turn your $10,000 into $20,000 (money that you take away from the closing table), you have to buy the house at $216,000. Depending on the pace of the local marketplace, start your negotiating between $198,000 and $210,000. (Use the higher number in a faster market.)

These numbers are not precise, of course. We haven't even factored in federal taxes. But you get the idea.

The fixer-upper playing field calls for tough, professional-grade negotiating. There's no room for tears. Be prepared to walk away before you'll go above your top price of $216,000. And don't worry too much about someone else stealing the house from you. You crunched the numbers, and you know $226,000 is not a good deal unless the person intends to live in the property for a number of years. And if someone does, you will find another property. There are too many fish in the sea to cry about the one that got away.

THE BEST AND THE WORST RETURNS

Rarely does everything go as planned; rarely do we get to do everything we want. So it works in the MONOPOLY game, in the real estate marketplace, and in our lives. In the Fixer-Upper Game, those words are in the rulebook!

Unless you plan to make the fixer-upper you buy into your home and do the improvements over a long period of time, you are going to have to make choices. Sure, with unlimited funds you could make the *place* into a *palace*. (It only takes one extra "a" to make the difference in the two words!) But get real! A palace might not fit into this neighborhood, and you will want to do the improvements that will bring in the best return on your time and money. Let's look at some examples.

Low Cost with Probable High Return

If you want to spend minimal dollars but improve the property enough to make it attractive to prospective buyers; if you want them to be willing to pay a price close to or even above neighborhood market value; if you want to speed up the resale time, then consider the following projects.

- **Exterior and interior painting:** Painting is said to return its cost outlay tenfold. Choose neutral colors.

- **Cleaning and landscaping:** Cut back overgrown everything. Fill in bare spots on the lawn and remove toys, teenage cars, and mops. Curb appeal still counts.
- **New kitchen floor:** Why? I don't know. Perhaps people still think of the kitchen as the heart of the home. The new laminates are relatively inexpensive and inevitably elicit *ooohs* and *ahhhhs*.
- **New wall-to-wall carpeting or refinished hardwood floors:** There's something about dirty flooring that really turns off buyers; maybe they imagine themselves going barefoot. Anyway watch for sales or check out the large carpeting warehouses. Often rolls large enough to do your whole house are considered remnants and are sold for 50 percent off and more. Choose neutral colors.
- **New lighting fixtures:** Light is a subliminal source of security. Make the house bright and stylish. Lighting doesn't have to cost a lot; it just has to look appropriate.
- **New faucets:** Rusting, pitted plumbing fixtures are repulsive to most buyers. Give them shiny new ones.

High Cost with Higher Return

OK, everyone else in the neighborhood has upgraded his house decades ago. You just bought the dwarf, the orphan, the poor relation. And you want to turn it into a Matt Damon or maybe even a Nicole Kidman (well, on a bad hair day). What should you do? Start out by doing all of the improvements under "Low Cost with Probable High Return" above and add the following:

- **Kitchen remodeling:** Often buyers judge the quality of a house by its kitchen and bathrooms. This is an expensive project but it can turn a 1950s' mediocre ranch into an oh-I've-always-wanted-a-kitchen-like-that bestseller. You must do it all (cabinets, countertops, and appliances), because partial jobs look patchy.
- **Bathroom remodeling:** Consider ceramic tile flooring, new fixtures, new cabinets, new mirrors, and new lighting. Installation of a full-wall mirror behind the sink-cabinet can make an older bathroom look, well, WOW!

- **New windows:** One of the biggest incentives to a sale is the replacement of all old single-pane windows and triple-track storms with new insulating windows. Get a name brand; you'll be surprised about how impressed buyers will be.
- **New roof:** No one will climb up and say, "oh, how beautiful!" But buyers do appreciate the words "new roof" on the listing sheet. The new roof is invariably used in negotiating and it invariably increases the offer. (Perhaps because buyers recognize and fear this large out-of-pocket expense.)
- **Addition of a bathroom:** Even a half-bath counts! No one wants to buy a one-bathroom home if they can possibly help it. Even new senior-citizen one-bedroom condos now have two bathrooms.
- **Addition of a garage:** A garage is more important in the north with its ice and slush than in the south, but a garage is a plus everywhere.

Costly but Little or No Return

People expect that a fine restaurant will have tablecloths, linen napkins, and a courteous wait staff. It would be fruitless, however, to advertise those features to help justify the high prices for the food. In the real estate marketplace, buyers also expect that certain structural elements and systems will be functioning properly. If they aren't, your prospective buyers may be scared off.

Fix the problems, but don't bang drums and toot horns about what you have done. And don't increase the asking price to cover your costs! Advertising that certain major problems have been repaired will actually hurt your deal. Document the repairs when they were done, who did them, what they cost, and all warranties that continue after change of ownership. Use this information to your advantage at the negotiating table.

- **Bracing, buttressing, or rebuilding the foundation:** If necessary, you really have to do the job, but don't talk about it more than you absolutely must. Buyers get very nervous about foundation problems.
- **Radon remediation, lead paint or asbestos removal, or elimination of other health hazards:** Keep the paperwork. You'll need to prove

what was done and that the provider assures that the problem has been solved.

- **Decontaminating soil around a once-buried oil tank:** Twenty years ago buried oil tanks were definitely *in!* Consider that you could bury 1,000 gallons of oil in the in-ground tank, and save all that garage or basement space needed for storage tanks. Then it was discovered that some of those huge tanks started to leak after a while. And the oil contaminated the soil, sometimes the soil near wells or water supplies. The federal government got into the act (the Environmental Protection Agency), and the nightmare is still growing.
- **Termite damage repair or termite eradication:** Buyers don't even want to *hear* the word *termite.* Most exterminators give a written guarantee.
- **Ant infestation:** Especially in warmer climates, carpenter ants or red ants may have built a whole colony behind the walls. Hire an exterminator if you see them coming out of cracks or places where the moldings join. Spraying with grocery-store-shelf ant killer just won't do the job.
- **Regrading to eliminate water seepage and/or waterproofing the foundation:** Water can do a great deal of damage, and it is insidious in its ability to find new ways into a basement. Buyers are suspicious of wet basements. If you are asked about it, explain what has been done and why.
- **New well, pumping equipment, filtration system, and storage tank:** Buyers will want to know what was wrong with the old one, but most will be happy to have a new system. Don't expect a jump in fair market value, however.
- **New septic tank, dry well, or leech lines:** Same as new well.
- **Chimney repairs:** Everyone loves a fireplace, but not everyone wants to pay extra for it. Most home inspectors will catch chimney problems, and they need to be attended to.

SOME GOOD DEALS ON FINANCING

As I mentioned in Chapter 7, REOs are a good source for extraordinary financing, not from a loan shark but from a reputable lender. And do you see that tall guy over there in red-and-white-striped

COMMUNITY CHEST

Never bend your head. Always hold it high. Look the world straight in the eye.

> —Helen Keller (1880–1968), American author, lecturer, and advocate for persons with severe disabilities

If you are caught with high-cost, no-financial-return problems, buckle down and do what has to be done. Playing Cover-up usually leads to more problems. Following are some places where you can get good advice.

Asbestos
OSHA: U.S. Occupational Safety and Health Administration
www.osha.gov/SLTC/asbestos

Lead paint
HUD offers information on the lead paint disclosure rule at
www.hud.gov/offices/lead/disclosurerule

Radon
Call the National Radon Information Line at 800-767-7236.
Or go to the EPA Website where you can read online "A Citizen's Guide to Radon" at www.epa.gov/iaq/radon

pants and a star-trimmed top hat? He has money to lend for fixer-uppers even if you don't have a penny for the down payment and no money for the cost of repairs. Sound too good to be true? It's your government at work!

The Department of Housing and Urban Development (HUD) in cooperation with the Federal Housing Administration (FHA) sponsors a fix-up lending program called 203(k). It is available through many national and local lenders. You can get their names and more information about the details of the program at *www.hud.gov*. Go to the link for 203(k) loans.

Essentially 203(k) lenders will let you borrow the purchase price plus fix-up costs for a one- to four-unit house. The loan amount is based on the property's probable fair market value *after* the renovation or rehab has been completed. The maximum loan-to-value ratio is about 95 percent for owner-occupants. It's a bit lower for investors.

Here's how it works:

- Find a house that needs work with a price tag under the local FHA limits.
- Make a list of all the repairs and improvements you intend to do.
- If your plan includes an addition, go to an architect or home designer and have drawings made.
- Get professional estimates for the completed work on all the improvements. This figure can include repairs outside the structure itself such as garages or landscaping.
- Then present everything to a 203(k) lender. The lender will give your plans and estimates to a professional appraiser for a written projection of the property's value when all the repairs and improvements are completed. You can borrow up to 95 percent of that figure.

Recently Fannie Mae, Freddy Mac, and some private lenders have been considering similar programs and some are being offered to the public. Talk with your real estate broker or a mortgage broker or banker. You can also search around on the Web under Home Financing, but there are so many offerings that it may take you forever to sort through them.

MORE THAN MONEY

There really are easier ways to make money than playing the fixer-upper game. If money were the only motivation, I don't think so many people would be in line at the playing field.

There's something else. We're living in a techno age, where almost everything starts at the touch of a button, where we must conform or we won't get the right screen, where so many people live in units so much like everyone else's, where trying to get the *right* answer can cancel out all possibility of creative thinking. In this age of conformity, many people take pleasure in doing something that is all theirs. Turning a rundown house into a home that stimulates admiration, if not awe, is an act of the independent spirit and an expression of individual creativity (and perfectly legal, too).

RULES AND STRATEGIES

- Fixer-uppers can be purchased for homeownership or investment. The considerations are somewhat different on each path.

- The fixer-upper playing field is demanding.

- You can hunt for fixer-uppers among properties about to go up for auction or among REOs, but in fact they exist at every price level and the owners are not always in financial trouble.

- Carefully crunch the numbers *before* you make your first offer.

- Some improvements that you make to a fixer-upper have greater return on time and money invested than do others.

- Financing for the fixer-upper is surprisingly easy to find.

CHAPTER 9
Leisure-Time Real Estate

Give me the luxuries of life and I will
willingly do without the necessities.
—Frank Lloyd Wright (1869–1959), American architect

This *could* be a boring chapter. After all, leisure-time real estate is just real estate. It comes in all the same sizes and shapes that we see in other areas of the marketplace. It comes in every ownership form. It can be found in virtually every part of the country. It can be rented, rehabbed, auctioned off, and passed down from one generation to another. I can't say I'd blame you if you're thinking that I'm probably going to slog through a lot of repetitive stuff.

But think again! You're more likely to be captivated, not bored, by the twenty-first-century vacation home marketplace. Leisure-time property is luxury property. Yes, that now-a-bit-rusty trailer you placed on your land in the Oregon woods is luxury property. It is something you keep for your comfort and pleasure. You don't *need* it. You don't even begrudge the money you spend on it. And yet . . . And yet sometimes it occurs to you that the sale of just half the land may pay your kids' way through college.

Some of you may not be quite so romantic. You bought your leisure-time property with every intention of getting an excellent

WORDS TO *GO!*

In the financial marketplace, *liquidity* means the speed at which an investment can be converted into cash. Real estate is considered a nonliquid investment, which is not exactly true because virtually everything will sell at a price. Leisure property can be very liquid or virtually frozen depending on the demand in the area, competing development, and the pace of the economy in general.

return on your investment. Or perhaps you saw a place to spend winter or summer vacation days that was also a safe haven for your retirement, someday. Some of you wanted a family gathering place, others an exchange token to be used for travel around the world.

Let's look at some vacation home opportunities and see how they measure up to your ideas of luxury, **liquidity**, and portfolio building— oh, and contentment, too.

WHAT WILL FIT YOU?

Do you have preferences for properties on the MONOPOLY board? Are you drawn to the purple deeds at $60 each or to the other side of *GO!*, where a royal blue deed will cost you $350 or $400? What do addresses like St. Charles Place and Pennsylvania Avenue say about their owners?

Believe it or not, some people do buy property just for the address. A hundred and fifty years ago Lenox, Massachusetts, and Newport, Rhode Island, were among the best vacation addresses. Today Ocean Reef, Florida, and Park City, Utah, are recognized status hangouts. Can you judge what vacation property is right for you by the location?

You can't really—or at least not completely. Shopping for leisure real estate is a little more like going shopping for clothes. You've got to find the stores and the sections within them that are right for you.

(Petites? Big and tall? Business suits? Jeans and casual wear?) And you should choose *where* you will do your shopping *before* you spend time looking through the racks.

When you think you know what kind of leisure-time property you want to buy, it's usually a good idea to try it on: that is, to rent a similar property once or twice before you commit your investment money. For example, you may *love* the privacy of being the only house on one of the Thimble Islands off the coast of Connecticut. But after a few weeks, bringing in gallons of drinking water by boat gets a bit tiresome. You may *love* the golf community in Green Valley, Arizona, until you spend a few weeks of summer there.

Out by the Edge of the World

Let's say you're a freedom and clean air type of person. You want to listen to the grass grow, feel the wind in your hair, and smell the scent of pines, and you don't mind sleeping in a tent. Remote land is still available, relatively easy to find, and relatively inexpensive. But real estate agents probably won't list much of what you might buy because undeveloped land is the slowest-moving segment of the marketplace.

If you want your own private retreat, skip the Main Street brokers and go instead to the town records offices in your area of choice. Spend some time looking at the tax maps. Make note of who owns large tracts and then contact the owners directly. Ask if they are interested in subdividing off a portion of their property. If the piece they are willing to divide off is **landlocked,** be sure you get the seller to give

WORDS TO *GO!*

A *landlocked* parcel of land does not front on any established road. Access must be through an easement over an adjoining property.

you a written easement that will give you access to your land. Also be sure to have it filed with the deed.

Already established landlocked lots that you might find on town tax maps are often your best deal, because they are hard to sell and require a significant amount of time and effort before closing. In order to assure the ability to get from the road to your land, you should make your offer contingent upon your being able to get an easement over one of the abutting properties. If you can negotiate it with the people who will be your neighbors, make the easement equal to the minimal width required for a road. (Thirty feet is common, but your requirement will depend on the town and its planning board.)

"Why do I need thirty feet?" you ask. "It's just me, my family, and our sports utility vehicle."

The answer: because life goes on and change is inevitable. What if you decide to build a house after camping out on your land for four or five years? Will a narrow-path easement allow the builder's trucks and equipment to pass legally over your neighbor's land? And what if, ten, fifteen, twenty years down the road you wish to subdivide your land and give a piece to each of your children? It's unlikely the town will allow you to do that without an adequate access road for, let's say, four houses.

And finally, consider your investment. The market value of land changes in response to the use of land around it. For example, let's say you start out with ninety acres in the New Hampshire foothills (seven miles from the nearest state road and about a twenty-minute drive to Nashua, the state's southernmost city). Then someone puts in a private landing strip in a town adjacent to yours and McMansions begin to go up. Then the governments of Massachusetts and New Hampshire approve a commuter rail line to be built between Boston and Nashua and Manchester. (All this has actually happened.) What do you think will happen to the value of your ninety acres? If it's landlocked, don't you think you might want access to a road?

Instead of an easement, you might want to try negotiating to purchase a thirty-foot-wide strip from one of your neighbors. It would connect your land to an established road, legally, with

CHANCE

There are always some risks in buying remote land. Water is a major concern. If you are going to put a cabin on your land, you will need a well, and it must pump potable water. Go to the town records office before you buy and gather information on the water-test results in the area. Those numbers do not guarantee the quality of the water under your land, but they will give you a good idea of what your neighbors have. You can also stop in at some of the neighbors' houses or into restaurants or other small businesses in town and in adjoining towns and ask about the local water. Real estate agents are another good source of information; they must deal with water questions on every sale.

Beside drinking water, another major water problem is drainage. You will need a waste disposal system, and much of its cost and effectiveness will depend on the character of the soil. You can have it tested with a percolation test. Also be aware that environmental protection laws have become stringent. Your waste disposal system cannot drain into a lake or water supply or threaten the water supply of a neighbor.

fee-simple ownership. It would certainly cost a bit more than an easement, but it would be an investment in an unthreatened future. And remember, everything is salable at a price.

OK, we're into dream time. Let's keep going for just a while. What if a huge theme park opens in the next town? Land in central Florida has made one of the most significant price jumps in history. Orlando has become a major city with a major airport; the traffic-laden interstates cross over and under each other, and developers are still buying up land.

A little less dramatically, the relocation of a major corporation can increase the value of leisure-time real estate within a 200-mile radius. Development of active-adult communities near your land will also increase its value, especially if some or all of your land can be used for commercial or recreational purposes. Hilton Head, South Carolina, is an excellent example, as are Sedona, Arizona, and Escondido, California.

DON'T GO TO JAIL

Before you buy a seaside, lakeside, or riverside cottage with the intention of razing it and building something "more suitable," check in the town hall. You may be required to build the new dwelling ten or more feet above ground level in order to comply with new building codes and to get flood insurance. Congress created the National Flood Insurance Program (NFIP) in 1968 to reduce flood damage through floodplain management and to provide homeowners with insurance. The program is managed by the Federal Emergency Management Agency (FEMA).

Just a Good Place to Hang Out

Forget undeveloped land! You do *not* like ants in your cereal. I can understand that. What you really want is a place to have fun. You want to be near other people; you want a lake, or an ocean, or a mountain, or a national park nearby; and you don't want the house to be too expensive.

You're in the majority. That's what most other Americans want too.

Until the late twentieth century, communities around lakes and seaside grew up bit by bit. Individuals purchased lots and built houses to suit their needs. Zoning and building regulations were minimal. The result was a hodgepodge of housing. Today, a one-bedroom artist's cabin may stand beside a 3,000-square-foot architect-designed "cottage." In other words, there often is something for everyone in older communities around our lakes, seashore, and other recreation areas.

In areas where the most recent building has been rather upscale and the majority of the older buildings are little more than shacks, some buyers are buying the shacks and tearing them down. They want the location. Other buyers choose the smaller houses because they can live in them while they do renovation or expansion work.

Living the Good Life!

Development of resort-style recreational communities has been rapidly increasing during the past decade. Some of these are age restricted (55+), but most are not. Generally, their location is anchored by a recreational feature or features such as golf, boating, horses, the use of college campus facilities, or hiking. The communities are homogeneous in price and general style. They may, however, contain several ownership styles such as condominiums, single-family houses, or multifamily units.

In addition to the primary recreational feature, most of these communities also have a clubhouse, at least one swimming pool, tennis courts, bocci, and the like. Some have their own restaurants, small shopping centers, and even movie theaters.

Generally there are few bargain properties in these planned communities, except perhaps on resales in very slow markets. But because of the homogeneous nature of the entire community, your investment dollar is protected. No one will build a Burger King or a bait shop next door.

Castles—with or without the Moat

I don't suppose that a whole lot of people who can afford shopping sprees at the international auction houses will be reading this book; they'll have a staff member do it for them. But just in case you just won the lottery, there really are recreational palaces available in today's marketplace. Most of them are secluded, however, and you will need the help of a specialized agent just to find out where they are.

At one time, however, the rich had their "cottages" lined up near their rich friends. Think of *The Great Gatsby* and the Newport, Rhode Island, mansions. Some of these "castle cottages" have been turned into museums and tourist attractions. Some are for sale. And a few have been converted to timeshares.

THE TRUTH ABOUT TIMESHARES

Twenty-five years ago Cancun, Mexico was a spit of sand; today it is a strip of luxurious resorts that might even rival Las Vegas, if one loves the sea. Who owns these sumptuous buildings? Some are hotels, but many are timeshares populated by Americans, Canadians, the French,

Brazilians, Japanese, and myriad people from all over the world, each of whom owns a week or two or three.

Interval ownership first became available in the late 1970s and early 1980s. No one thought its popularity would last more than a decade. Today there are thousands and thousands of "resorts" all over the world, and new ones are still being added. Conde Nast would award some of them five stars; others are failed motels from the 1950s that have been converted to timeshare apartments. Some are new and some rather old trailer communities, some are former estates, and some are hunting and fishing camps. At the other end of the scale, big names like Marriott, Hilton, and Disney have gotten into the interval ownership business.

As originally conceived, timeshares were condominiums in which ownership was divided not by units but by units *and* weeks. So unit C-101 could theoretically have fifty-two owners, one for each week. In reality, the condo association usually keeps two weeks in the off-season for maintenance.

In the early 1980s trading associations came into popularity. Resort Condominiums International (RCI) and Interval International (II) are currently the best known. These large corporations made it possible for an owner in Hawaii to "bank" his unit for trade and choose a unit in, let's say, Scotland for a week any time within two years.

What a great idea! Travel the world with no responsibility other than paying the annual maintenance fee for the week you own on Paradise Island.

Like most great ideas, it has gotten a bit out of hand. Ownership periods now range from "quarter shares" (thirteen weeks every year) to owning one week every two years. (You can choose odd or even years.) And some people who buy into timeshares don't own any real estate at all.

Timeshares are "sold" in different guises. Following is a brief summary.

- **Fee simple:** You take title to the interval, let's say unit 312, the third week in February every year. You have a deed, title insurance, maintenance fees, and taxes, just as you would if you owned any other condominium.

CHANCE

Timeshare sales promotion programs offer free vacation weeks, cruises, helicopter rides, TVs, and many other "gifts" as incentives. All you have to do is come and listen to the presentation. The sales pitch starts low and works into high pressure. Prices are very negotiable.

If you go to a timeshare presentation, be aware of what "ownership" style is being offered. And don't be afraid to say "No, thank you." You will still get the prizes and incentives that have been offered.

- **Right to use:** The length of the "ownership" term for right-to-use vacation property is usually twenty or twenty-five years, but in fact you do *not* own anything. What you have is a kind of lease. For twenty-five years you can use *this* apartment during *this* week. Or you can trade it. At the end of the ownership period, you have no share interest in the resort. Many resorts that were sold in the 1980s are now converting to hotels or single-owner-per-unit condominium ownership, and all right-to-use timeshare "owners" can no longer claim their weeks.
- **Membership share:** There is usually no real estate ownership when you buy into one of the big multiresort leisure management companies such as Marriott or Fairfield Resorts. You do not get the same unit or the same week each year. You buy share use in the corporation that owns the resort. For your purchase dollars you are assigned a certain number of "points" in the system. If you wish to revisit "your" resort each year, you must call for a reservation. You can, however, trade your points through the international trading companies. Many large hotel chains such as Marriott and Hilton are selling timeshares in this manner and allowing members to trade their points at the franchise hotels around the world.

Generally, timeshares are not a good financial investment. Units often resell for $1,000 or $2,000 a week even when their owners paid $15,000 to $25,000 or more for the interval. Maintenance fees are generally high. If you multiply out the $400 to $500 a week that is customarily charged, you'll come up with $1,600 to $2,000-plus a month. Think of that against the customary and usual monthly maintenance fees for year-round condominium ownership. And annual membership fees in the international trading organizations are moving ever upward. And that's not all. Members in RCI, II, and other groups must also pay a fee for each trade that is made. The trading fee is now well into the hundred-dollar range.

If you wish to buy a timeshare, promotional sales offices are *not* the place to go. Instead, you can go to the business office of a timeshare that you like and ask if there are any repossessions (foreclosures) for sale. Many people, unable to sell their units, just stop making maintenance payments. Often you can buy these repossessed units for the unpaid balance of maintenance fees. If the condominium office is overrun by sales agents, ask for a list of the board of directors for the condo association. Simply call a board member and ask if there are any units in foreclosure.

Many units are also available on the Web. Independent groups like Timeshare Users Group (TUG) not only list units for sale by their owners, they also include reviews from members on the quality of the resorts. The big Internet trading organizations like eBay have thousands of timeshares for sale every year. Many sell for $1. Be aware, however, that you don't *buy* the unit on the Web. Buyer and seller are simply put in touch with each other; you must go to an escrow company to arrange for a closing and the transfer of funds.

AMERICAN GOTHIC—DOWN ON THE FARM

Do you know the famous painting by Grant Wood? The one with the dour farm couple—he with the pitchfork, she in the flowered apron? It sure is a long way from Mr. MONOPOLY, isn't it! Yet many Americans fantasize about a farm as their leisure-time property.

"You've got to be kidding!" you say. "A farm is nothing but work!"

COMMUNITY CHEST

Perhaps you love the smell of tomatoes on the vine, or perhaps you want your children to see a calf being born, or perhaps you long to keep and ride horses. If you don't mind a few hours' drive to get to your farm every time you want to visit, you should start your farm property hunt. Sometimes the best way is to spend a few nights at local bed and breakfasts or stop in at barns or farmhouses and talk with the owners about who might want to sell in the area.

Uncle Sam can help, too. The Farm Service Agency makes direct and guaranteed farm ownership and operating loans to family-size farmers and ranchers who cannot obtain commercial credit from a bank. Check the U.S. Farm Service Agency (FSA), which is a division of the U.S. Department of Agriculture on the Web at *www.fsa.usda.gov.*

That's true, but what if you own the land and let someone else farm it? There are several ways to arrange to be a gentleman farmer, a farm owner who comes by for weekends and perhaps the summertime.

Think about the possibilities. If your farm is contiguous to another farm, you can keep the farmhouse and out buildings for yourself and lease the use of the land to your neighbor. If your farm stands alone, you can build a second home on the property for your use while keeping the original house and land for use under the direction of a manager and his or her family. Or you can lease the land to a large agricultural corporation, reserving a few acres for your own use.

Many people fantasize that they will use the farm while their family grows and then (let's say twenty years later) they will sell it for a profit. Their dream goes like this: by the time they are ready to sell, suburbia will have moved outward from the city and the land will be ready for development. It will be time to harvest the huge profits!

That does happen, sometimes. It is happening right now on the outskirts of Montgomery County, Maryland, where the suburbs of

Washington and Baltimore are soon going to bump into each other. But it doesn't happen nearly as often as dream investors would like. If you want to buy a farm and can afford it, do it! But don't count on the sale of that land to pay your kids' college tuition.

ON LEASED LAND

Buying or building a house on leased land is risky business. Often seaside or lakeside land is so valuable that families keep it generation after generation, allowing leisure-time buyers to build on it and pay for a lease. But there are land leases and land leases.

I have a friend—let's call him Paul—who fell in love with a small waterfront house that he had rented for several years on the Jersey shore. The owner wanted to sell, and the price was very reasonable. Only one hitch: the house was on leased land, *a one-year lease that had to be renewed each year!*

"Don't do it," I cautioned.

"Oh, come on," he replied. "This family has been renewing that lease for forty years. There are twenty-three waterfront houses on the land. The owner is not about to change anything."

Paul bought the house. Three years later, the father (the patriarch who owned the land) died. His kids got a handsome offer for the land from a condominium developer. They served notice that the leases would not be renewed.

In the courts, Paul fought with all that he knew, which was considerable. He managed to delay property transfer to the condominium developer for two years, but in the end he lost. In fact, all twenty-three owners lost their vacation homes. (The only alternative was to pay to have the houses professionally moved and the question was: *to where?*) That's the worst end of the leased-land story line.

The other end is the 100-year prepaid lease. This kind of arrangement is sometimes used when a deed for a large piece of land has restrictions that forbid the sale and/or the subdivision of the land. The long-term prepaid lease sometimes causes problems with financing (lenders don't like to deal with leased land) and may decrease resale speed and sometimes the market value of the house. But the ownership

WORDS TO *GO!*

Equitable title is a less than fee-simple interest in real estate. In the case of a long-term lease, the buyer does not hold the deed to the land, but he or she takes possession of it and assumes all risks and responsibilities of ownership including maintenance, taxes, assessments, etc. Unless there is a clause in the lease that forbids assignment, the buyer can sell the house with the lease in tact.

is secure for 100 years; the owner does not have to make any additional payments and in fact holds **equitable title**.

THE INTERNAL REVENUE SERVICE (IRS) AND YOUR LEISURE-TIME PROPERTY

Now we leave the location and ownership style of your vacation home and turn to everyone's favorite topic: taxes. Do you think of your vacation property as a second home or do you think of it as an investment property that brings in a good return while providing your family with a drop-in place for a couple of weeks a year? How you use your leisure property will determine the attitude of the Internal Revenue Service when they review your federal income tax return.

To Qualify as a Second Home

You, the owner, your spouse, or a blood relative *must* use the property at least fifteen days each year *or* more than 10 percent of the number of days that it is rented at fair market value in the area, *whichever is greater*. This means that if you rent out the property for the summer months, let's say sixty-five days, you must use it yourself for fifteen days. If you rent out the property for the academic year, let's say nine months, or 270 days, you must use it yourself for twenty-eight days. Which means you could spend the summer there.

If you choose to treat your leisure-time property as a second home, you will be allowed to deduct property taxes and mortgage interest on your income tax return. If the property is rented to a tenant at fair market value for *no more* than fourteen days in a year, no deduction can be made for maintenance costs but the income from the rental need not be reported. The property cannot be **depreciated** and it cannot show a tax loss.

To Qualify as a Rental Property

You, the owner, your spouse, or your blood relatives can use the property *no more than* fourteen days each year *or* 10 percent of the total number of days that it is rented at fair market value, *whichever is greater*. So if you rent the property for 300 days, you cannot use it for more than thirty days in that calendar year. If the property is vacant for most of the year and then you rent it for thirty days, you cannot use it for more than fourteen days.

When you declare that your leisure-time property is a rental property, you can deduct mortgage interest, property taxes, and maintenance expenses allocated to the rental period against the rental income. The amount of deductions can legally exceed the income, creating a tax loss. The property can be depreciated for tax purposes.

WORDS TO *GO!*

When we talk about investment real estate, *depreciation* means the decrease in value (often a paper decrease for tax purposes) of buildings and improvements because of deterioration or obsolescence. (More about investment properties in Chapter 10.)

CHANCE

More than any other type of real estate, leisure-time property responds to the economic moods of the nation. When times are good, prices go up, sometimes spiraling; when times are bad, prices not only fall, but most property becomes difficult to sell. Worse yet, rentals fall off when money is tight. "No tenants" can cut off the income that was paying the mortgage!

Few lenders like to foreclose, but they *will* foreclose eventually. With foreclosure looming, some leisure-time property owners will sell their leisure-time property well below market value. The same is true after a hurricane or other natural disaster. Bad times are often good times to buy leisure-time property (*if* you have the money!).

FINANCING THE PROPERTY

Financing leisure-time property is pretty much the same as financing other types of property. Sometimes the lender charges a higher interest rate for remote or seaside property or for what is considered a **subprime** mortgage. Some buyers who have considerable equity in their primary homes purchase their vacation homes or land by refinancing their home. That tactic usually leaves heavy financing on the primary home and little or no financing on the leisure-time property. In difficult times, such an arrangement might allow the owner to offer the vacation home for sale with seller financing, which would definitely help in the marketing process.

Rather than refinance, other buyers choose to keep their first mortgage intact and take out a second mortgage on their primary home. Interest rates are usually higher on a second mortgage, but the principal is smaller than it would be in a total refinancing. This plan works well if current interest rates are higher than the original first mortgage rate on the primary home.

Some developers of large leisure communities and condominiums offer below-prime-rate financing as a purchase incentive. This is accomplished through a bank deal called a **buy-down**. The below-prime rate usually lasts for a short time (two or three years) and then the mortgage interest rate reverts to going rates, which can mean a rather large jump in payments.

If a developer is offering you financing with a low interest rate for the first few years, you can use that offer as a negotiating tool. Since the developer *pays* the lender upfront cash for the reduced rate, you can simply make a lower offer on the purchase price and say that you will arrange your own financing. As I said, you can refinance your primary home, or you can seek out financing more to your liking such as a thirty-year fixed rate, or an adjustable rate mortgage with a longer term between adjustment periods and better caps.

If the seller of a vacation home offers to take back a purchase money mortgage (nothing down, lower-than-market rate, perhaps), read the mortgage-loan contract very carefully. Many such financing arrangements are interest-only mortgages with balloon payments scheduled within five to ten years. If you don't have the money or you can't refinance when the balloon payment comes due, you could lose the house.

PRECONSTRUCTION CONTRACTS

One currently popular way to invest in vacation-area condominiums is the preconstruction contract. Here's how it works.

Builder Dreamscrapes Inc. gets planning board approval for a 140-unit waterside community with boat dock facilities. Even before ground preparation begins, the company sets up a sales office (a trailer with a lot of flags flying around it) and begins to advertise on billboards near major roadways. Prices have been set, economic times are good, and the "units are selling like hotcakes!"

Most of the units will not be habitable for at least two years. Why are they selling? What will the real estate market be like in two years? The investors who are buying these "paper units" are counting on prices going up, way up. Traditionally, as portions of a condo community

WORDS TO *GO!*

Charles Darrow and the Parker Brothers probably never heard of *subprime* mortgages when they put their MONOPOLY game on the market in 1933. But subprime loans are being made everywhere today (seventy-five years later), and they are the cause of much financial concern because they have a significantly higher default rate than conventional loans.

A subprime lender is one who lends to borrowers who do not qualify for loans from mainstream lenders. Be aware that some are independent lenders, but some are affiliates of mainstream lenders operating under different names. Often subprime buyers do not qualify under traditional guidelines because of bad credit scores or because they wish to carry larger loan amounts than they are qualified for. (Your loan on your primary home is considered in your qualification data when you apply for a loan on a second home. You have to be able to carry both.)

A *buy-down* is a one-time cash payment made by a seller, a buyer, or any interested party such as a relative to a lender in return for a lower interest rate during the early years of a mortgage agreement.

are completed and some landscaping is done, the builder raises and re-raises the prices.

The investor/preconstruction buyer reserves the unit at the original price that is stated in the contract with an escrow deposit of (usually) 10 percent. Many investors wait a year or so and then assign (sell) their contracts-to-purchase for a fee. For example, you are under contract to buy a condominium for $400,000. You have $40,000 being held in escrow. A year later an identical unit is selling for $487,000. You assign your contract for a fee of $80,000. You get your escrow back (it becomes the buyer's escrow) and you double your investment. The buyer of the contract gets to buy a unit he or she wants and pays $7,000 less than the going price.

DON'T GO TO JAIL

If you consider getting into preconstruction contracts, negotiate to have your escrow funds held by a fiduciary party. Many developers want the funds released to them to use toward building costs.

Also be sure to check out the reputation of the developer. If Dreamscrapes goes bankrupt before they get to your building, you have a contract on nothing.

THE HANDYMAN SONG

Maintenance time and work is one of the main reasons that most new construction in the leisure-time housing industry has been structured with condominium ownership. Most potential leisure-property buyers just don't want to take on more work.

But there are some of us who enjoy the family trip to the shore cottage to open up after winter. Some actually enjoy the physicality of the fix-up work and the creativity of making a place newer and better. Some of us like owning something we have made a little different from what everyone else has. One neighbor of mine at a beach community painted her two-story waterfront cottage hot pink. It had been a wedding gift from her parents, and she hung out a sign to name it: TICKLED PINK.

Others of us choose to spend leisure time having fun. If you choose the condo option for your vacation property, little maintenance effort will be required. Seasonal closing up will be all interior work. All of the exterior maintenance work will be done by the condo association. You can lock up and go away for six or even nine months, and not worry.

If you choose the remote cabin or an established (older) lake or seaside community, you must be prepared to dedicate some time to upkeep. Coastal properties are affected by corrosion caused by the salt-laden air, not to mention hurricanes. Lakeside communities often have drainage and septic system problems. Cabins in the woods are susceptible to invasion by termites, bats, squirrels, or other rodents. If you live some distance from your leisure-time property, you will probably want to hire a local person to check on your house periodically.

RULES AND STRATEGIES

- It is important to choose leisure-time property that fits your particular needs and goals.

- Ordinarily, timeshares are not a good financial investment.

- Uncle Sam might help you buy a farm.

- Some leisure-time property is built on leased land. The safety of your investment depends on what is written in the lease.

- Check with the IRS on how to treat your leisure-time property on your federal income tax return.

- Subprime mortgages and creative financing are common in the vacation-area marketplace.

- Maintenance demands should influence your choice of leisure-time property.

CHAPTER 10
Landlording

Look ere ye leap.

—John Heywood (1497–1580), English writer and playwright
from *The Proverbs of John Heywood,* 1546

MONOPOLY landlording! Isn't it great? Every time anyone lands on your property and you have little green houses or a red hotel sitting there, he or she must pay you rent. There's nothing for you to do besides haul in the cash. So you begin to muse . . . *Wouldn't it be love-er-ly! We could buy this building with no money down and the government would give us the money to fix it up. Then we could live in the nice unit on the first floor and the rent we collect from the other three units would take care of our mortgage payments, taxes, and insurance too! We'd be living for free! We could even save money and buy another building like this one and then another. We'd be rich! We'd be landlords!*

Yes, all that is possible. But it might be a good idea if you looked around carefully, both physically and mentally, and learned a little more about what you were getting into before you sign any papers. In the *real* real estate game, being a landlord, especially a live-on-the-premises landlord, can be financially rewarding but also time consuming and, sometimes, emotionally trying. Let's look at some factors in choosing the property that will make you a landlord.

WHAT MAKES A GOOD INVESTMENT?

In this chapter we'll be talking about multifamily homes, mixed-use buildings, and investment condominiums because these three investment vehicles are within the reach of most people who have only recently entered the real estate marketplace. (In this game, you're a novice for at least five years!)

If you want to play on this playing field, you'll be moving up into a new league. You'll need to know everything you've learned in *The House Hunt* version, the *Fixer-Upper* version, and the *Foreclosures* version—and you'll need to learn some real estate–specific business and management skills. This is a marketplace where your opponents (other buyers and sellers) are not interested in being comfortable and happy; they are interested in profit. They are both investors and property managers. You will be, too.

Look for Positive Factors

As in every real estate marketplace, location is the most important factor in estimating the probable **appreciation** of a building. Look at how the land around a building is being used. Is it the **highest and best use** that is possible in the given circumstances? Are buildings and their usage changing in the area? Is there any land available for new development? Is the state or local government involved in urban renewal? The answer to each of those questions should factor into your choice of a rental investment property.

In a nutshell, the most important factor in investment real estate is neighborhood. And neighborhood is a crucial factor in both the price of the property and the rental income it will generate. On the MONOPOLY board, properties are color coded. You can buy purple properties at the lowest prices on the board ($60 each) or you can go to the other end of the road and buy royal blue properties (Park Place for $350 or Boardwalk for $400). Why not buy just the cheap properties? Because different neighborhoods generate different rental rates. (The owner of Mediterranean Avenue, for example, collects $2 rent when a player lands on undeveloped property, $10 with one house, and $160 with four houses. The player who lands on Boardwalk, however,

WORDS TO GO!

As mentioned in Chapter 5, *appreciation* and *keeping pace with inflation* are two different factors in real estate. Appreciation is *added* value in real (adjusted for inflation) dollars. It occurs because *demand* for the property increases. Increased demand can be caused by factors in the environment (better commuting opportunities, new recreational facilities, safer streets) and/or the improvement of the building through better appearance and facilities.

Highest and best use is a phrase commonly used in real estate purchase and development, especially at planning and zoning board meetings. It refers to the most profitable single use for a property or the use most likely to be in demand in the near future. The *highest and best use* must be a use allowed by zoning laws, financially feasible, and physically possible (you can't put a parking lot oceanside). Planning and zoning boards will discuss the probability of maximum benefit to the community.

pays the owner $50 if it is undeveloped, $200 with one house, and $1,700 with four houses.

When considering an investment property, you must evaluate the town, neighborhood, and lot because all three affect value. In fact, knowing the area is so important that I recommend you invest only in areas that are familiar to you. Future property-value perception is a sixth sense to be developed. Only over time and with studied sensitivity can you get a feeling for what is *probably* going to happen in a town or neighborhood.

"Is the future of a town or neighborhood important?" you ask.

It's the key to creating value. Knowing the direction of town growth, management, and character can help you to evaluate the desirability factor of a property. It's almost like having a crystal ball—an especially glittering one that predicts money-making potential.

The following are some windows into that crystal ball. They peek into the economic health of a community.

- **Look at the master plan and land-use maps for the area:** Ask the town clerk about recent changes. What type of land use and development is being encouraged? Commercial development? Recreational facilities? Shared-space housing? Active adult (retirement) communities? Go to zoning board meetings (they are open to everyone) or read the transcripts in the local library. What are the pending issues and appeals? Look for dedicated park space or open-space land. How does the town stand on environmental issues?
- **Get current population and employment statistics:** Dig into some statistics with your real estate agent or on the Web. What is the total population? How is it broken down by age groups? By industry, what is the employment profile in the town? Unemployment ratio? What are the income range and median income of the employed population and per household?
- **Study community growth trends:** Is there any new industry in the town or nearby? What are the population changes over the past ten years? What is the prediction for the next ten years? (Increasing population will increase demand for housing.) What new housing is being planned? (Too much housing growth will diminish demand for rental property.) Is new school construction planned? (This usually increases taxes.) Are new retail centers planned for the town? Look at the tax records for the past ten years. What is the current tax rate? How has it changed over the past ten years? How does it compare to neighboring towns? What is the projection for the next ten years?
- **Consider the character of the community:** Include climate, topography, ethnic makeup, age of the citizens, educational opportunities, cultural attractions and opportunities, recreation, transportation, medical care, crime rate, emergency services (police, fire, and ambulance), and historic significance, if any.

Although the economic health of a community is the major factor in determining the ability to *create* future value in your investment property, **cash flow** often determines its viability. Unless the building can sustain itself, you won't be able to own it long enough for significant real appreciation in value. Remember, you will be collecting rents but you will also be paying maintenance expenses, debt service, insurance, and

WORDS TO *GO!*

Cash flow refers to gross income from the property minus the money used to pay property taxes, insurance, all operating expenses, and the debt service. *Positive cash flow* means extra cash the owner can spend; *negative cash flow* means the investor must add out-of-pocket dollars to meet costs.

taxes. Will you *really* be making any money on a month-to-month basis? It all comes down to numbers.

When considering a property, you should ask the seller to provide you with net operating income (NOI) records for at least the past two years. The NOI is the gross income minus management fees, accounting and legal fees, property taxes, insurance, utilities provided to the tenants (heat, electricity, water, cable TV, etc.), and maintenance costs. The NOI does not include debt service (your mortgage and interest payments), which you will have to subtract to see if there will be any cash in the kitty at the end of each month.

DON'T GO TO JAIL

NOI is not a gnat to be brushed away when considering a purchase in the hundreds of thousands of dollars. If your property loses money every month and you can't raise rents without losing tenants, you will eventually be unable to pay the bills. The dark clouds on the horizon are tax delinquency, foreclosure, and inadequate maintenance; the storm is bankruptcy.

COMMUNITY CHEST

Bankruptcy: a player who is bankrupt, that is, one who owes more than he can pay, must turn over to his Creditor all that he has of value, and retire from the game.

—George S. Parker (1866–1952), Founder of Parker Brothers, from Rules of MONOPOLY, 1935

Don't Overlook Negative Factors

Prolonged vacancy or nonpayment of rent in one or more of your units can significantly affect the investment's cash flow. Of course you can't predict rental activity, but you can collect information on occupancy rates in the town and in the neighborhood. Your real estate agent can get this information for you and it will help you to evaluate not only probable cash flow but also probable appreciation. If the vacancy rate is low, it means demand for housing units in the area is high. Unless you live in New York City or one of the few other places where rent control is still in effect, a low vacancy rate usually leads to higher rents.

If the vacancy rate is high, you should ask *why*. Has there been overbuilding in the area so that there are more units than people who want them? Has the crime rate risen? Is appearance and maintenance in the neighborhood poor? (This will affect your property even if you keep the building in pristine condition.) Has a major employer left the area? Is the building you are considering rundown but located in a neighborhood that is generally well maintained? (If so, negotiate for that bargain price and fix it up! This problem is easy.)

Are any major changes being considered in the zoning that would negatively affect future value? This question is just as important as evaluating the possibility of appreciation. Some investors blithely forget that it really is possible to lose money in the real estate marketplace.

Ask yourself: *will this property become less desirable during the time I plan to own it?* Here are some considerations:

- **Physical deterioration:** Will the effects of time decrease value? Is the problem curable or incurable? Curable problems are those that can be repaired, and the cost of the repairs will increase the property value proportionately. (Exterior painting is a good example.) Incurable problems are those for which repair costs will exceed the added value to the property. (The need to replace the plumbing infrastructure is an example.)

- **Functional obsolescence:** Are physical design features outmoded or unacceptable? If the feature (old and broken bathroom fixtures, for example) can be remedied without costs that exceed the increased value, the obsolescence is curable. If the feature (adding central heating) would require an expenditure greater than the potential added property value, the obsolescence is considered incurable and reduces the market value of the property. But don't turn away from a property because of a functional obsolescence. Make your offer low enough to cover the costs of fixing the problem and you will add value that you didn't have to pay for.

- **External or economic obsolescence:** Are there negative factors not intrinsic to the property and beyond the control of the owners that are affecting the value of the property? Are some buildings in the area being abandoned? Are boutique and service shops moving out because of crime-family or gang pressure? Has a sewerage treatment plant been built at the end of the street? You get the idea. External obsolescence is always incurable because the owner cannot remedy the problem. It is what you look for and choose to avoid when you evaluate a neighborhood. Some property may not be a bargain at any price.

The Master Plan

It is essential that you visit the town records office and look at the **master plan**. (It is likely to be kept in the planning and zoning board office, if the town keeps a separate room.) You want to know particularly if major highways or other public transportation will be built near or through your property. (*Near* could increase or decrease value.

Through could mean you will no longer own the property when road development begins.)

Since zoning and municipal planning became the responsibility of municipal government, that government has held the right to seize private property (after paying fair market value) when there is a need for change for the greater good. This process is called **eminent domain** and it has most often been used when road or railroad development necessitated creating pathways through cities and countryside.

However there is a new danger/opportunity for property owners. Some will be angry at the loss of ownership; others will rejoice at being paid for their property at market value. Today, municipalities can seize whole areas of a town and sell them to developers who can demolish the buildings and build others. You may consider such a sale a grand opportunity to be paid cash and move on. Or you might consider it an infringement of your constitutional right to hold property.

COMMUNITY CHEST

In 2005 the U.S. Supreme Court heard the case of *Kelo v. New London* (Connecticut).

They ruled that government may use eminent domain to condemn private homes and transfer the land to developers who want to demolish and replace the homes with privately owned shopping malls, hotels, or convention centers. There was a great outcry at the decision. Critics shouted that the Court had sided with a town government that was seeking additional tax revenue. The question is: *was that decision for the greater good of the community as a whole?* The new development will certainly bring in more tax dollars, and more money for schools and recreation. It might positively affect property values in other parts of town. But it would also displace many people from their homes. And it would probably line more than a few pockets with exquisite white ermine.

THE IRS AND RENTAL PROPERTY

You've passed over the "Luxury Tax" square many times in your MONOPOLY games, always with a faint sigh of relief. And (hopefully) you've given a respectful nod to tax issues as you've read through these chapters so far. But now you've landed on the square. No more bits and pieces of Internal Revenue Service involvement in real estate ownership. Let's dive into a little more excruciating detail.

Yes, you can skip this large section and turn "taxes" over to your accountant if you like. But tax decisions are an important part of real estate investment planning. If you don't know the basics of the tax laws, you could make decisions that will needlessly cost you money.

How Depreciation Works

A true story about me: As a newly married couple more than forty years ago, one of our first knock-down, drag-out arguments was about **depreciation**. *He* was trying to get me to understand that we had to depreciate the property. *I* was trying to get him to understand that the property had *appreciated* by at least 15 percent over the past year. There was no communication because we were in different ballparks: he was in taxes and I was in real estate. *And* we were both right.

Property often appreciates in value while owners can legally deduct depreciation on their tax returns. That's one of Uncle Sam's little gifts to real estate investment. On paper the value of your investment goes down, down, down . . . no matter what.

As of this writing, residential investment real estate (single-family houses, multifamily houses, condominiums, and apartment buildings) must be depreciated over its economic life (sometimes called the *recovery period*) of 27.5 years. You must use the **straight-line depreciation** method, which means that at the end of each full year of ownership you declare $1/27.5$ (that's about 3.64 percent) of the price you paid for the property as a loss on your federal income tax return. The depreciation loss for the first year is partial, prorated according to the proportion of ownership time in that year.

If you invest in commercial (nonresidential) property such as a store, warehouse, or office condominium, the recovery period for your

WORDS TO *GO!*

Master plan is the municipal government term for a comprehensive map for the development of the entire community. Ideally, the plan will allow for orderly growth or change that is economically, socially, and ecologically sound. Most cities and towns, even small towns, have a master plan.

Eminent domain is the right of the government to acquire property for the public good. Fair and just compensation must be paid to the owner.

On your federal tax return, *depreciation* means a paper loss in a building's value that is created by an accounting procedure. Remember land is not depreciable.

Straight-line depreciation reduces the value of the building by set equal amounts each year over its established economic life.

property will be thirty-nine years. That's a deduction of $1/39$ of the price you paid for the building or unit (about 2.5 percent per full year of ownership).

Hold on! you're thinking.

I know your question. You've recognized that there are two different schedules for commercial property and residential property and you're wondering what happens when a property can be classified as both.

It's a common occurrence. We call it mixed-use. And yes, when you own mixed-use property, some problems stick their little heads up when you go to fill out those endless income tax forms.

If you buy a mixed-use property, you must establish the proportion (you can use square footage for a ratio, for example) of each type of use in the building and then calculate two depreciation schedules accordingly. If you keep a part of the building as your home, you must establish the proportion of the building that you are using. You cannot claim depreciation on your personal living space. (But remember the lovely homeowner's tax exemption! You're not losing money by living

CHANCE

Forget about such realities as the actual age of a property. The IRS is *not interested*. Every time ownership changes, the property is said to be *put in service* and the depreciation schedule starts all over again. Remember *depreciation* is accounting paperwork. It has *no* relationship to the decreasing or increasing value of the building.
        (Until you sell it. More in a bit.)

in your mixed-use property, even if the building includes a store, an apartment for rent, and your home.)

How Depreciation Lowers Your Annual Federal Income Tax Liability

Let's keep this as simple as possible for this demonstration. Let's say you bought a two-unit house for $350,000. Your municipal tax bill estimates the value of the land at $50,000. Your **basis** for tax depreciation purposes therefore is $300,000. Each year you are allowed to depreciate $1/27.5$ of the basis. So $300,000 divided by 27.5 equals $10,909.09, which is your annual depreciation deduction.

Let's make up some numbers for a tax return:

Annual rental income:	$14,000.00
Deductible expenses (mortgage interest, taxes, maintenance, services):	$11,000.00
Positive cash flow:	$3,000.00
Depreciation	−$10,909.09
Taxable income	(−$7,909.09)

For federal income tax purposes you show a loss this year of $7,909.09. The tax loss (up to $25,000) can be applied against ordinary income to reduce tax liability for those who are actively involved in the management of their real estate investment. This law does contain a few complications. Be sure to talk with your tax accountant before you claim your deduction.

Capital Gains When You Sell

Profit from the sale of investment real estate held for a year or more is considered a long-term capital gain and taxed as such. Wouldn't it be nice if it were that simple? This is where I must warn you: *keep accurate records!* It's the law.

Besides keeping records with military precision, I'll also recommend again using an accountant if you own investment property. No matter how much you know, it's amazing how easily a significant item can be overlooked. Sometimes you overlook obvious factors simply because you are too close to the action.

Our next stop is a summary of the major tax calculations that must be done when you sell investment property. It proceeds step by step and may seem quite clear to you. Don't assume! Make an appointment with your accountant; *you* bring the coffee and doughnuts.

DON'T GO TO JAIL

Paperwork! Paperwork! Sometimes we feel as though we're being both over-stuffed and suffocated by it. But if you really want to buy, manage, and sell investment real estate, try to grin (grimace?) and consider recordkeeping as your hobby. Make nice neat piles (or files) of all your receipts, bills, and payments. No matter how friendly your IRS agent is, he or she will not believe that you spent $15,000 on new windows unless you can prove it.

WORDS TO GO!

Basis is the dollar value of the property that is to be used for determining depreciation and tax liability.

The *adjusted basis* is the figure used for computing capital gains on investment property.

A *capital improvement* is work done to extend the useful life of a property and/or add to its value. A new heating system is a capital improvement; painting the interior of an apartment is a maintenance item. Capital improvements can be depreciated according to MACRS; maintenance items cannot be depreciated, but their cost can be deducted from the gross income.

MACRS is the IRS's Modified Accelerated Cost Recovery System which allows you to depreciate capital improvements on a separate schedule from building depreciation.

- **First, determine your adjusted basis.** That is your purchase price minus the depreciation that you have claimed over your years of ownership, plus the cost of **improvements**, minus the depreciation you have claimed on those improvements according to **MACRS**.
- **Next, determine the adjusted selling price.** Take the sale price on the contract and subtract from it the real estate commission, closing costs, and all other expenses associated with the sale, such as inspections, or tests for radon, lead paint, etc., and the repairs that were specifically required before closing title.
- **Finally, subtract your adjusted basis from the adjusted sale price.** Now you have your profit (as the government sees it, anyway).

Naturally the actual tax laws are more complicated than this streamlined version; why else would the government need to hire so many tax specialists? So do get one of your own. He or she might even help you to put off paying any taxes for quite a while. There is a way.

Later, Uncle Sam!

Homeowners are not the only ones so loved by Uncle Sam that they get big hugs and kisses, like not having to pay taxes on the profit from the sale of their primary residences, with some strings attached, of course. (You've already read about them in Chapter 8.) The tall guy in striped pants also loves his real estate *investors*, although perhaps not quite as much. Players in the landlording game can *put off* paying taxes on the profits from the sale of their properties.

Under the tax-deferred exchange laws, you can legally continue not to pay taxes on your investment-property capital gains until you sell one and do not buy another. But don't run off to find a good bottle of champagne in your wine cellar! You'll need all your brain cells on alert for this game. Starker, or 1031, exchanges are complex and have lots of rules that call for elimination of your eligibility if you don't abide by the letter of the law.

Named for the section of the Internal Revenue Code that describes them, 1031 exchanges *must* be done through a neutral third

COMMUNITY CHEST

Here's a rule not yet incorporated in the MONOPOLY game. When on the real estate investment playing field, *1031 exchanges,* sometimes called *Starker exchanges,* allow for the postponement of capital gains tax payment when one property is sold and another property of *like-kind* is purchased within a specified time period.

Like-kind may sound as though you'll be stuck driving one type of investment vehicle as long as you're adverse to paying taxes. But the IRS has defined *like-kind* as any property held for business, trade, or investment purposes. That generous interpretation means that you can use a 1031 exchange when you sell your investment multifamily house and use the profit to buy a gas station/convenience store, and vice versa.

CHANCE

You must *not* touch the money you will make when you plan to do a 1031 exchange. If you actually hold the profits from the sale of your property, even for one day, the exchange is disqualified. The IRS will expect your check come April, and yes, April is the cruelest month.

party called a *facilitator, exchanger,* or *qualified intermediary.* To qualify the exchanger *cannot* be a relative, a business partner, an employee, your real estate agent, or your attorney.

Most important, when you sell you must *plan* for an exchange. First, you sign an agreement with an exchanger stating your intention to do an exchange. You arrange to have the proceeds from the sale held by the exchanger in an escrow account. When you close on the property you are selling, you have forty-five days to identify a new property for purchase. You must close on the new property within 180 days from the date of closing on your old property. No exceptions.

To avoid paying any taxes, you must acquire property that is of equal or greater value and equal or greater in debt (mortgage loan or loans) than the property you sell. If you withdraw equity from the exchange, you must pay taxes on the amount that you take. Exchanges of property in the United States for property in another country do not qualify.

How to Build a Pyramid, Legally

Many people around the world have become very rich through real estate investment while abiding by the laws of their land. Sometimes the wealth is generated by land development, but much more often it is a factor of the number of properties owned by the investor. It's a little like putting up little green houses on the MONOPOLY board: the more houses, the higher the rent. Look at Pennsylvania Avenue for example: with one house, you collect $150 rent if someone lands there, but with four houses you collect $1,200!

Would you like to start with one multifamily house, go on to owning three, change that to four, and then own seven positive cash-flow properties by the time you retire (at about age forty-nine)? It's an inverse pyramid balanced on its point. Yes, there's risk, but it can work and has worked for some savvy and persevering investors. It's one of the "unique, secret, insider" plans sold by the TV gurus. And it's really quite simple.

The plan is predicated upon an ever-expanding economy with real estate values going ever higher over the long run and mortgage money easily available. Of course this economic good health is not guaranteed. Like the stock market, the real estate market does have price increase periods and then "adjustment" periods. Mortgage rates go up and they come down; money is easy to get, and then hard to get, and then easy to get again. But if you look at the whole of the twentieth century, the trend is definitely upward on property value. You may have to wait or search for a good borrowing time or place. The security of owning property and our government's benign taxation attitude toward real estate ownership makes this pyramid plan feasible.

It's all about leverage (explained in Chapter 5). The pertinent taxation fact is that you are *not* taxed on the equity you withdraw from a property if you do not sell it. For example, suppose your property has appreciated by 50 percent. (Don't blink, this has happened a lot in the last two decades.) You want to buy another property but you don't have a lot of spare cash lying about. So you refinance the investment property or take out a second mortgage on it.

You withdraw enough equity to make a down payment on another property. Even if you take out more money than you originally put into the property, you are not taxed on the money you withdraw. Now you own two properties. Inflation and appreciation continue, rents go up, soon both properties are showing good positive cash flow. And if you like what you are doing, you can do it again.

Is this the hen that lays golden eggs? Not quite. Remember that the IRS computers have very big memory banks. You will eventually pay the taxes you owe. But by the tally-up date, hopefully, the equity that you withdrew will have grown to a positive return many, many times the amount of taxes to be paid on it.

Is there a downside? You will have to have the perseverance and funds to live through (or work through) periods of economic downturn. And, you will be in the property management business, a kind of work that some people simply don't like. Let's talk about that.

IT'S ABOUT REAL ESTATE WITH *PEOPLE* IN IT!

The biggest factor that makes multifamily houses and mixed-use buildings management-intensive paths to making money is the *people* housed in the real estate. Investment condominiums escape this classification because they are managed by the condo association's management company, as are most of the properties owned by professional-grade investors who have expanded and diversified. For the most part, beginning investors manage their own buildings and often that management period is the test hurdle for success in the landlord game.

Multifamily Houses

Financially, one of the easiest ways into the Homeowner's Club is the multifamily house. In your qualification considerations for a mortgage, the income from the rental unit or units is considered right along with your income from salary, commissions, or other sources.

Emotionally, however, owning and living in a multifamily is sometimes more daunting. You are sharing the building that contains your home and, at the same time, you are running a business. You sometimes become good friends with your tenants or sometimes you, at the least, try to be friendly. But you also collect the rent each month. You are wearing two very different hats. You set the rules: like how many cars can park in the driveway and how late the teenage band can practice. But you also fix the clogged toilet and mow the grass. More different hats!

The answer to the dilemma of too many hats is quite obvious: *pick good tenants.*

"Great idea!" you say with a wry smile. "Could you tell us exactly how to do that?"

I hate to admit it but Lady Luck does play a role in the landlord's game. So give her a nod and take control beyond the roll of the dice. Create a good application form. Consider the following.

- **Credit history:** You can ask permission from prospective tenants to run a credit check but you are not legally obliged to do so. Landlords can initiate credit checks on prospective tenants by contacting a credit information agency. Key *Credit Reporting Agency* into a search engine or check your local Yellow Pages. There is a fee.
- **Employment history:** Ask how long the applicants have held their current job. Try to get a reference letter. Who were their previous employers? How long at each job? Steady employment rates more stars on your evaluation chart than high pay.
- **Relocation history:** Ask how often your prospective tenants have moved in the past five years. Long-term leases are far more profitable than month-to-month arrangements.
- **Good references:** Employers are good as references but previous landlords are the best.
- **Positive vibes:** You should "feel right" about the people who will be your tenants.

COMMUNITY CHEST

Did you know that a predecessor to the MONOPOLY game was patented in 1904 by a young woman named Elizabeth Magie? She was the first person in American history to apply for and be granted patent protection for a board game. And, you guessed it! She called her creation: The Landlord's Game.

Source: *Monopoly: The World's Most Famous Game & How It Got That Way* by Philip E. Orbanes, DaCapo Press, 2006

DON'T GO TO JAIL

Being a landlord is not being King of the Hill. You too must obey the laws of the nation, state, city, and condominium association. The federal *Fair Housing Act* and *Fair Housing Amendments Act* prohibit discrimination in housing for race, color, religion, national origin, physical or mental disability, gender, or familial status (which includes families with children under eighteen and pregnant women). Some state laws add other factors.

When you are the owner/*occupant* of a multifamily house, however, you can refuse a prospective tenant for any reason. They own a black cat, for example. Or they drive a red pickup truck. Or for no reason. But you cannot state that you are refusing tenancy for a reason that is protected by law. This is a fine line. The law allows you to choose the person or people who will occupy another unit in the house that you live in.

Everyone, all tenants and all landlords, should sign a lease before occupancy. Like a purchase contract, it should spell out the agreement between the two parties. Included should be the amount of rent, date by which it is to be paid by each month, the penalty for late payment, the length of the term of the lease, the penalty for breaking the lease, and the amount of the security deposit, where it will be held, and the terms for its return when the tenant vacates. The security deposit must be held in an escrow account. Once the tenant takes possession, both parties should abide by the rules.

Mixed-use Buildings

It may not actually be true, but owning and managing a mixed-use building sometimes feels a lot like double jeopardy. You have the problems of managing residential tenants and the problems of managing commercial tenants. And if you decide "to live above the store" yourself, you also have to deal with all the emotional connotations of *home, privacy, us and them.* On the other hand, the building has the potential to support itself, even bring in some positive cash flow, while providing both a site for a startup business and a place to live.

Everything said about multifamily building tenants is pretty much true of mixed-use buildings too. There is an added challenge, however, in melding the needs and concerns of people doing business and people being at home. Parking, quiet time, smells, sounds, water usage, and trash disposal are just a few of the problems that come up. The habits and needs of children are often a major point of contention.

The lease is another major difference between residential and professional or commercial tenants. Nonresidential leases are usually written for longer terms than residential leases and they come in three different types: the net lease, the net net lease, and the triple net lease.

Under a net lease, the tenant pays all operating expenses (heat, water, and electricity) but not the real estate taxes or insurance. Under a net net lease, the tenant pays all operating expenses plus insurance premiums. Under a triple net lease, the tenant pays for almost everything: all operating expenses, insurance, real estate taxes, and in some cases even the mortgage payments.

One of the best starter investments in mixed-use buildings are the stately post-Victorian mansions that still stand on well-kept streets in many American cities and towns. You will often see the street-level space converted into professional offices, day care centers, or business uses such as real estate agencies. Meanwhile the upper level or levels are used for residential apartments.

With a sharp eye, you may be able to find spacious older houses that could be converted to mixed-use property. You may have to apply for a zoning variance and a nonconforming use permit. The main concerns in investing in such properties are adequate parking and separate commercial and residential **access**. Unless you can show that both are feasible, the zoning board is likely to turn down your request. The other major concern, of course, is future development. What will the neighborhood look like in ten years?

If you are considering the purchase of a mixed-use property or a conversion into one, consider carefully. These properties can be very

DON'T GO TO JAIL

When you choose to be a landlord, you take on responsibilities. It may even feel as though your chances of landing on the *Go To Jail* square of the MONOPOLY board have increased. And in a way, they have. You just have to deal with it using the best possible decisions and strategies. Consider the following elements of American law.

Police power refers to the power of the state to overrule the individual in questions of safety, health, and the general welfare of society. In real estate law, it is the basis for building codes and zoning laws. You must know them in order to comply with them.

The implied warranty of habitability refers to the landlord's responsibility to provide livable premises when a housing unit is rented and to maintain that condition throughout the tenancy. Every state requires that rental properties meet minimal structural, health, and safety standards. Specific requirements vary from state to state. Contact your state's attorney general's office and get a printed copy.

No nuisances. (No joke!) In rental real estate law, a *nuisance* is anything that is dangerous to human life or detrimental to human health. Insufficient lighting in common areas (hallways, backyards) and inadequate heat and ventilation in rental units are good examples. Nuisances are defined and determined by local housing codes. If they are not corrected, landlords are subject to fines and penalties. Do a monthly check.

Attractive nuisances are to be avoided. According to municipal law, *attractive nuisances* are conditions that might attract inquisitive children or other people in unusual circumstances such as homelessness. Some examples are abandoned vehicles, discarded appliances, wells, scaffolding, or excavation. If someone is hurt through contact with an attractive nuisance, the landlord is liable. Keep your property adequately insured.

WORDS TO GO!

Access in the real estate world means more than the ability to approach or enter. When you consider access to a commercial or mixed-use property, you must evaluate the surrounding area for its effects on your building and location. Consider traffic patterns and traffic load at different times of the day, parking availability, highway exit systems, the topography (steep is not good), streams and bridges and other hazards, stairs, sidewalks, handicapped ramps, and even evacuation routes.

profitable but they usually take longer to sell than strictly residential properties. All the considerations of other investment rental real estate are valid in this vehicle, but more so. Check and double-check location, physical characteristics and condition, legal constraints, a local market analysis, and your personal analysis of your investment goals.

Investment Condominiums

Investment condos can be either commercial or residential real estate. Commercial are usually office space in large buildings; medical and legal offices are obvious examples. Residential condominiums are now one of the leading building types being constructed in the United States, surpassing both McMansions and rental apartment buildings by far. They are appealing to investors because they usually bring positive returns on the invested capital without the management demands of multifamily houses and mixed-use buildings.

"Sounds nice," you say. "Good return on my money, no work!"

Yes, but . . . The two people problems in investment condos are choosing the tenants and dealing with the homeowners' association. In condominium construction, **deed restrictions**, bylaws, and house rules are established with the master deed (sometimes called a *declaration*) and you must choose tenants who are willing to comply with them. Some condo communities are restricted to age 55+ and the rule extends to tenants as well as owners. Other **covenants, conditions, and restrictions (CC&Rs)** and bylaws concern pets, parking, use of recreational facilities, and maintenance of common areas.

If a tenant does not comply with bylaws and house rules, a member of the board of directors will usually speak with him or her. But if a cautionary word does not have the desired effect, the board will call the owner. Noncompliance can result in eviction of the tenants. It is the condo owner who takes the financial blow.

The term of rental leases also can be restricted by the bylaws of the community. In some areas of the country where living-space demand is seasonal, such as Arizona golf country and the Florida coastline, many condo bylaws require a minimal three-month rental period. The idea is to prevent high-turnover, hotel-style usage.

You're probably thinking: *Is that legal? Isn't it an unfair restriction of American property rights?*

It's legal. When you buy into a condo community, you agree to abide by the bylaws that were established in the master deed. If the bylaws say no pets, you must not plan to smuggle in Fluffy. And if you do and she is discovered, she can be evicted. If you are unwilling to do that, you can be evicted too, even if you own the place! The bylaws of a condominium community—like municipal laws, and in fact, state and federal laws—establish the limitations within which citizens must agree to live.

WORDS TO *GO!*

Covenants, conditions, and restrictions, commonly called *CC&Rs* or *deed restrictions,* are limitations placed on property in the deed. They remain with the property through all changes of ownership. CC&Rs are a part of every condominium master deed, but they may be included in the deed to any property.

RULES AND STRATEGIES

- Evaluate rental property by its potential for both appreciation and positive cash flow.

- Consider the economic health of the community in which the property is located.

- Get NOI figures from the seller for at least the past two years.

- Ask yourself: *will this property become less desirable to tenants during the time I plan to use it? Why? Can I do anything about it?*

- Before you buy, not just before you do your federal income tax return, learn the IRS laws regarding rental property. Abide by them.

- Keep your property records carefully. You will need them.

- Remember that as a landlord, you are dealing not only with real estate but also with people. You are in a management-intensive corner of the playing field.

PART III

GETTING OUT

CHAPTER 11
Fixing to Sell

Like the Victorians, we want our homes to be havens
in a rapidly changing, complicated, uneasy world.
—Winifred Gallagher, American writer and author
from *House Thinking: A Room-by-Room Look at How We Live*

I overheard two men talking about real estate at a barbeque recently. One was about to put his house on the market and was bemoaning the amount of fix-up work he still had to do.

"Don't worry about it," said the other. "You've got a water view. The location will sell your house no matter what's inside."

It took a steel zipper on my mouth to keep me from breaking in on their conversation. I wanted to say, "That's not true; or it's only partly true. Location will sell the property, but the time on the market is likely to be longer and the sale price lower if the house has not been prepared for marketing."

"Why?" you ask.

Maintenance and appearance are more important in the sale of a home than in investment real estate sales because there is an emotional element in homebuying that can often outweigh all the facts and statistics. Most buyers want to feel comfortable, secure, and at least a bit proud of their homes, but they don't want to clean up someone else's mess to get that comfort, security, and pride. Add to that the baggage they carry.

When house hunting, each prospective buyer carries within his or her psyche acknowledged and unacknowledged memories of "home." Those memories affect choices. Sometimes a real estate agent will hear "Oh I love this kitchen, the window over the sink looks out on an apple tree just like the house where I grew up." The agent usually starts planning a negotiating strategy.

Sometimes the emotional reaction is less overt. Imagine this scenario: A couple is viewing a two-story colonial; they like everything. Last on the tour is the basement. It is spotlessly clean. Shelves hold tools and maintenance items all lined in rows. Nails and screws are stored in glass jars, each labeled for size. Two carpenter's saw-horses stand to one side with a hand-saw and a short piece of molding lying across them. The woman buyer admires the neatness and the strictly ordered arrangement of everything. The man moves away. Staring up at the floor joists, he walks about the perimeter of the basement. Then, without another word, he begins to climb the stairs. The couple leaves the house quickly. They don't buy.

Perhaps the man saw something unacceptable that no one else had noticed—a high water mark maybe? Was it real or imagined? Or perhaps he recognized a personal emotional trigger in that basement. Or perhaps he didn't know what was bothering him and just had a feeling: too rigid, too disciplined. It doesn't matter which. He couldn't (or wouldn't) buy that house.

Keep these two very different stories in mind when you start wondering about seemingly inexplicable buyer behavior. And remember also that it's just as important to recognize your own home-based emotions and to try to keep them out of the marketing plan and the negotiating for your property.

OK, enough theory for now. Let's turn to what you can do to influence the perceptions of prospective buyers. It's a fine line to walk. You are selling a home as well as a house. You want to make your product feel "homey" but you do not want too much of your "hominess" to show through. You want your prospective buyers to feel comfortable and

WORDS TO *GO!*

By law in most states, a seller must *disclose* in writing any conditions, malfunctions, or other problems that might adversely affect the monetary value of the property or that might endanger the health or safety of future occupants.

relaxed while in your house. At the same time you want them to be interested, curious, maybe just stimulated enough to start mentally placing their furniture in the rooms.

The rest of this chapter is about how to do just that.

NECESSARY REPAIRS

Fifty years ago, a conscientious real estate agent might have installed an octagonal red sign at every street corner of the real estate marketplace. Instead of STOP, it would read CAVEAT EMPTOR (Latin for "let the buyer beware"). That safety tactic won't work in the consumer-protection-oriented and litigious twenty-first century. Today the seller must take care to reveal all the hidden problems in every piece of real estate that is for sale. It's called **disclosure**.

What and How to Disclose

Most states have preprinted forms for seller disclosure. You can get them from your real estate agent or you can call your state's real estate commission. If you want to go on the Web, try keying in [*name of your state.gov*]. Go to the real estate commission site and then hunt about for the disclosure form. You can print it without permission.

Most forms are several pages long, consisting of Yes or No answer boxes arranged in columns. The questions are grouped in categories such as roof, plumbing, foundation, and so on. There is also always space for "Other."

The most important phrases on the disclosure form are "to your knowledge" and "during the time you have lived in this house." The state does not expect you to hold competency certificates in plumbing, construction, wiring, roofing, and all the other homebuilding and home-maintenance trades. The form provides space for you to acknowledge what you have experienced in the house and what you know about the house.

For example, let's say that three years ago you saw termites swarming in the spring and you had your house inspected. An infestation was discovered under the garage. You paid to have the entire house termite proofed and paid extra for a ten-year warranty that included annual inspections. In response to the question *have termites been discovered in your house during the past five years?* you check the Yes box. Either in the margin or at the bottom of the page, you note the

DON'T GO TO JAIL

Usually it's not what you disclose that causes problems in a transaction. It's what you omit. Let's say that you are selling your house in August and you don't tell the buyer that the upstairs bedroom in the northeast corner of the house never seems to get enough heat. Long before you listed the house for sale, you complained to your oil company. They said you may need some new ductwork. And maybe a bigger capacity furnace would help, too. But you decided to live with the problem and you didn't mention anything about it on the disclosure form.

Your buyers choose the northeast corner room as their nursery. The baby is born in November, and they can't keep the room warm enough. Has your lack of disclosure endangered the health and well-being of a future occupant? Most courts would say yes. You could be slapped with a lawsuit to cover the cost of a new furnace and new ductwork. We won't even talk about pain and suffering.

date of the extermination work and you attach a copy of the company's ten-year warranty to your disclosure form.

Follow the same procedure for any other major repairs or replacements you have done during your ownership period such as new windows, a new roof, grading and waterproofing to prevent water seepage in the basement, and the addition of water-softening equipment. Other material facts might include the age of the water heater or a septic tank that sometimes backs up in very wet weather.

Answers to the questions about disclosing other problems and situations that might affect the health or well-being of the occupants have many shades of gray. Disclosure of high radon readings is considered absolutely necessary. But is the fact that your house is in an approach flight pattern to a major airport a hazard? What if you know there's a church-sponsored "halfway" house for released drug offenders four blocks away? And the big question: what if you know that a convicted sex offender lives within a mile of your property? Whether you add such information to a disclosure sheet is a matter of personal conscience. Some forms even ask if there has ever been a murder in the house.

Water Works

Buyers worry about water. I've watched many a house hunter tighten the faucet handle in an attempt to stop an ever-so-slow drip. Serious lookers turn on the shower and flush the toilet simultaneously to see how well the drainage system is working. And virtually every prospective buyer who walks into a basement checks the walls. They're almost always looking for cracks and a high watermark. So it follows as clearly as night follows day that you should start your fixing-to-sell program by checking the condition of everything that has anything to do with water.

Sinks that have tan-shaded gullies worn in the porcelain from years of a slow drip should be replaced. The buyers will notice the wear and they will think "old house, needs work." Stained and pitted bathtubs aren't so easy to replace, but they can be quite successfully resurfaced. Shower stalls may require some high-powered cleaning solutions, a stiff brush or two, and gloves for your hands. Retiling is inordinately expensive.

Everyone notices toilets that leak; you know, those little glug-glug bubble sounds. If you have one, replace the inner works. There are kits available at local hardware stores; it's not a huge job. (Don't forget to turn off the water before you start work.)

If a toilet's flushing system is idiosyncratic, leave a little sign on the toilet back that reads something like: hold handle down for three seconds before releasing. That may sound a bit silly, but plumbing problems are fear factors to most buyers. I once lost a deal when a woman buyer took her child to use the powder room. She could not get the toilet to flush. All of us, her husband, the other Realtor, and I, could hear her pushing and repushing the handle. The solution was simple—wait for it to fill and then hold the handle a bit longer—but no one wanted to intrude on her privacy. Finally she left the toilet unflushed, came out of the door with her child by the hand, and left the house as though there were a half-price sale around the corner.

Under the kitchen sink is another place where interested buyers do contortions to get at "the truth." Even in the most well kept homes, this area is hardly pretty. So whadda-ya-gunna do?

Make it uncluttered, clean, and neat. Let the buyer believe he or she can see everything. First of all, take all the "stuff" out, line the base of the cabinet or the floor with shelf paper, and then replace only the absolute necessities such as dishwasher detergent. The ant and roach killer aerosol can, the air freshener, the drain opener, the cleaning rags, and the old pot scrubbers simply must go. (Store them in a closed box out of sight, if you must keep them.) The drainage pipe usually looks "aged" even when it doesn't leak; just wipe off loose dirt.

Next, check your water heater. It's probably covered in dust, soot, and cobwebs. Clean it up and check underneath to be absolutely certain that there are no pinhole leaks developing. If the water heater is more than fifteen years old and you think it might be starting to leak, replace it. It will cost you a lot less for the new appliance than the amount that the buyers will negotiate off the price when the inspector's report comes in with the notation: aging water heater, likely to leak. And besides, you can put your own notation—brand-new water heater—on the listing.

If a municipal waste disposal sewer system has recently been installed in your area, get the balance on the **special assessment** from the town records department. It should be noted in your listing information. You can use payment as a negotiating point or you can simply state that the balance will be paid in full at closing. If you have a septic tank, have it pumped before you list the house. If gnats often gather over the **leach lines**, consider some new top soil and seeding.

Electric Company

In the MONOPOLY game, the Electric Company is a good buy at $150, especially if you can get Water Works too. In Selling Your Home, electricity is the next item on the Must-Repair list.

First of all, leave no exposed wiring anywhere in the house. If switchplates are missing, worn, or discolored, replace them. If you

WORDS TO *GO!*

A *special assessment,* sometimes called an assessment lien, is a municipal tax lien charged to a property for an off-site improvement such as sewers or street lighting. Payments are often scheduled over several years and can be assumed by a buyer. Most buyers, however, do not like that arrangement since lenders often add enough dollars to the monthly mortgage payment to cover the annual or semi-annual assessment payments. As an alternative, you can arrange to have the balance of the assessment paid at the closing from the proceeds of the sale.

The words *leaching fields, leach lines,* and *leach trenches* all refer to methods of removing liquid waste material from sewage by filtration through sand, gravel, tiles, stones, or other means. They are used in reference to private sewerage disposal systems, also known as septic tanks.

COMMUNITY CHEST

A ground fault indicator, or GFI, is a relatively modern safety device that cuts off power to a socket or switch if water causes a short circuit. It is a required part of new construction in bathrooms and kitchens. The device looks like a tiny colored or raised square button between the sockets or switches. You can restore power to the circuit simply by pushing on the button.

Even in older houses, most inspectors will note that GFIs are missing. You can easily install them or have them installed; kits are available at any hardware or home maintenance store. This is a very small expense that can prevent another issue when the inspection report comes in.

don't already have ground fault indicators (GFIs) at all sockets near water access, either install them, if you have some experience working with electricity, or have them installed by a professional. In the same safety vein, if you don't already have one or more smoke detectors, install them. If you do, check that they are working.

Check that every lightbulb in your house lights. Be especially mindful of outdoor walkways, hallways, and basement lighting. In basements, increase the wattage of the bulbs so that there are no dark corners.

Broken Glass

That basement window has been cracked since your toddler (now seven) kicked a soccer ball into it. It's only a small crack, at the corner. Who cares?

It would be a good idea if you do. Broken glass is another item that sets off alarm bells in buyers' heads. All they can think is: poor maintenance.

And besides, they don't want the bother of fixing it, just as you didn't want it so many years ago.

Survey all the windows and storm windows in your house. Replace those that are cracked or have chips out of the corners. This may seem like an annoying chore, usually more annoying than expensive. But you do not want "broken windows" to be a negotiating item. The same goes for storm doors and screens. If you have sliding glass doors, be sure they do not stick or scrape when being opened and closed.

Be especially diligent about replacing cracked mirrors. It's amazing how much superstition still exists, unspoken, in this age of technology. If the mirrors on bathroom medicine cabinets are cracked, it is best to replace the entire cabinet. (No rings and stains to pass on to the buyer. And believe me, the would-be buyers will look inside.)

Heating and Cooling

Take your vacuum cleaner to your furnace area and vacuum up all the soot. Then have your heating contractor (oil or gas company) come in and do a maintenance check. He or she will give you an efficiency rating. The decision is yours as to whether you should replace an old and inefficient furnace or let it be part of your negotiating.

If wall-unit air conditioners are built in, they remain with the house. Window air conditioners usually go with the seller, but they are negotiable. If you have central air conditioning, consider the age and efficiency of the unit. Again, whether to replace it or include it in negotations is your decision.

If you have an older dial thermostat, replace it with a new digital model. The cost is small, but the perceived improvement can make a difference in the perception of the property.

The Roof over Your Head

Most people don't think much about it, but like everything else in the world, a roof can wear out. If yours is fifteen years old or older, it may be feeling its age, even if there are currently no leaks.

If your roof is leaking, you should consider taking out a credit line on your home to finance a new one. "Leaking roof" on a disclosure sheet will often be a deal breaker. If you don't disclose the problem,

DON'T GO TO JAIL

Here are a few more items that could be grounds for a lawsuit:
- Attic space must be vented. Check to be sure that squirrels or other visitors have not made nests that block air passage.

- Bathrooms and heating systems are vented through the roof. Have the chimneys and their flashings checked.

- If a deck has been added to a house, be certain that it is not pulling away from the building.

- Check the fireplace flue. It should have adequate draw. If not, have the chimney cleaned.

most likely it will be picked up by the inspector, and that will cost you either big negotiating bucks or a walkaway by the buyers.

On the other hand, the words *new roof* on the listing will improve the salability of the property because roof repair is not a task new homeowners want to take on. This improvement, however, may not recoup its total cost in added value. It's one of those things that buyers expect will work, but when they discover that it doesn't work, they negotiate for double or more the actual cost of the repairs. Think of the repairs not as money to be made but as money saved.

If your roof is aging but not leaking, it is better to make a mental note of the fact and prepare yourself for its appearance as a negotiating item. Get your own estimates on the cost of a new roof and put them aside. Since the roof is not currently leaking, you can negotiate an allowance for a portion of the estimated cost of a new roof. The logic is that the roof probably won't leak for a number of years, so you should not have to deduct the entire cost of replacement from the agreed-upon price for the house.

On a lighter note, be sure you have all gutters and downspouts cleaned before you put your house on the market. If there is a pull-away from the eaves anywhere, have it repaired. And if you don't have concrete spillways at the bases of your downspouts, put them in. You can buy them at home maintenance stores.

CURB APPEAL

According to the National Association of Realtors, 20 percent of home-buyers buy a house that first caught their interest because of a FOR SALE sign at the curb. Wow! In this age of computer searches for everything, a good number of us still drive around to see what we can see.

So put yourself in the shoes (well, on the wheels) of a buyer and try it out. Get in the car and drive by your house, slowly. Drive around the block and approach from the other direction, stop, take pictures if you like.

How does your house fit in with the neighborhood? The houses around you determine value and salability more than any other single feature. The drive-by appearance of your house should be neat and appealing but not imposing or extraordinary.

Here's another story: In an office where I once worked, a relatively new agent had listed a house that was two stories high, plus an attic, in a neighborhood of Cape Cods and ranches. "Different from the neighborhood" is a negative selling point, but actually not too bad in this case. Except! Except that the big house was painted lilac with bright white trim and a deep purple door. No one could miss it, but it took a long time to sell.

While you're out on the road looking at your house as a buyer might look, ask yourself if you can really see it. Sometimes overgrown landscaping not only hides the structure but also darkens the interior. If you feel comfortable with pruning, trim foundation plantings to just below the bottom edge of the front windows. If plantings have grown over the path to the front door, cut them back or take them out. (You don't want your prospective buyers fighting through the pachysandra vines or around cactus arms.) If plant discipline is difficult for you, just hire a landscape service to prune on a one-time basis.

With or without a landscape service, be sure to keep the grass cut and trimmed. And if it's not perfect grass (let's say there's a weed or

CHANCE

If you are selling your home during the winter in a northern climate, be sure to keep all pathways shoveled and sanded. If you have an appointment scheduled soon after a snow or ice storm, it may be better to postpone it to a later date than to risk a house hunter or a real estate agent slipping. You are in fact legally responsible for the physical safety of buyers and agents who are inspecting your home. Talk with your insurance agent to check on your liability coverage.

two mixed in), cut it short and cut it often. Weeds are much less recognizable when they are only stubs.

If you have exterior paint that is fading, chipping, or peeling, give your house a face lift. A new exterior paint job is the fix-up activity that has the best financial return when you consider added value in relation to cost. It can increase the market value as much as ten times its cost. On the other hand, if the siding is in good condition but the trim is chipping and peeling, have just the trim painted. Don't assume that no one will notice the few spots under the eaves that no longer have paint. Buyers will judge worn-out paint in even the smallest area as an indication of poor maintenance. Some of them won't even bother to come inside.

Beyond the overall color and appearance of your house, your front door is the exterior focal point of your home. If it looks weary and the hardware is pitted and darkened, consider replacing it. If you don't wish to replace the entire door, you can give it a coat of paint and replace the door handle and locks. A tasteful wreath or other seasonal door decoration is usually perceived as warm and inviting.

If you live in a rural area with a curbside mailbox, be sure that it too is in good condition. You don't want a rusty mailbox to be the first thing buyers see after the FOR SALE sign. And if you have a fence, hire Tom Sawyer and Huck Finn and make it look like new.

LET BUYERS FEEL COMFORTABLE AND RELAXED

In her book, *House Thinking: A Room-by-Room Look at How We Live,* Winifred Gallagher points out that people regard home as either a refuge from the world or a vista from which to look out upon the world. Frank Lloyd Wright identified the two human attitudes as nesting and perching.

"Sounds plausible," you say. "But what has all that got to do with selling my home?"

If house hunters feel comfortable and relaxed when they walk about inside your home, they have stepped over the line that divides prospective buyers from potential buyers. They are looking not at your home but at a house that they could make into *their* home. Some may see it as a refuge and some as a vista, but in either case each potential buyer will consider it in terms of his or her own needs. Your goal is to create the interior space that best lets house hunters do that. Preparing your house for sale is very much a work of art.

Moving You and Your Family Out

No, I don't recommend selling an empty house. In fact, vacant properties usually hang around longer in the marketplace than any other type of property except new construction. What I do recommend is a focused effort at depersonalization. You may be very proud, and rightly so, of your collection of family photos dating back to 1947, but

COMMUNITY CHEST

Simplicity and repose are the qualities that measure the true value of any work of art.

Space is the breath of art.

—Frank Lloyd Wright (1869–1959), American architect

you do not want house hunters examining them as they climb the stairs to the second floor.

Take down from the walls or take off the shelves and tables all the family photos. Carefully wrap them and box them and put them into storage. (Or if you are lucky enough to live near family, beg a little storage space at their house while you sell.) Next remove and box all the trophies and ribbons that you might have on display, even the big blue one that Dozer won at Westminster!

Are you crushed? It gets even harder. You're going to have to make economic decisions about rock-group posters, school projects, octopi on the bathroom shower curtain, and mushrooms on the walls of the kitchen.

Kids' rooms, especially teenagers' rooms, are often very personal-ized and very unappealing to house hunters, unless those house hunters just happen to have similar kids. Sometimes it's really diffi-cult to get children and teens to understand how important clean and neutral space is to your sale. But you've got to get their cooperation. Let them continue to "own" their stuff by getting each young person his or her own moving box (you can buy them from move-it-yourself companies like U-Haul). Let each child help with the packing, and promise that he or she can put everything back up in the new house. You might even add the temptation of adding some new wall decorations in the new house.

Among the "mature" décor you have chosen for your home, wall-paper is definitely an item of personal taste. Unfortunately, as such, it can put off many buyers who happen to have different (not necessarily better, mind you, just different) taste. Also unfortunately, wallpaper doesn't always strip from the walls well and the remnants can be dif-ficult to paint over.

Condo owners have a special problem with wallpaper because there are often many apartments for buyers to choose from that are exactly alike except for the location and the decorating. Wallpaper that is unacceptable to them can deter a sale. Many condo buyers (and house buyers, too) don't know how to wallpaper, and professional wallpaper hangers are expensive. (So is new wallpaper.)

CHANCE

Michael Corbett, real estate and lifestyle expert on NBC's *Extra,* and author of *Ready, Set, Sold!* (Plume, 2007), writes: "What happens when you avoid doing the work and give your buyer an allowance instead? You will corner yourself into accepting a lower offer because your house doesn't look 'buyer perfect'—and you'll still pay the allowance!"

So what should you do? If you are a handyperson, allow yourself a couple of weekends. Room by room, strip away the wallpaper that looks faded or worn or is particularly unique to your taste. Then either paint over the walls or repaper with a neutral-colored textural paper. If you are not a do-it-yourselfer, or if you do not want to pay for a wallpapering job, be sure the room is clean and uncluttered and hope that a buyer will like what's already up.

More Space than You Ever Thought You Had

Things take up space. Now, I know that doesn't sound very profound, but perhaps you'll think a little differently if you consider that space is what you are selling. Usually, the less space the potential buyer perceives, the less money he or she is likely to offer. So your next job is to make more space. You do that by removing unnecessary things.

We live in an age of "more is better," and most of us tend to accumulate. Aunt Millie's needlepoint footstool stands in front of grandma's rocker, and no one ever sits there except on Christmas morning. Many of us have not one but three or four television sets, each having its own DVD player or other add-ons. All about the house, any number of electronic gadgets, athletic gear, games, books, and magazines lays stacked on every available horizontal surface. And we don't even notice the stuff is there!

OK, pick a room. Take everything out. That includes all easily moveable furniture and wall hangings. Now look at the room from its entranceway. If you were an artist or an interior decorator, what would you put into this space to make it inviting and comfortable? You may need only half the furniture you currently have in the room. And perhaps only half the plants. As Frank Lloyd Wright said, leaving open space is the essence of art. The appropriate use of space creates focus. The feeling of enough space creates a sense of comfort.

To the extent that it is feasible, do this exercise for every room. In the bedrooms, the bathrooms, and the kitchen, also put away as many of the "things" on horizontal surfaces as you possibly can. Remove as much extraneous furniture as you can. Rent a storage facility or impose upon your relatives. If you plan to leave any particularly large items when you sell (perhaps an entertainment center or bookcases that are more or less "built in"), include them in your listing. Technically, they are called **chattel**.

Wall-to-wall carpeting is one of those items that often comes up in discussions of what stays. Most people see it as an installed item; however, there are those who maintain that it can be removed without permanent damage to the floors beneath it. Whether it stays or not can be negotiated, especially if the buyers do not like the carpeting and are looking for another way to lower the purchase price.

WORDS TO *GO!*

The real estate legalese for personal property is *chattel*. Generally speaking, if something in the house isn't nailed down or otherwise installed, it is considered personal property and not included in the sale. But nailed down seems to have quite a few interpretations. It is always best to write everything, going or staying, into the contract.

CHANCE

Most sellers feel more than a twinge of pain when they think of paying for large fix-up expenditures just before selling. But try to get past the very normal feeling of resentment for not getting to enjoy the new stuff you put in. Let thoughts of lowering inspection/negotiating anxiety be your Get Out of Jail Free card. Your bill for most refurbishing is likely to be considerably lower than what the buyers would negotiate off the price when they or the inspector found something unsatisfactory.

Wall-to-wall carpeting is the most common example. Buyers in general do not like the thought of walking over someone else's worn and soiled floors. (Pet owners take note!) Sometimes, the condition of the floors kills a deal. Always, it is a major negotiating issue.

If your carpeting has obvious walking patterns or stains, have new wall-to-wall installed. Buy a neutral color. You'll be surprised at the selection of sale carpets. Often at the larger carpet stores, you can charge your purchase with delayed payments and no interest for a year or more. You may be able to pay the entire bill from the proceeds of the sale and never take a dollar out of your wallet.

Storage Space, Cobwebs, and Dirt

Most people do not like change. If you don't think that's true, just try asking any person to change his or her living habits. Or try it yourself. Psychologists will tell you that it's a tall order. (Resistance to change is one of the reasons that 95 percent of weight-loss diets fail over the long run.)

But unless you are an extremely neat and orderly person, you and your family are going to have to change your daily habits during the time that your house is on the market. In the sixteenth century, Machiavelli saw resistance to change in the state of the state; in the twenty-first century, you are about to experience it in the state of your home.

COMMUNITY CHEST

Announce to your family that in addition to the living areas, the garage, the basement, and all the closets and cabinets in the house must be cleaned and organized, and kept that way, every single day, until the house is sold. Your proclamation is not likely to get an enthusiastic reception. But try to explain how important (and temporary) this condition is: we're talking about the buyers' perception of space.

Every homebuyer wants a lot of storage space. But no one wants to clean up someone else's storage space. The following are some tips to enhance buyer perception.

- **Start in the garage or carport.** Toss or put into storage everything you are not currently using. When finished, if you still have a lot of stuff, consider buying some metal shelving from a nearby home maintenance store. It's inexpensive, and you can take it with you for the next garage. Thoroughly sweep or vacuum up the floor. There should be no dead leaves or debris. Increase the wattage in the light-bulbs so the space does not look dim. If the garage has a window, clean it!

- **Declutter the basement.** Basements collect stuff, sometimes a lifetime of stuff. Prospective buyers are very put off by stacked boxes and old, broken, and unused furniture and toys. And most people, even if they won't admit it, are afraid of spiders. Soot and dirt around the furnace suggests a lack of care, and old paint and solvent cans are considered a combustible danger. If you have a teen or children's "rec" room in the basement, light it well, take out or organize the extras, and keep it clean. If you have a cat litter box hidden somewhere, clean it often.

- **Photograph your linen closets for *House Beautiful.*** I first suggested this strategy almost thirty years ago in my second book (*Selling Your Home*), and it still holds true. Prospective buyers are going to open all the doors. If the linen closet is full of rolled-up towels and sheets that have been stuffed in wherever there was a space, the buyers will be quite positive that their linens simply won't fit in that closet. Fold each towel and piece of bed linen neatly, stack by color and type, with the fold to the door and the open edges to the inside of the shelf.

- **Skip the California Closet organizer.** But do lighten up on the load. A customer of mine once opened a bedroom closet and had a bag of knitting supplies fall on his head. No harm was done, but he wasn't about to buy that house! Reduce and reorganize everything stored on closet shelves. Clear the top shelves enough to make them appear ready to hold much more. Remove all the off-season clothes from your closets and put them in storage so that the racks look as though there is plenty of space. Don't leave shoes in a jumble on the floor.

- **Virtually empty the foyer guest closet.** You can leave a few coats just to be sure the buyers know that this is a guest closet, but what you really want is pretty much empty space and some hangers so that the buyer/guests can hang up their coats if they wish. Don't leave your vacuum cleaner, broom, or mop in the guest closet: it will look as though you have no other place to put these cleaning tools.

- **Organize your pantry and kitchen cabinets.** As I've said, buyers will open doors. It would be far worse than the knitting bag incident if a soup can were to fall from a cabinet shelf and hit someone. Try to use up some of your stored food before you list the property. You will want to make the shelf space appear ample. For aesthetic appeal, group items by type.

- **Survey your bathroom cabinets.** No matter how "nice" your neighborhood, it's not a good idea to put temptation in the path of your buyers. Remove all prescription drugs into a safe place that is unlikely to be opened.

COMMUNITY CHEST

She keeps the house so clean you can eat off the floor!

—Polish/American immigrant saying

Yes, as the old adage goes, cleanliness is next to Godliness. Especially when you are selling your home. Think how you would feel if you walked into a hotel room and found crumbs on the floor and stains on the walls. Would you "buy" the room, even for one night? Again, your prospective buyer is considering the quality of the space being offered for sale.

Become a Painter

Like exterior painting, interior painting brings a huge return both in higher market value and in a quicker sale. A coat of paint will cover the bangs and scrapes of everyday life and offer a fresh new start. Before putting your house on the market, repaint wherever you can. Choose neutral colors.

"But I'm not a beige person!" you cry.

Your buyers probably won't be either. And they may eventually paint over your work with more vibrant colors of their own choosing. But they will be pleased with the clean and unimposing color on the walls when they first see the house, and they will not feel pressure to redecorate immediately upon moving in.

If you have the time and the skills, also consider painting the ceilings, especially the kitchen. No one will notice the job you've done. What they will notice is how bright and clean the rooms look. Another job for those who have a long lead time before actually putting the house up for sale is painting the inside of closets. The original builder's white that is put onto the inside of closet space turns to yellow-gray after so many years and looks dingy, even if there isn't a mark on the walls. A fresh coat of paint will make the space appear bigger and better.

LET BUYERS FEEL INTERESTED AND STIMULATED

Am I contradicting myself? First I tell you how to make buyers feel comfortable and relaxed, and now I'm going on to tell you how to make them feel interested and stimulated. Hmmm, maybe I should try my hand at romance novels.

Can you really do it? Yes! Possibilities are what make buyers interested. They imagine themselves using the rooms. They begin to think what they can do with the space they see.

To help them imagine positively, fill the rooms with as much light as possible. Keep draperies open and blinds either pulled up or in open position. In the evening or on rainy days when you leave the house for showing, leave with lights on in every room. You don't have to have all the lights on, just enough to warm the atmosphere of the room.

I've also suggested that you take all personalizing elements out of your house. Now put some personality back in. Flowers on the table or a bowl of fresh fruit will add a bit of color. A few recent magazines on the coffee table, a filled candy dish, a large plant or two in appropriate locations, all add a lived-in feeling. If you have an enclosed porch or another place for a convenient game table, a partially completed jigsaw puzzle or a game of chess often causes a stop, a smile, and an idea for the buyer's own use.

It's Like Perfume, Only Different

Odors are sometimes even more powerful stimulators than visual perceptions. The brain registers perceived smell in the limbic system, which is a nonverbal and sometimes unconscious but powerful emotional motivator. The scent of your house, therefore, can influence its sale.

The old cliché of home selling is: bake bread. And yes, the smell of bread in the oven whispers "home" to many people. But apple or pumpkin pie, brownies, cookies, or even a turkey can stimulate an unspoken desire to stay.

COMMUNITY CHEST

The limbic system is the area of the brain most concerned with emotion . . . its influence on behavior is unbelievably extensive . . .

—Richard M. Restak, MD, American neurologist and author of eighteen books on the human brain

Cooking odors often take us back to childhood memories. If you like to cook, you can use your craft quite effectively. Avoid permeating the house with strong smells like fried fish or boiled cabbage, however, or with strong spices like garlic and turmeric. On the other hand, don't walk around your house spraying fruit-of-the-fields room freshener in every room just before prospective buyers are scheduled to arrive. Too much artificial scent can be as big a put-off as last night's trout bones left in the kitchen wastebasket.

One of the worst scent offenders in the real estate marketplace is the cat litter box. People who don't live with cats can find the box by scent alone; people who do are only rarely bothered by it. Mustiness is another problem. Especially if you are selling a vacant house, be sure to open the windows frequently and get some fresh air.

The Sound of Silence

Sounds too can affect a buyer's perception of a property. I once showed a house with two rottweilers locked in a downstairs storage room. They barked constantly from the second we set foot in the door. The prospective buyers did not stay long enough to see the entire house.

. The sound of a barking dog, especially a large one, frightens many buyers, even if the dog is crated or otherwise restrained. A dog barking in the backyard or in a locked garage has the same effect. Try to take your dog with you when you go out for an hour or so while the house is being shown.

And what about music? If you have a good sound system in the house, there's no harm in leaving some easy-listening CDs playing during the perspective buyers' inspection. But don't leave the TV or the radio on; it makes both buyers and agents nervous that someone is still at home. You definitely don't want a tour of your house to start off with a nervous reaction.

If you usually have a lot of street noise at the time of a showing appointment, close the windows and run the air conditioner. The buyers will deal with the street noise later; you just don't want it to color their first impression. The same goes for children playing computer games with dramatic sound effects or old-fashioned Cowboys and Indians. Telling them to play quietly won't do any good; take them out for an ice cream.

Other Stimulants

If you wish to further stimulate interest in your home and your town, you can also leave flyers and brochures on a table or countertop. Choose those that describe groups, services, and things to do in the local community like civic groups, libraries, childcare, and recreational opportunities. (More about this kind of marketing in Chapter 13.)

And if you wish to hit on taste along with the other four senses, you can leave a full coffee maker and coffee cups on the table and

DON'T GO TO JAIL

If there is a sewage treatment plant a mile or so from your home, or perhaps a landfill, or an industrial plant, any of which can occasionally (let's say once a month) permeate the air with an unpleasant odor, you must reveal its presence on your disclosure form. If you don't, the buyer would have the right to sue because the odor could be interpreted as a factor that reduces the value of the property.

perhaps donuts or crackers. Many brokers put out quite a spread for open houses. Most sellers don't bother to do so for showing appointments. They wait until they have an appointment for a second showing. That's when you want to encourage the potential buyers to sit down for a bit and have a cup of . . .

INVESTMENT REAL ESTATE

Just about everything in this chapter applies to investment property, but not always to the same degree. Emotions play a much smaller role in this marketplace, as they should.

If you are about to list a rental property, for example, you should still try to make the building and living quarters appear clean and well maintained. But questions of fix-up come down to two perspectives: Should I do the renovation or rehab in the expectation that it will bring me a higher price? Or should I sell the building "as is" and accept the lower price as a tradeoff for all the work I didn't have to do and all the money I didn't have to put into the property? The answers to those questions often depend on the mood of the marketplace (see Chapter 14) and the goals of the investor.

One of the biggest factors in the successful sale of investment property is often the tenants. If one day your tenants see a FOR SALE sign on the front lawn and they have had no notice of your intention to sell, they may well become fearful of eviction. Fearful or resentful tenants can make selling extremely difficult. For example, the tenants can refuse to show their apartments. Or, even worse, they can vandalize improvements you have just made. And when asked simple, conversational questions by prospective buyers, some tenants will tell lies about the living conditions.

It is usually best to inform tenants of your plans. You can either write leases that will survive the transfer of property or you can settle on a payment amount (often it's the security deposit) as a release from the remaining term of their rental agreement. A cooperative tenant is a definite plus factor in this marketplace.

RULES AND STRATEGIES

- Prospective buyers need to feel comfortable and relaxed while viewing a house, but they also need to become interested and stimulated.

- Most states have laws requiring written disclosure by the seller of factors or material faults that may affect the market value of a house.

- Think about water. Buyers are concerned with all aspects of a house that obtain it, contain it, or dispose of it. Be certain that everything works as it should and looks clean and appealing.

- To draw a top-dollar offer, a house must appear to be well maintained. Pay attention to details.

- Buyers first see (and get a sense for) a house from the road. Curb appeal should be a primary concern of every seller.

- New paint (outside and inside) has the best return of all fix-up expenditures.

- Simplify, depersonalize, and neutralize all rooms.

- Clean and organize closets, cabinets, garage space, and the basement and/or attic.

- Sounds and smells can unconsciously affect buyers and influence their attitudes toward the property.

- Tenants can and do affect the marketing of investment property.

CHAPTER 12
What's It Worth?

*I get so tired of listening to one million dollars
here, one million dollars there, it's so petty.*

—Imelda Marcos (1929–), First Lady of the Philippines,
quoted in *The Times* (London) June 22, 1990

Indiana Avenue at $220. Marvin Gardens at $280. Connecticut Avenue at $120. Some things never change. The price of each property is printed on the MONOPOLY board and that is the price you pay to buy it from the bank. Maybe the real real estate marketplace should take note. In the twenty-first century, maybe houses for sale should come with bar codes. Imagine how easy it would be: just run the scanner by and pay whatever the computer says you should pay.

Can you hear the proponents shouting? *Faster! More efficient! No need for extra service people! Equality for all!* And thus another of America's few remaining negotiating opportunities would bite the dust.

Is that a wry smile I see? Are you about to ask, perhaps with tongue in cheek, exactly who would do the programming so that every house would scan at exactly the right price?

Good question! I think, however, that you know the answer: all the buyers and sellers currently in the marketplace would each have a say.

Impossible? Yes, and no one could ever be really sure that the bar code reading was the real price. At best, even in this brave new century, a bar code on a house for sale could only establish an asking price.

Fair market value in the real estate marketplace is still determined by what a ready, willing, and able buyer is willing to pay and what a ready, willing, and able seller is willing to accept. Despite the easy availability (in town hall records and on the Web) of the exact price last paid for virtually every house in the nation and despite the numerous Websites and local real estate agency offers to give you a market-value figure for your property, the worth of each and every property is determined at the negotiating table.

HOW TO PUT A PRICE TAG ON YOUR HOME

Even acknowledging the need for negotiating space, pricing is harder and more important than you may think. You want to name a figure that will attract prospective buyers enough to convince them to look at the interior.

Your asking price should not intimidate buyers into imagining a worst-case negotiating situation. Some buyers won't even go inside a house they think is too far overpriced because they fear not being able to negotiate to a price they think is fair. And some buyers fear that if they love the house or need the house, they might overpay. On the other hand, you do not want to set the price so low that the house sells the first day on the market and you spend the rest of your life wondering if you could have gotten more.

Using the Web

Market evaluations at the touch of a computer key were not so easily available even ten years ago. Sellers either depended on real estate agents to name a price or just took a guess (usually too high) at market value.

But that was then and this is now. It should be much easier now. And in some ways it is, but it's also easier to make a mistake.

I can hear you thinking: *How can you make a mistake? Why not just take the market worth numbers from several sites and average them out and then add 5 to 10 percent for negotiating room?*

COMMUNITY CHEST

There are now many Websites that will give you an estimated market value for your home and there are new ones being created almost every day. You can go to a search engine and enter the words *home value* or *home price* and choose among them. Following is a list of some of the most popular sites.

www.homeadvisor.com

www.homes.com

www.homesdatabase.com

www.iown.com

www.owners.com

www.realestatebook.com

www.realtor.com

www.zwillow.com

Let me answer that question with another. If you, or your son or daughter, were applying to college, would you like it if every college announced a one hundred point range for acceptable SAT scores? If an applicant fell below or above the numbers, they didn't get in. No appeals.

"Hang on," you cry. "What about all the community activity a student does? What about talents, sports, and motivation? What about test-taking skills or lack thereof? What about the interview?"

You're absolutely right. Not even the most carefully researched and substantiated numbers can evaluate worth. There are intangibles, both positive and negative, in every home that simply cannot be factored. What is appealing to one buyer may be repellent to another. For example, the fact that a school playground abuts the back line of the property for sale might be appealing to a young family and anathema to a newly retired couple. Seller and buyer preferences such as a desired short or long escrow time before closing are also factors that are unavailable to the computer. Included or excluded decorating items, appliances, and built-in furniture are still others. And finally, the pace of your local marketplace always has an effect in determining the most appropriate asking price. (More about that in Chapter 14 and in just a bit.)

Be aware that I'm not advising you *not* to get market figures from the Web. Do research such numbers online; they are very helpful. Just use them as a starting point rather than your final answer. Average the numbers to establish a ballpark figure for home value and work from there. If you are selling investment real estate, Web figures can still be helpful, but you will be playing a different, more demanding version of the real estate game. We'll get to that later in this chapter.

If you do not have access to a computer, you can do your setting-the-price market evaluation the old-fashioned way. Go to your town hall records department and look up the transaction prices listed in the tax records of your neighbor and of houses similar to yours elsewhere in town. The more recently sold, the more likely that the number has relevancy to your market value. You can also look at the tax assessments for your neighborhood. Is your house assessed for more or less than those of the neighbors around you? Have any of those houses sold recently? If so, consider the ratio of the selling price to the assessment. Your working estimate of probable selling price for your home should be about the same ratio to your assessment as the comparable house.

CHANCE

If you call in three or more real estate agents to give you a market evaluation on your home, you will learn a lot about the pace of the local market, get a suggested asking price and a probable selling price, get suggestions on how to improve the presentation of the property, and hear a pitch from each agent as to why his or her agency is "the best" in the area. If well trained, each agent will ask for your listing. *Don't sign anything!* Instead, listen and ask questions. *Why does the agent think his/her agency is right for your home? What will the agency do for you?* (More in Chapter 13.)

Whether you spend time with the local tax records or not, you should still get a professional evaluation of your home's market worth, by a person, not a machine. To do so, call agents from several different real estate agencies asking each to do a comparative market analysis (CMA) on your home. The service is free and I highly recommend you take advantage of it.

Using Realtor Opinion

When doing their CMAs, real estate agents will use the same Web-sites available to you plus a few more private subscription sites. So why bother to invite them into your home for a viewing and waste the time taken up in getting their opinions?

Because theirs are *professional* opinions. Realtors know what has recently sold and at what price, and most important, *why*. They know what specific factors affected sale price. For example, there may be too many look-alike condos for sale in one neighborhood to stimulate any competition; or perhaps the need of a particular seller for a delay of four months to closing kept some prospective buyers from making offers; or perhaps the beautiful new kitchen counters, cabinets, appliances, and floor in a 1950s ranch increased its sales appeal. A real estate agent who is actively in the business can tell you what factors made a recently sold house comparable to yours sell more quickly or less quickly, at a higher price or a lower price than expected. With that knowledge, you can refine your estimate of both market value and salability.

Realtors also are working with the pace of the *local* marketplace. (That can be quite different from the figures on national TV.) They know how long the average house stays on the market. They know how much difference there usually is between asking price and actual selling price in your area. This information is invaluable in determining the amount of negotiating dollars to add to your own market-value estimate. (More in Chapter 14.)

And finally, because they accompany house hunters from room to room, real estate agents know which factors are appealing to local buyers and which are not. A good real estate agent can advise you on what

CHANCE

Beware the Wily Witch and Merlin the Magician in the real estate marketplace! You will recognize them disguised as the "special-powers" real estate agents who tell you they can get you any price you want and/or sell your home in seven days. These "super people" also have special skills to bend numbers on a CMA to show value at 10 to 20 percent above everyone else's estimates.

Signing a listing contract at an excessively high price with "magical" agents can put a home out of the showings-included range of other similar houses. It will sit on the market, unvisited for months. By that time, it is considered a "dog on the market" by neighbors and other agents alike. The effect is negative; some agents forget the house is still on the market, and buyers who might be interested ask, "what's wrong with it?" Unsuccessful marketing will also increase your frayed nerves and decrease you already wavering self-esteem. An unrealistic asking price is a home-selling mistake that is often anxiety provoking and sometimes difficult to correct.

furniture or wall decorations to remove or rearrange, what wall colors seem to get the best response, and how to change lighting for maximum effectiveness. Perhaps most important, a good agent will advise you on what needs to be included when you fill out the disclosure form.

Choosing Your Numbers

You must choose *one* number as your listed asking price but there is always a range from which to choose. So what's next? How do you pick the number?

Calculate. And listen. Take the average of all the Web estimates and compare that figure to the real estate agents' CMAs. Consider the pace of the local marketplace and *your* pace. Do you want to sell as quickly as possible or would you like time on the market while you look for a new place or perhaps have a new house built for you? Then decide.

Your next step is to write down three numbers: what you think is the probable selling price, the absolute bottom figure that you would accept if you had to, and your dream figure that you'd really like to get if you could. Don't show these numbers to anyone, especially not to your real estate agent. Just put them away in a safe place that you'll remember when you need to consider them again. Then list at a price somewhat above the probable selling price to give yourself some negotiating space. More about the other two numbers in Chapter 14.

THE EQUITY FACTOR

"The equity factor? What has equity got to do with setting the price?" you ask. Many experts say *not much*, and, if that's true, why bother to discuss it? Because the amount of real money (useable cash) you have in your home may very well affect not only your asking price but also your plan for future moves in the real estate marketplace.

When you put your home on the market, the asking price must come from four factors: the value of the property as compared to others like it in the vicinity; the value of the unique aspects of your property; the pace of the local marketplace; and the pace for your selling plan. The pace for your selling plan depends on what you want to do next. In order to calculate how much you can afford to pay for another house, for example, you must know not only a probable selling price but also how much equity you have.

CHANCE

Most sellers like numbers with nines, like $459,000. And buyers are quite used to them. But not too many nines; $459,999 looks about a dollar short.

To calculate your equity, call your mortgage holder, give them the number of your account, and ask for the mortgage balance. Put that number aside for just a minute.

Now take the probable selling price and calculate the real estate agency commission (usually 6 percent, but that is negotiable). Note that figure. Then ask your real estate agent for an estimate of your closing costs. He or she won't be able to give you an exact figure but closings are a part of their jobs and they will be familiar with customary and usual costs. Then make a list of any liens or second mortgages on the property.

When you have all of these numbers in hand, deduct them from the probable selling price. Here's a made-up sample:

$500,000 probable selling price
− 260,000 first mortgage balance
− 30,000 real estate commission
−   5,000 closing costs
− 20,000 second mortgage balance
_____

$185,000 the cash amount you have for your next down payment

OK, now comes the kicker. The next, very important, question is: *can you afford to buy your wish-list house?* Unless you do this exercise *before* you sign a contract to purchase, you may find yourself under contract to buy and then discover that you do not have the down payment money you expected. As an experienced homeowner with good credit, you may still be able to get a mortgage. But the less-than-optimum down payment could mean a higher interest rate, a bigger mortgage, a choice of Netflix or Blockbuster for your weekend entertainment, and hot dogs and beans or pasta for dinner three times a week. Not for months but for years. Or at least until your income goes up and your living costs go down.

If you are forced to move because of career or personal issues, you should buy the best housing you can with the numbers you get. If, however, you are choosing to move to get more space, a more gracious house, or a better location, consider your numbers carefully. Selling and moving is costly, both financially and emotionally. Check to see if the move is worth the cost. Would postponing the sale a year or two allow the next house to be closer to what you really, ultimately, want? Sometimes balancing time and money can make a huge difference in comfort.

HOW TO PUT A PRICE TAG ON INVESTMENT PROPERTY

Setting the asking price is a little different on the investment side of the playing field. Comparables are still important, of course, but there aren't always a lot of comparables around. Most multifamily houses on

WORDS TO *GO!*

An *appraiser* is a licensed real estate professional who is paid for his or her opinion of property value.

You can get more information about the appraisal industry from their many trade associations. The Appraisal Foundation is a good source for names, numbers, and Websites. Contact them at: 202-347-7727 or *www.appraisalfoundation.org*.

When talking with your appraiser you will also want to recognize the following terms:

Capitalization rate is a method of estimating property value for income-producing buildings. The expected return (yield) is used in evaluating worth.

Effective gross income in a rental property is the potential gross annual income minus a correction for vacancies and nonpayment of rent.

Annual operating expenses include management fees, accounting and legal fees, property taxes, insurance, maintenance fees and supplies, security fees, and the utilities provided to tenants (heat, electricity, water, cable TV, air conditioning, etc.).

the market today were built long before the homogeneous suburban neighborhoods of the 1950s and onward that make it easy to find comps. Multifamily houses are often on city and small town center streets, and few are exact copies of each other.

So what should you do about pricing your investment property? If you are a beginning investor (less than three properties bought and sold), you should find an agent experienced in the type of investment property you have chosen and work closely with him or her. Or you can pay for a professional appraisal. We can learn a lot about market value in investment property from the methods used by **appraisers**.

The three most commonly used procedures are:
• The market data method, which is the same as doing a CMA;
• The replacement cost method, which also factors in depreciation;
• The income analysis method, which relies on rental rates in the local area.

Don't be afraid to ask your appraiser which method or methods he or she is using and how the numbers were determined.

THE ROLE OF THE REAL ESTATE AGENT

To be comfortable in all areas of the real estate marketplace, it's important that you recognize the role of the professional agent in selling property. In the next chapter, I'm going to talk about marketing and showing property, which is what agents do every day. But before we go there, let's look a little more closely at the agent's role in setting the price of a property.

Let the agent help you set the price using all the numbers and knowledge at his or her disposal. A house or investment property originally listed at too high a price will languish. At too low a price, it will usually sell quickly (there are always sharks swimming about) but the seller will lose money. There is a professional skill (an art, if you like) in taking all the numbers available and mixing in nontangible factors like presentation, the mood of the marketplace, and the reputation of the neighborhood, and then adding seller needs and concerns to come up with a marketing figure that will bring the best return.

COMMUNITY CHEST

Most, but not all, really competent agents are Realtors. The National Association of Realtors (NAR) does acknowledge experience, excellence, and continued study with several trade designations. If a real estate agent has earned this recognition, it will most likely appear on his or her card.

Certified Residential Specialist (CRS) indicates varied experience and specialized course work in residential listing and sales. "Residential" includes single-family houses and multifamily houses. Most CRS agents do not work extensively with apartment buildings, office buildings, or complex mixed-use buildings. They do, however, handle building lots suitable for dwellings and small tracts of land that might be subdivided for houses. For more information, go to www.Realtor.com.

Certified Commercial Investment Member (CCIM) is conferred by the Commercial-Investment Real Estate Council, an affiliate of the NAR. Earning a CCIM requires extensive course work, documentation of experience, references, and a written examination. Only 6 percent of the estimated 125,000 commercial real estate practitioners in the United States hold the CCIM designation. For more information, go to *www.ccim.com*.

The *Society of Industrial and Office Realtors* designates membership with the acronym SIOR. This association has more than 3,200 members, 2,500 of whom hold the SIOR designation. Candidates must demonstrate knowledge, production, and ethics. For more information, go to *www.sior.com*.

Not a part of the NAR, the *Urban Land Institute* (ULI) also offers many courses and seminars in real estate–related subjects. You can contact them at *www.uli.org*.

COMMUNITY CHEST

So choose your agent carefully. If you are selling a home, get several CMAs and interview each agent. If you are selling an investment property, it is essential that you work with an agent who has extensive experience, or even a specialty, in your kind of property. Finding and choosing such an agent may take a little extra time, but that time will be rewarded with insider knowledge that can only be acquired by experience. Many larger real estate firms have separate offices that specialize in investment property. Ask.

THE ANXIETY DEMON

Anxiety is one of the most destructive demons in the real estate marketplace. Like MONOPOLY, selling real estate is a game that plays out over a period of time. The effects of the moves and decisions you make may not become apparent or make a difference for what seems like an eternity. And then you start thinking: *Did I price it right? Should I do a price reduction? Should I offer extras? Why isn't this property selling? Is my house unappealing? Why aren't more people coming to see it? Is the real estate agent doing a good job?*

I have lived the experience of such anxiety (my husband and I have bought, lived in, and sold eight different homes) and I have witnessed it in clients and in readers seeking advice. I wish I could tell you to take two pills or read two chapters and it will go away. It won't, because we create it from within ourselves.

When you are playing the real estate game (whether it's *real* real estate or MONOPOLY real estate), remember that Lady Luck is always hanging around the playing field. And she is a fickle being! Things will happen that are beyond your control. To survive with your sanity still intact and without needlessly losing money by prematurely reducing the price, you must believe that you have done all the research, all the fixing, and all the presentation cosmetics that could or should be done. You must believe that you set a marketable asking price. You must believe that you chose a dedicated and competent agent and agency. (There's no harm, however, in keeping communication and evaluation lines open with that agent.) You must believe that the right buyers for your property are out there; they just haven't shown up yet. And you must try to court the favor of a marketplace goddess; her name is Patience. Sometimes she's fickle too.

I'm going to talk more about the Anxiety Demon in the last chapter. Let's think now of getting through the on-the-market stage. Much anxiety comes from within yourself. But many experienced buyers and some unscrupulous agents will attempt to increase your anxiety level by asking probing (and often irritating) questions. Try to stay calm and use their questions to get insight into their motivations or their particular demons. Read the quotation in the Community Chest sidebar for insight from a very down-to-earth man.

RULES AND STRATEGIES

- Many Websites will assign a market value to your property and also to all of your neighboring properties.

- There are intangibles in every property that must be factored into a market evaluation.

- Beware real estate agents who claim they have special powers that will enable them to get more money for your property than anyone else.

- Putting a price tag on investment property requires lots of numbers and a cool head.

- Do not give in to the Anxiety Demon.

CHAPTER 13
Marketing Matters

Life is painting a picture, not doing a sum.
—Oliver Wendell Holmes, Jr. (1841–1935),
American Supreme Court Justice

This is the penultimate chapter. (Next to last!) It is also one of the most important in the book.

"Why?" you ask.

Because in order to make the home-selling process more effective, I'm going to give you some advice that seems to contradict the past twelve chapters where I've been saying *keep your head in control.* (That's how you win at MONOPOLY, right?) But now, in the *real* real estate game, I'm going to advise you to play on some heart strings a bit.

Home Sales is the only corner of the vast real estate marketplace where emotion is recognized as playing an important role. I mentioned in Part I that you as a homebuyer should "love" a prospective purchase, at least a little. Now, as a seller, whether you choose to use an agent or not, it is your job to entice a buyer by presenting your property as "loveable."

WHO IS YOUR BUYER?

Even in high school business classes, students are taught to identify their target market. Usually the first question both for students who are learning to sell and for business executives who are developing a product is *Who is your probable buyer?* The piece of property you have for sale is your product. Ask yourself *who* is likely to be interested in buying your house and *why*. The answers will help you focus your marketing plan. Following are some things to think about.

Cave or Vista?

As mentioned earlier, the world-class American architect Frank Lloyd Wright identified two basic human needs in housing that he called *perching* and *nesting*. The nesting person seeks the security of a cave-like retreat. He or she sees the home as a place of refuge, a place to get away from the demands and risks of the world. The perching person is more outward looking and wants a home from which he or she can evaluate prospects (which is indeed another kind of security). Perchers seek a vista on the world.

Some houses can easily be categorized in the cave mode, some in the vista mode. If one or the other is apparent in your property, emphasize security and privacy or emphasize accessibility and view. You will attract your type of house hunter.

This is a nice concept, but it's not quite so easy in the day-to-day working world. Some houses provide both cave and vista spaces. Some buyers are couples; one is looking for security and the other is seeking vista. And some individuals want both at the same time.

Of course you're not going to advertise "cave house" or "vista house" in the newspaper or in your flyers. Instead you'll be aware of the concepts and use them not only in your advertising but also in your presentation. For example, if you have a dark bedroom, don't apologize or turn on lightbulbs totaling 5,000 watts. Arrange furniture and lighting to be secure and relaxing rather than stimulating.

To give you a few more short examples:
- *If you think you have a vista house,* pull all window treatments to the side or tie them back so that a house hunter will feel the contact with

the outside world. You want to create a sense of freedom and possibilities with an invitation to look outside the home.

- *If you think you have a cave house,* keep window treatments drawn part way and turn on interior lights. You want to create a feeling of warmth and comfort, a sense of being safe from the demands of the world.
- *If you have one or more rooms that seem to be vista rooms and other rooms that seem to be cave rooms,* play to the concept appropriate to the room. Many people want public rooms that are vista areas and private rooms that are secluded cave areas.

Status

At the beginning of the twentieth century, two great American novelists, Henry James and Edith Wharton, used descriptions of characters' houses to depict both social status and inner personality. Today, despite the importance of the car that a person drives and the quality of his or her cell phone, we still see houses as reflective of both position in our society and the characters of the people who live there.

If your property is located in a "desirable" town or neighborhood, market the location. If your house is architect designed, of historic significance, or otherwise notable, market its unique appeal. If you are located on the edge of one neighborhood but close to another of higher housing value, market the closeness. If you are located in a turnaround or revitalization community that is becoming more and more desirable, market the upward-moving value! Remember, you are

COMMUNITY CHEST

Think of what you can do with what there is.

—Ernest Hemingway (1899–1961), American author

DON'T GO TO JAIL

Be especially careful not to discriminate in your advertising. Even when home selling without a broker's involvement, discrimination on a personal basis is against federal law. For example, do not advertise "Executives-Only Neighborhood." But you can say "The Best Neighborhood for the Best People."

marketing to the person conscious of his or her position in the community (and that of the children too).

Money

Money motivates! If your property is a particularly good value for any reason, be sure you make prospective buyers aware of it. You may be the smallest house in the neighborhood and therefore asking the lowest price. You may have an addition that cannot be seen from the road and are offering more bedrooms than any other house in the neighborhood. You may have done a renovation that includes new windows, a new roof, and central air conditioning and are offering more comfort and security.

Especially when value factors cannot be seen from the road or in a photograph, you must tell your prospective buyers about them. You are marketing to the bargain hunter. (And don't we all have a bit of *that* characteristic?)

If you are willing to hold the mortgage at an interest rate that is a bit lower than the going rate, you will attract many house hunters. Even a buy-down or a second mortgage offering can be attractive. Also when putting together a brochure, be sure to name any major extras such as kitchen appliances, lawn furniture, or even a riding mower that you are including in the purchase price.

Above all else, avoid red flags in your advertising. Phrases like *Must Sell!* will indeed bring out bargain hunters but they will also prompt extremely low offers. Your prospective buyers will believe that you are negotiating under extreme pressure to sell and that is negotiating without any power.

Security

There are only a few people around nowadays who don't bother to lock the doors of their homes. Security is a major factor on most buyers' "wish lists." If you live in a gated community, in a high-rise with a doorman on duty 24 hours, or in a private association of home-owners with its own security force, make it known. If you have an alarm system installed in the home, leave the details of the type of service and its monthly cost on a counter or table. (No passwords!) If your town has a particularly low crime rate, make that known too.

Security is an intangible plus that can affect the speed of your sale and the price you get. If you can promise security *and* privacy, you have a hot package.

Maintenance and Time-off Activities

One of the major attraction features of condominium and co-op communities is the freedom from exterior home maintenance chores. And, of course, it's even better if freedom from maintenance comes with fun-time opportunities.

Community recreation facilities should always be made known to prospective buyers. But don't forget to include the cost of membership and maintenance. When freedom from maintenance chores and recreational opportunities are motivators, you are indeed marketing to busy people or seniors with time to enjoy their homes. Never forget, however, that money is still an important factor among both groups.

SOMETHING LIKE AROMA THERAPY

In December of 2006, when home sales in Florida were just about dead in the water, I met an interesting house seller at a cocktail party. He was currently a corporate executive but he had once been a Realtor and a marketing manager. He talked with me about his efforts to sell a new house near Orlando that he had bought as an investment under a construction contract. He had signed the purchase contract when the marketplace was red hot. But while the house was being built, the Florida "BUY NOW!" fire went out. And now he wanted to get his money out of the investment!

Since prices had actually slid a bit, he thought he could cut some of his losses by saving money on the real estate commission. So he listed the property on seventeen different Internet real estate sites, paying each a fee and being promised various levels of "help" when prospective buyers appeared. He got "hit counts" from several sites but, over the course of four months, not one person showed up to look at his property. My "new friend" told me he had decided to list with a top local agent who was associated with a national franchise office. Later, I found out from mutual friends that the new full-service agent had sold the property in six weeks at very close to asking price.

Why the long story? Because I really want you to be aware that few houses sell from Internet listings, newspaper advertisements, or open houses. Does that surprise you? According to the National Association of Realtors, only 1 percent of homebuyers buy the house they first saw at an open house, and only 3 percent buy the house they saw advertised and called on. Twenty percent of homebuyers, however, buy the house they found through a sign on the property, and 40 percent buy a house that was selected by a Realtor. *What* is going on?

To paraphrase the Oliver Wendell Holmes quotation at the beginning of this chapter: home selling is art and drama, not adding and subtracting numbers. Web listings don't usually work because people skim through them, and after a while all the numbers get jumbled and all the houses look alike. Getting potential buyers *to the site of and then inside* the property is the key to success. All the pretty pictures, real-time VistaVision, statistics, facts, and promises don't have anywhere near the effect of being there and feeling the essence of the home.

Every professional real estate agent will tell you that house hunters who have listed their wants and needs quite often see and buy a house that doesn't seem to fit the lists. Instead it fits more important subliminal needs. That is why the most important function of a real estate agent is to get to know the properties on the market and to get to know the prospective buyers. The best agents can grasp the concept, the *whole*—whether it be property or personality—and still have a sensitive awareness to the details that may make a difference.

When the right buyer is connected to the right house, there is magic in the air; call it pixie dust, if you will, or call it the mysticism of *home*. That's why signs on the property work better than advertisements. Even when buyers are very anxious to buy, there is always a certain reluctance to go into an unknown occupied house—perhaps it's a cultural reticence, perhaps an inertia that keeps one from making the first appointment.

They're probably quite obvious by now, but perhaps I should stop a second here to acknowledge my personal preferences. I believe that traditional real estate agents do the best job for the home seller. In my opinion, a seller should have personal contact with an agent who honestly thinks that he or she can sell the property in question and who is willing to put in the time and work necessary to do so.

Although it theoretically saves the seller money, selling *by owner* has some very real risks and drawbacks. And quite often, it doesn't save any money at all. Using discount brokers invariably means discount service, although it can work in a hot market. It works less well in a cold, or buyers' market. Let's talk about the possibilities.

FOR SALE BY OWNER

One would think that more owners are selling their own houses in this Information Age. The fact of the matter is that by-owner sales are actually decreasing! As of this writing, 2005 was the most recent hot sellers' market and the National Association of Realtors has reported that only 13 percent of home sellers sold their homes without a broker in that year. The NAR did not say how those home-sale prices compared with similar houses sold by professionals, but they did say that only half of that 13 percent said they would consider going solo again.

By-owner home selling is tough. Consider the following reasons:
- **Telephone tag:** The person who answers the phone can make or break the possibility of an appointment to show the property. Real estate agents are trained to put a positive spin on their responses and

to encourage a showing. The phones are answered during extended business hours. It is a rare home seller who is willing to stay at home to answer a phone, or even commit to answering a cell phone whenever it rings. On the other hand, answering machines prompt hang-ups, and sometimes the caller does not leave a message and never calls back.

- **Showing on demand:** House hunters want to go a-hunting at what seems like every possible hour. Weekends, dinner hours, and late mornings are among their favorite times. Are you willing to cancel your plans? *Can* you make yourself available at the buyer's convenience?
- **Being afraid:** Fear can affect one's poise and one's attitude, and it is one of the major problems of selling on your own. There is no intermediary to meet, qualify, and accompany prospective buyers in by-owner and most discount-broker situations. Sometimes there is only one homeowner available to do the showing and he or she is expected to show all the rooms including the basement. Some owners are obviously and justifiably anxious because they have little or no identification information on the people who arrive at their homes.
- **Negotiating:** Face-to-face negotiating is difficult. You can find some suggestions to facilitate a meeting of the minds in Part I, Chapter 4. But getting buyers to make a reasonable first offer is usually the hardest part. Most of today's buyers are Internet savvy; they have checked out the market value of comps. They also know that you are not paying commission on their deal, so they deduct the commission

CHANCE

If you must show your home solo, arrange for a friend to call you during the time you will be doing the showing. Then call that person back when the house hunters have left.

money and then make an offer well below that price. They do this even if you explain that you have already adjusted for the commission in the asking price. Most buyers come to a by-owner property sale with the attitude of *this is a chance to get a real deal.*

- **Legal language:** Most homeowners know little or nothing about purchase contracts, contingencies, home financing, and closing procedures. Many homebuyers are also at a loss when asked, "What's your next step?" Taken together, no information and misinformation can make for treacherous bumps and perilous curves on the road to a completed transaction.
- **Expenditures:** For-sale-by-owner is not cost-free. Yes, you can put up flyers in the church basement or the club foyer, or even distribute them to your neighbors, but the responses are usually few and far between. Newspaper advertising is rather costly when extended over weeks and months, even if you limit yourself to sparsely worded print ads with no highlights. Internet site listings are still another expense, as are signs. And don't forget to put some kind of worth tag on all the time you are spending.

CHANCE

Be sure to put a limit on your for-sale-by-owner efforts. Newspaper and Internet advertisements are most likely to attract local buyers who are looking for a bargain. Most, if not all, of your active buyer pool will have seen your ads within three to five weeks.

During that period you will also get many, many phone calls from real estate agents trying to get your listing. Invite them over, show them the property, ask their opinions, and interview them. But be wary! When an agent tells you he or she has a customer from out of town who would just love this house, offer to sign an **open listing**. *Do not sign an exclusive listing during your self-marketing time!*

WORDS TO *GO!*

An *open listing* is an agreement between a property owner and a real estate broker in which the owner agrees to pay a stated commission if the real estate agency sells the property at acceptable price and terms. However, *the owner retains two rights*: the right to sell the property himself/herself and not pay any commission and the right to enter into an open listing agreement with any other broker. A seller can have concurrent open listing agreements with each and every broker in town. Open listings do not appear on the Realtor Multiple Listing Service.

You can write and sign an open listing agreement for just one showing. Or you can write it for a month or more with a provision for cancellation at any time by written notice. Real estate agencies generally do not advertise open listings. They make their sales by taking people who call on similar properties to see the open listing.

Do you still want to give for-sale-by-owner a try? OK, I'll give you the best advice I can. Some of these suggestions are procedural or logistic and some are insider bits and pieces that will help you get the job done.

How to Put Together an Information Sheet
As a by-owner house, your property will be in direct competition with every other similar house on the market in your local area. Most of these will be professionally handled and you must provide the same information for your property that is on the MLS printouts that are currently being circulated.

Why? Because buyers expect it. It is difficult to keep the properties seen in a day's house hunting separate in one's mind. Questions come up: *How old was that house? Did the brick house have a fireplace? What were the taxes on the split-level?* You as a seller will want your potential buyer to have all the necessary information at hand.

(A photo helps too so the buyers can remember which house has all those nice features.)

To do this effectively, get some copies of listings currently on the market in your area. Set up your information page to be as similar as possible to the Realtor Board listings. This puts you on an equal footing because the serious buyer who has been out looking does not need to hunt for information. Be sure you provide *all* the necessary facts, including tax information and the size of each room. (You can buy large-size tape measures in any home improvement store.)

If you use a computer you can print your information give-away sheets yourself. If you would like to stand out a bit, choose a colored paper. If you don't have a computer, you can make one master and take it to a copy store. Leave a number of these listings (six to ten at a time) on a kitchen counter or on a hallway or dining table. Be sure that your house hunter takes one home.

If you are good with the computer, you may want to do a separate sheet or even a folded brochure with some color photos of the exterior and/or the interior. This extra should not replace the information sheet in the Realtor format. Don't forget your name, address, and phone number in an obvious place in the brochure. You can also add bits of text that point out some of the plus points of your property. You can include something about the schools, recreation facilities, activities of the neighborhood association, or perhaps the best commuter routes into "the city."

How to Advertise Your Property

Local newspaper ads get the best response. If you live in Holmdel, New Jersey, don't spend your money for ads in the *New York Times*. As I said earlier, very few out-of-town buyers bother to run down for-sale-by-owner ads. If you advertise on the Internet, be sure the Web-site groups the listings geographically.

Always include the price in your ads. Research has shown that the majority of buyers won't bother to call on an ad without a price. And don't say "asking" unless you want to generate low-ball offers; just print the price. Include your phone number, but do not include the address beyond the name of the town. It is better to make phone contact between seller and buyer, to become real people as it were, rather than to have house hunters just drive by and decide in a glance that they don't want your home.

Other necessary items in advertisements are the number of bedrooms, the number of bathrooms, the total number of rooms, the style of the house (Cape Cod, ranch, colonial, etc.), the size of the lot, and any special features that set it apart from other houses being advertised. Don't forget the price and your phone number.

A FOR SALE sign in front of your house is another good way to let the immediate world know you are selling. For a single-family or multifamily house, you should create a sign that is at least two feet by three feet, with the same information on both sides. The essentials are your phone number and the words *Shown by appointment only*. Stick-on, weather-proof vinyl letters and numbers are best for this information since they will not fade or run.

Set the sign into the ground near the curb, perpendicular to the road, so that it can be read by people passing in either direction. If you are in a condominium community where curbside signs are not allowed, you can place a somewhat smaller sign in your window.

Some home sellers try to compete with real estate agents by placing an "information tube or box" at the curb near the sign or the driveway entrance. They place their printed information sheets inside, ready for the taking. I personally do not recommend this procedure. You are providing too much information to anyone who wishes to open the box. It is far better to e-mail or fax the information sheet to a person who calls after seeing the sign. (*And* the extra step provides you with his or her name, phone number, and e-mail address.)

How to Answer the Phone

When the phone rings, you must be ready to answer questions and give directions. The call is usually your first contact with a prospective buyer. Of course, you want to make a good impression, but more important, you want to encourage the caller to look at the property. Keep a copy of your information sheet at every phone. Also keep a copy of clear

CHANCE

Many callers on by-owner ads will ask for the address and directions and say that they would like to drive by. Encourage them to make an appointment and do it all in one trip. If they insist on the drive-by, let them know that you will *not* show the house without an appointment.

The same goes for people who stop by because they saw the sign. It is simply too risky for you to answer a ringing doorbell and then respond to "Oh, we just love it! Can we come in now?" with an unqualified "yes, of course." If the house hunters are really interested, they will make the appointment. A set appointment time greatly increases the security of the person doing the showing.

directions from several major crossroads. You can also put these directions on your computer and offer to e-mail them to the caller.

If children or teenagers answer your phone, instruct them not to give information. If you are not at home, have them get a name and phone number and say that their parents will call back shortly. If you are at home, have them call you to the phone.

When you first answer the phone, the prospective buyer is likely to start asking questions about the house. Answer a few and then interrupt yourself with something like:

"Oh, almost forgot! My name is Martha Seller. May I have your name?"

If the caller will not give his or her name, you do not want to pursue the conversation much further. You could be talking with a real estate agent trying to get your listing, you could be talking to competing sellers, or, worse case, you could be talking with house thieves.

Always, you should also ask for the phone number, "just in case I need to call you back." Once you have the phone number, one easy way to do a little honesty probe is to call the number back a while later and ask for the caller. Why? Because you forgot to tell him or her something.

How to Show Your House

If possible, always have at least two adults in the house when you are showing. Decide who will be the "seller" and let that person do virtually all of the house talking. The other person can stay back and quietly follow along, or just keep "busy" in a den or kitchen. It is very disconcerting to house hunters when husband-and-wife sellers talk over each other, correct each other, and point out features at opposite points in the same room at the same time.

If there are two house hunters and they decide to split and go in two different directions in your house, one adult seller should accompany each. If that is not possible, simply ask the sellers to stay together. As I've said, it is a good safety precaution to ask a friend or family member to call you about ten or fifteen minutes into the appointment time. You can preset a code phrase for trouble that most likely would not be detected such as, "Oh yes, Fluffy is just fine. Our vet got rid of all the fleas." And of course, no answer to the phone call is also cause for concern by your caller.

When you greet the house hunters at the door give each a copy of the information sheet. Then take them on a tour of the house. Do not say "This is the living room" or "This is the kitchen." It's obvious. Instead, point out some interesting extra in the room that is included in the price, such as window treatments, or mention the room's dimensions, or the view, or the nice neighbors whose windows you can see next door.

If you have a two-story house with a basement too, always go from the first floor to the second. When you return to the first floor, ask the house hunters if they want to see the basement on this visit or on a return visit. If they are serious, they will look at the basement. The same is true of the yard and walking the property limits. If you have a survey map of the property, make copies of it. If the house hunters want to walk about on your land, give them a copy of the survey. They are interested buyers.

Answer all questions honestly, but do not take out your disclosure sheets until an offer has been made. Let the house hunters bring up the topic of closing date; it is a negotiating tool. Be prepared to answer questions about schools, taxes, municipal services, commuting, and security.

DON'T GO TO JAIL

Be sure to restrain or confine your pets when you are showing your property (even if Caesar has never bitten anyone in his whole life). Dogs and cats are wary of strangers who may be walking about in private areas of the home. They can sense fear and anxiety in the house hunters or in their owners and may respond inappropriately to a sudden move.

There are also special problems when house hunters bring along their children. You want to protect your pets from being squeezed or chased, and you want to protect the children from being scratched or nipped. And you don't want a lawsuit.

Don't encourage house hunters' children to play with your children's toys. Items often disappear and cannot be retrieved. Believe me, your children will know their "stuff" has been tampered with. Having their personal playthings exposed to whomever passes through will certainly increase their anxiety level, already high because their home is for sale.

When your house hunters are ready to leave, thank them for coming and encourage them to call if they have any questions. If they seem genuinely interested, you can also ask: "Would you like us to call you if we get an offer or decide to list with a broker?"

Why *Not* to Hold a By-Owner Open House

Most home sellers are pleased and excited when their real estate agent tells them he or she has arranged a public open house on a Sunday afternoon. They shouldn't be! Open houses are an invitation for anyone who is interested to wander through your house, most often unattended. And open houses add little or nothing to the marketing of the property. Remember the National Association of Realtors reported that only 1 percent of homebuyers buy the house they saw at an open house.

So why do open house ads fill the Sunday real estate sections of newspapers across the nation? It's the business. Open houses are a good source of customers (house hunters) for the real estate agent who is "sitting" the property for two or three hours. The by-owner seller, however, gets *no advantage* from the open house because he or she has no other houses to sell.

If you feel that you *must* run an open house during your for-sale-by-owner time, please take precautions. Put away everything of value, especially small items generally kept on tables or other horizontal surfaces. Take all prescription drugs out of your bathroom medicine cabinets and put them beyond reach. Get as many adult family members as possible to assist you during the open hours—ideally, one for each room. At an open house, house hunters (and often a good number of just plain nosey people) expect to be allowed to wander around unaccompanied. It is an intrusion on your privacy at best, a risk for theft at worst.

How to Put the Deal in Writing

If you are fortunate enough to attract an interested buyer, first follow the negotiating tips in Chapter 4, switching them to a seller's point of view of course. When you come to an agreement, take a sheet of lined paper and write down all the things you have agreed to. Make a copy for the buyer.

However, do not sign anything and do not exchange money. At this point, you need professional help. Without knowledge of real estate law, you do not want to commit yourself on paper to the deal. Ideally, you will already have a lawyer or have contacted one in advance to review the terms of your deal and draw the papers for you. The buyers may or may not use another attorney, which is their choice. Set a time limit (three to five working days is good) for the contracts to be drawn and fully executed.

But you're not done yet . . . At this point in a by-owner transaction, the seller must take over the role of the real estate agent. You must take on the job of monitoring the contingencies and supervising progress toward the closing. Have the buyers applied for the mort-gage? Do they have a commitment from a lender? Was the inspection done? Will the inspection results affect the terms of the contract? Where will the closing be held? Who will do the title search? Will there be title insurance? The list goes on.

COMMUNITY CHEST

There's a saying in the business that for-sale-by-owner ads are simply sellers in search of an agent. There's truth in the old saw, but don't let that stop you from inviting the scouting agents to your home. Meeting many agents and showing them around your property is a great way to gather a well-rounded view of the local marketplace and to get a feel for the competency and commitment of each agent who is after your listing. Here are some strategic questions.

- Ask each agent if he or she thinks your asking price is appropriate to the local marketplace and why. Ask about recent comps. Has the agent sold a similar property recently? What was the most important factor in that sale, and what made the house more attractive than the competing properties?

- Ask if he or she thinks there is anything you can do to the interior or exterior of your house to make the property more appealing to more people.

- Ask "why do you want this listing?"

- Ask why the agent thinks his or her company is the best choice to market the property if you are unable to sell it by-owner.

- Ask the agent how long he or she has been in the business, full-time or part-time, and what kind of property he or she usually sells.

- Write down the answers, staple the agent's card to the sheet, and add a few words about your response to and evaluation of the agent.

PROFESSIONAL HELP

I'm sure you too have heard someone say, "I think I'll work in real estate part time. I love looking at houses."

I guarantee anyone who thinks that way will never make it professionally. The real estate marketplace is one of the most competitive and demanding of all sales careers and "looking at houses" is the equivalent of a few pebbles on its road to success. A good real estate agent will not only market your property effectively but also protect your property and your interests as a seller. Let's take a closer look at what they do and what they can do for you.

The Listing Contract

The real estate brokerage business is built upon listings. Advertising houses to sell brings in customers looking to buy. So the listing agent wants your listing and he or she wants you to be pleased with the service that is given. In other words, the agents want to sell your property quickly and for top dollar. Your job is to help and oversee them.

Be sure to read the listing agreement carefully and thoroughly. There are two types commonly in use: the **exclusive right to sell listing contract** and the **exclusive agency listing contract**. Choose the one that seems appropriate to your needs and expectations. The contract must:
- Be in writing
- Be dated on the day it is executed by all parties
- Name all the sellers and the broker who is taking on the listing (with addresses for both parties)
- Name the type of listing (exclusive right to sell or exclusive agency)
- Identify the property
- Name the commission (either a percentage of the sale price or a flat fee) and state at what time it is to be paid (usually at the closing)
- Name an asking price
- Have an expiration date
- Include permission to put a sign on the property and a **lockbox** (sometimes called a **keybox**) on the front door

In the small print you will usually find a clause that extends the listing conditions for two or more months if the property is sold to a buyer who was introduced to the property by a real estate agent. This clause prevents sneaky buyers who want to shave the price by playing behind-the-agent's-back games. One of the most common is for the buyers to call and tell the sellers that they will pay full price minus the commission after the listing expires. This action is illegal and in bad faith. The extension clause will hold up in court and the bills for court action will cost many times the potential commission saved.

Attached to or accompanying the listing contract will be pages of questions about the property. These questions are needed to fill in the listing form for distribution to other agents and potential buyers. Be sure that your agent supplies information, not just check marks. Buyers don't want to see: *dining room [x];* they want to see: *dining room 10' × 14' with built-in china cabinet.* It is the agent's responsibility to get the latest tax assessment on the property, the mill rate in the town, and any special assessments that might be attached.

Be sure you include on the listing form all items that are included with the property such as window treatments, carpeting, stove, and dishwasher. Also include a list of items that specifically do NOT "go with the house" such as a chest freezer, washer and dryer, shelving in the garage, and so on.

Finally, there is always a "comments" section on the listing form. Help your agent to point out the special appeal of your home. Be sure he or she includes more than some banality such as "three spacious bedrooms." Go back to the notes you took when considering *buyer motivations.*

COMMUNITY CHEST

The palest ink is better than the best memory. —Chinese proverb

WORDS TO *GO!*

An *exclusive right to sell listing contract* gives the right to sell the property to one real estate broker or brokerage company. This is the most common type of listing contract used for listing on the Realtor Multiple Listing Service. These listings are available to all other Realtors but the listing agency receives an agreed-upon share of the commission no matter who actually sells the property. When an agent outside the listing office sells the property, the commission is split between the two agencies according to a preset agreement. During the term of an exclusive right to sell listing agreement, the listing broker will collect the agreed-upon commission even if the owner sells the property to a relative.

An *exclusive agency listing contract* names one real estate broker or brokerage company as the exclusive agent of the seller, but the seller retains the right to sell the property by his or her own efforts to any buyer who has not been made aware of the property by a real estate agent. Most brokers advertise and share exclusive agency listings on the MLS.

A *lockbox* or *keybox* is a locked container for holding a house key. It is usually in the form of an oversized padlock and slipped over the front door knob. The Realtor can open the cover of the box with a special key or a special code.

While you have the broker or the broker's agent in your living room, discuss the firm's advertising policies. Make some suggestions for features you'd like mentioned. Say that you'd like to be consulted about which photos of the house should be used. And ask for a scheduled weekly report in writing regarding what agents have shown the property and what the response of each house hunter was. Get all these agreements in writing.

Finally, no matter how enthusiastic your agent is, try to avoid having a public Sunday open house. Unless, of course, you are just itching to help the company acquire new customers. As I've said, open houses rarely bring in a buyer, and there is definitely risk to your belongings.

Speaking of which, many people also hesitate to use lockboxes for fear of having strangers in their homes. It is possible to ask that your agent be present for every showing with another broker, but this restriction complicates showing schedules. Some selling agents simply won't bother to make the appointments if they know that they will have to wait for the listing agent to show up.

Unlike open houses, I think lockboxes or keyboxes are a good idea. The newer ones are electronically controlled and can give readouts that will tell you who visited and at what time. Even if your agent does install a keybox, however, be sure to print on the listing notice that your house will be shown by appointment only.

Open House for Agents Only

After you choose your agency and sign the listing contract, one of the first and most important things to do is prepare open house tours for the other agents in your brokerage company and for the real estate business community in general. Your listing agent will make the necessary arrangements.

These Realtor open houses are one of your prime marketing tools. As I've said before, it's really hard to generate genuine buying

DON'T GO TO JAIL

A century ago *net listings* were still in common use. Under this type of contract, a seller would name a price that he or she wanted for the property. The broker could then sell the property at any price above that figure and keep the excess dollars as his or her commission. Net listings are illegal in most places now. It is an arrangement that invites scams and slippery deals. Stay away!

enthusiasm from statistics on a listing sheet or even from photos on the Internet. You want as many real estate professionals as possible to actually see and tour your property. Once they've done so, they will be able to answer telephone inquiries and to speak of the house to their customers more accurately and with more specifics. NAR research shows that fully 40 percent of buyers are introduced to the houses they buy through the suggestion of a real estate agent rather than advertising, signs, or the Internet.

The first open house is usually for the agents working in the firm that took the listing. One day each week most agencies go on "caravan" by doing a carpool tour of all the new listings the firm has taken. Some firms allow other agencies to share in their caravan open houses, some don't. The second open house is for all Realtors and it is at a set time (say 11 AM to 1 PM) and advertised on Realtor sites. Often the listing agent serves coffee and goodies and agents discuss the property with each other. Some listing agents leave a bowl or box on the table asking for anonymous guesses at what the selling price will be. This is just a way of rechecking the market value estimate that was done.

Snags and Loopholes

What if you decide that your broker is not doing the job you expected? Can you get out of your listing contract?

Yes, but . . .

The first step is to sit down with the agent, broker, and/or office manager and air your complaints. Sometimes changes can be made that will fix the problems. Or sometimes there is a mutual agreement to part company and the listing can be terminated.

If the broker is unwilling to let you out of your listing contract, you can file a complaint with your state real estate commission. The problem in this procedure is that you have to prove that your broker was not making good, sufficient, and professional efforts to sell your property. By the time you get someone to listen to your complaint, the listing may have expired anyway.

A much better way to prevent the possibility of dissatisfaction is to list for a shorter rather than longer time. Many agents ask for a

COMMUNITY CHEST

If you've been transferred by your employer and you wish to try selling your home with your own agent before turning it over to the company, be certain that your listing contract includes a corporate rider. This clause will allow you to turn over your property to your employer's agent without paying a commission to the broker you chose for your marketing time. Some companies simply continue to use the employee's chosen broker, others don't.

listing term of six months or even a year. I believe the best listing term is three months. This time period gives the agency an opportunity to show you what it can do. If you are satisfied, you can renew the listing. If you are not, the commitment is over and you can list with another agency.

If you are dissatisfied not only with your broker's efforts but also with the activity of the market in general and would rather "wait till spring" or some other time, you can withdraw your listing. You will no longer have strangers walking about in your bedrooms, but be aware that you will not be able to sell the property during the term of the original listing without paying commission. Once you pass the expiration date, you can relist at any time, either with your original agency or with another.

Children and Pets

Home selling brings up anxiety in children of all ages. The very young have naps, feedings, and playtime interrupted. School-age children ask question after question: "But why? But what will happen? When?" Sometimes they find their toys or projects tampered with by the children of house hunters.

Teenage children tend to be resentful of the move, not wishing to give up their friends and activities. Some teens have been known to try to sabotage sales by making negative comments to house hunters or by leaving every possible inappropriate piece of anything in every inappropriate place. There is not much I can offer as advice here, except try to understand where the behavior is coming from and, of course, talk and listen.

Whenever possible try to have your home unoccupied for the showings. Buyers like to try out and try on rooms when they are considering a house. The presence of children is invariably distracting. Pets are even worse.

Barking dogs, even when confined in a dog crate, shorten the time a house hunter spends in a house. Cats usually hide, but well-meaning agents and buyers have let more than a few indoor pets out the door. Some sellers leave signs on the kitchen counter or print in their listing contract: *Do NOT let the cat out.*

If you have pets, be sure to vacuum the floors thoroughly before a showing. Many house hunters have allergies to cat or dog dander and will not inspect the house thoroughly if they start sneezing or have gritty eyes. The scent of a cat litter box has also been known to "encourage" house hunters out the front door. Pet stains on the carpet will cost you the equivalent of carpet replacement. While your house is on the market, try to prevent your pets from being seen, heard, and scented.

DO YOU GET WHAT YOU PAY FOR?

Twenty years ago I did a video commercial for a company called Help-U-Sell. They were one of the first national franchise discount brokers, and their concept seemed like a good idea to me. Unfortunately, the idea not only spread like dandelions in springtime but also seemed to be altered with each new entry into the game. Today there are Internet brokers who claim you never have to walk upon a property to buy it; there are discount brokers who will list your property on the Internet and then leave you to your own devices; and there are discount brokers who send over anyone who calls on an ad and then let you do the showing and selling. They come in for the negotiating, however, and for the closing and collection of the commission. There are also fee brokers who charge a flat fee up front. It must be paid whether or not they sell the property.

Everyone who acts as a broker in the sale of real estate in the United States must be licensed by the state in which they work. And they must meet the standards of the state real estate commission. So the discount firms are legitimate.

Do their tactics work? Do they really save you money? The answer is sometimes *yes* and sometimes *no*. When the marketplace is hot and houses are selling quickly and at ever-higher prices, discount brokers generally get the job done. But one wonders if for-sale-by-owner might not work just as well in those sellers' markets. When the marketplace is sluggish and houses are not selling quickly or for anywhere near full asking price, the number of discount brokers working in any given area seems to diminish. Do they close their doors for lack of business or poor success rate?

SELLING INVESTMENT PROPERTY

Virtually everything in this chapter so far has been focused on selling a home. But most of the information and strategy also applies to selling investment property, except that emotions (the voices of the heart) are rarely in control. That does not mean, however, that they are not heard, if perhaps only subliminally.

Just as wise and careful buying of investment property is heavily dependent on research and numbers, so it is with selling. You must be prepared to present income and expenditure records to a prospective buyer. You should know what improvements will soon be needed and what they will cost. And you should have verifiable estimates of how much, if at all, they will justify a rent increase.

Multifamily houses, small apartment buildings, mixed-use buildings, and land take longer to sell than your typical single-family home or condominium apartment. These investment properties are also extremely difficult to sell through by-owner marketing. In the investment property marketplace, the buyer pool is smaller and buyer motivation and specifications more focused. And if the owner doesn't live on the property, meetings must be arranged for showings and tenants must be notified.

COMMUNITY CHEST

Deals are my art form. Other people paint beautifully on canvas or write wonderful poetry. I like making deals, preferably big deals.

—Donald Trump, American real estate businessman, in *The Art of the Deal,* 1987

Unless you have unlimited time to get the property sold and more or less unlimited availability to meet with buyers, it is usually best to choose a real estate agent who works with the type of property you are selling and whose office is located within easy reach (short driving time) of the property. The listing contracts are the same types as those used in home selling, but they usually include occupancy and lease clauses. (Some leases survive a change in ownership.) The term of the listing contract is also usually longer. Six months is generally considered a minimum although that does not stop you from asking for a tryout three-month listing at the outset.

Turnaround fixer-uppers and vacation homes that are in season are more easily marketed and sold by owner, if that is your choice. Especially in "hot-market" areas or within planned communities where real estate agents have several homes similar to yours for sale, you can piggyback on their advertising and open house programs simply by putting out a sign. If you are in a condominium community, especially when construction of the whole master plan has not been completed, you will get many inquiries simply by putting a sign in a front window. In slow markets or off season, however, you will need the services of a good agent.

And finally, a few more words about those *voices of the heart.* Is there a successful real estate investor who has been able to ignore them? Certainly not Diamond Jim Brady, Donald Trump, or Mr. MONOPOLY. Even when we don't acknowledge it, we are influenced by memories, by beauty, by pride, by power, and by greed. Emotions speak to real estate buyers (actually to every person), sometimes in voices like sirens blaring in the brain and sometimes in inaudible whispers. That's why the cautionary words *keep your head in control* need repeating.

A neatly edged lawn, flowers in the window boxes, a newly painted and well-lit hallway, a laundry room in the basement that brings in a positive cash flow each month and a locked bike room that doesn't but pleases the occupants . . . It's hard to say exactly what will touch positive, emotional, I-want-to-own-this-property chords in an investment buyer, but it's quite certain that there are unseen factors in every deal. As a seller, try to keep your head in control but also regard your investment property as a creative endeavor that you are offering for sale, not as a balance sheet.

RULES AND STRATEGIES

- The first of all marketing questions is, *Who is your buyer?*

- Consider the goals and character traits that might be motivating your prospective buyer.

- It is important to get house hunters to come inside the house. Drive-bys and Internet images do not sell property.

- For-sale-by-owner is more challenging than most people think and usually saves considerably less money than anticipated. Be cautious.

- Never show a property without an appointment.

- Understand what you are agreeing to in a listing contract.

- Keep your head in control but acknowledge that there are voices of the heart in every deal.

CHAPTER 14
Hot and Cold Market Strategies

*The object of the game is to obtain
as much wealth or money as possible...*
—Lizzie J. Magie (1866–1948), Creator of *The
Landlord's Game*, from the U.S. Patent issued in 1904

O n September 19, 2007, a front-page headline in the *New York Times* read: "Fed Cuts Rate Half Point, And Stock Markets Soar." The author of the article, Edmund L. Andrews, summed up the anxiety of the nation in the first paragraph. "The Federal Reserve rolled out its most powerful interest rate weapon on Tuesday in a bid to stop the turmoil in housing and financial markets from bringing down the overall economy."

If you had any doubts about the economic importance of the American real estate marketplace, Andrews's observation surely answers them. Real estate is a major factor in our economic health. Like the stock and commodities markets, it responds to supply and demand, *and* consumer attitudes, *and* the availability of money, *and* greed. It just responds more slowly.

In the first five years of this century, home prices spiraled. One of the stimulants for the hot market was the availability of low-interest-rate mortgage money, easily given out to almost anyone, almost for the

COMMUNITY CHEST

asking. Recently that easy money has become much harder to get as more and more subprime loans are being foreclosed.

As of 2008 nationwide, the real estate marketplace has turned cold and some home prices have fallen. Analysts have said that this reversal was a necessary correction. One wonders, however, what *necessity* prompted millions of people to pay more than they could afford for housing. Was one factor the fact that lenders were willing to loan more money than was prudent in their desire to make more money?

In addition to the availability of money, a piece of real estate responds to the supply-and-demand economics of what is happening around it. An oceanfront, architect-designed house has little competition in the marketplace and little restraint on asking price beyond the availability of money. On the other hand, a condo apartment in a community where condominiums have been overbuilt and are abundant on the market will sell for virtually the same amount as every other similar property, or less.

Predicting value in the real estate marketplace is never unequivocally accurate; economics itself is not a science. A complex web of many factors determines future values in both fields. Historically, real estate prices have been marked by periods of expansion and periods of correction. There is virtually nothing any one individual can do to change this wave effect. As a buyer or seller therefore, you must deal with the marketplace in which you find yourself.

What you *can* do, however, is sharpen your awareness of the current competition and availability and learn how to deal effectively in either a hot or a cold marketplace. This, of course, is more easily said than done. But let me get you started with some basic concepts and strategies.

HOMES IN A HOT MARKET . . .

A high-demand, fast-paced real estate market is a sellers' market. Demand for houses exceeds availability; property tends to sell quickly; home prices leapfrog over each other; and actual selling prices tend to be relatively close to asking prices. Sometimes buyer competition stimulates **bidding wars** in which selling prices can exceed asking prices.

In the hot market of 2004–2005, some brokers near major cities such as Washington routinely used sealed-bid auctions for desirable homes. In these marketing formats, the listing price was not an *asking*

WORDS TO *GO!*

Real estate *bidding wars* occur when two different parties make offers on a property at about the same time. Counteroffers go back and forth between the sellers and two sets of buyers, each buyer being aware of and trying to out do the offer made by the other party. The results invariably favor the seller. In fact, bidding-war offers can easily surpass the asking price.

Sometimes, listing agents actually try to stimulate bidding wars by informing the agents representing every buyer who has expressed positive interest in the property that an offer "is coming in." When agents from different real estate brokerage firms bring in offers, the seller can negotiate with two (or more) buyers *at the same time.* If the offers come from sales agents working in the same firm, however, all parties in the dealing must agree that the agents become transactional agents—that is, they represent both parties equally, or more accurately, no one.

If you are a buyer in a bidding war, use the comps and market data to set your top price. Think twice (or more) before you exceed it.

If you are a seller in a bidding war, rejoice!

price but actually the *minimum bid price*. All potential buyers were required to tour and inspect the property within a period of about a week. Those who wished to buy it then had to submit sealed bids. On a given day, the sellers and the agents of all parties concerned opened the sealed bids. Each bid had to include an earnest money check and a signed purchase contract stating all the terms of the sale including a closing date *and* a mortgage qualification letter from an acceptable lender. The seller could then choose the buyer. Negotiating had become passé.

Since the asking price on sealed-bid houses started out at approximately market value for the neighborhood, this selling technique contributed to the further escalation of home prices. For buyers, sealed-bid auctions are not a value-oriented way to buy. Because buyers are responding to the scarcity of appropriate housing, they are paying a top-dollar price. Especially if the housing boom is soon followed by a correction period when the market slows down (and it always does), a considerable period of time will pass (sometimes years) before readjusted market value in the neighborhood catches up to the price paid for the sealed-bid house.

Fear and Greed are the silent demons of the hot real estate market for both buyers and sellers. Buyers are afraid "someone else" will get the house they want. Sellers tend to think, *if John and Suzie got $450,000 for their house just down the street, why shouldn't we get half-a-million for ours?* At the same time, there is a lingering fear that after selling their home, the sellers who did get $500,000 for their home won't be able to find a replacement at a price they want to pay.

Before You Put Your House Up for Sale

If you plan to buy and sell in a hot market, try to protect yourself from being forced to buy from the pool of available houses because yours has been sold. Before you list your home, spend time house hunting. It's a good idea *not* to take your checkbook along on these trips. You don't want to commit to buying on an emotional high. But do take your camera. Take pictures of houses you like and make notes on the listing information sheets. You will be working on your intuitive perception of market value.

Then work on your perception of market value for the house you want to sell. If possible, go to the open houses of properties on the market similar to the one you plan to sell. Talk with the agents you meet about the pace of the marketplace. Ask: "How close to asking prices are the actual selling prices for this kind of house? What is the average time on the market for houses like this?"

Prelisting house hunting will also help you to plan your selling strategy. Ask yourself: "What is it that makes some houses more attractive than others?" Note the indoor and outdoor features that are being highlighted by the broker. What facts about the town or neighborhood are being brought to the attention of prospective buyers?

Because the pace in a sellers' market is often very fast, adequate planning time *before selling or buying* is essential. It can and will save you time and money. It will also save you from a great deal of anxiety.

Sell First, Then Buy

"Sell first, then buy" does not mean that you should close on the house you are selling before you buy another, but only that you should have a fully executed contract on your house before you sign a purchase contract. There are always some financial and lifestyle risks when selling one house and buying another. You could end up carrying two mortgages or you could be forced to rent while you hunt for the right house.

Although renting is not necessarily expensive, it means shouldering the cost of two moves or putting your belongings into storage. If you have children in a school system, the classroom changes and the uncertainty about where their next home will be could contribute to emotional problems for the children—and, as a result, for the parents too.

Putting your house on the market and then waiting until it is under contract of sale before you sign a purchase contract to buy another house lowers all of those risks. Consider the following factors in choosing to sell before you buy.

- You can make a strong effort to set your closing date on the old house very close to the closing date on the new house. This proximity facilitates one move rather than two moves. You can avoid storage loading and unloading fees and the cost of renting temporary shelter.
- Because you are waiting to choose your new house and you have time on your side without pressure to meet a closing deadline on a house purchase, you can test the market for a little more money by setting an asking price higher than the normal negotiating space for the predicted fair market value of your home. If you don't get an offer at the higher price or if you come upon a house that you really want to buy and want to speed up the selling process, "price reduced" always stimulates interest in brokers' offices and sellers' wallets.
- By putting your house on the market and waiting for a buyer before you become a buyer, you will not be under financial pressure to sell your home at any price, or at least a price below optimum, because the closing date on the new house looms.
- You can give for-sale-by-owner a try if you want to. Do this only in a fast market and a selling situation when you do not need to move quickly. Try it for no more than six weeks; after that time you will have exhausted potential among most of the local buyers and you will need the help of an agent to bring in customers from a wider geographic circle.
- You will know exactly how much money the house will bring and how much you will have left after the closing.
- If you have chosen another house and it is available when you finally get a sale contract on your house, you will be able to negotiate for that house or any other house you choose with a stronger hand. Sellers always feel more comfortable when a prospective buyer already has a sale contract on the house they must sell.
- If you have not chosen another house when you get an acceptable offer on the house you are selling, you can set a distant closing date (four or five months or even more). This will give you time to house hunt, again with financial accuracy and a strong negotiating hand.

WORDS TO *GO!*

Bridge loan is the common marketplace name for a short-term interim loan in the amount of all or part of the equity in the home you are selling in order to make the down payment on the home you are buying. A bridge loan is often needed when the newly bought house closing must take place before the selling closing. It can be either *secured* or *unsecured*.

The availability of bridge loans depends very much on the availability of money in the financial marketplace. Some sources of bridge loans include home equity credit lines, second mortgages on the house you are selling or the house you are buying, credit unions and banks with which you have a long-term relationship, and mortgage brokers. Your real estate broker should be able to help you find sources of money.

A *secured loan* is backed by an asset or assets (your home, a boat, a car, or jewelry, for example) known as *collateral*. The lender can seize this collateral if you do not repay the loan as scheduled. Interest rates are usually lower than those for an unsecured loan.

An *unsecured loan* does not have an asset pledged as collateral. Essentially, the loan is made because of your good credit rating, reputation in the community, and track record with the lender.

- If you find another house quickly, you *may* be able to reset (move closer) the closing date on your old house. In the best of all possible worlds, you will arrange to close on your old house in the morning and on your new house in the afternoon. The money from the old house can be wired to your bank and then a bank check written for the closing on the new house.
- If you cannot change the closing date on your old house (the buyer needs the time, for example) and you *must* close on the new house before the old house closes, you will have an easier time getting a **bridge loan** because you already have a buyer under contract.

- You can put a clause in the contract on the house you are selling to have all escrow monies released to you as soon as the contract contingencies have been met. This money can be put toward the down payment for the new house, thus enabling you to take out a smaller bridge loan. Many buyers object to the release of escrow money fearing that they will lose it, but this money transfer is perfectly legal if it is agreed to in the contract. It can in fact be a negotiating point. The listing or selling broker, however, might object saying that the real estate commission should come out of the escrow money before it is released. You may need to sharpen your negotiating skills to make escrow-money release work, but it *can* be done.

Buy First, Then Sell

Because houses sell quickly in a hot market, some people choose to sign a purchase contract on the house they want to buy before they have a sale contract on the house they want to sell. This strategy assures that the *buy first/then sell* sellers will move into the home they want, but it does not determine how much money they will have to do so. It can cause painful financial problems if a hot market suddenly turns cold.

For example, if a major employer announces a plant closing in the area, you will suddenly see real estate agents reading their newspapers at their desks. There will be few buyers driving about looking for FOR SALE signs. And then there is the very real possibility that *your* house (the one that all the agents told you was a "sure thing") doesn't even have lookers, much less offers.

If buying a particular house is your primary goal in a hot market and you wish to secure it even before you have a sale contract on your old house, consider the following:
- Start your preparations early! Have your home completely prepared for listing on the market, even before you go out hunting for a new house. Decide upon an agent to handle it and carefully research the probable fair market value.
- Try to make your purchase contract for the new house contingent on the sale of your old house. Some real estate agents advise sellers not

to accept this clause. In a hot market, you can negotiate for its acceptance by showing the sellers of the new house that you will list your old house as soon as the purchase of the new house is secure. You can even show them a completed but yet unsigned listing contract for the sale of your old house. You use such a listing contract to show that you will list at a price near predicted fair market value and that you are prepared to list with a well-known broker in the area. If the sellers accept your offer, you must show them a signed copy of the listing contract. Very few sellers, if any, will accept a contingency on the sale of your current home if you say that you plan to sell by-owner.

- Price your home within customary and usual negotiating space to predicted fair market value. If you get a low offer, you can hold out for your price, but if you overprice by too much, your home could sit unvisited even in the hottest sellers' market. You will feel more and more financial stress as each day passes and you get closer and closer to the closing date on the new house.

- Try to negotiate for a closing date on the new house later rather than sooner. This will give you more time to sell. If your old house sells quickly, you may be able to move the closing date on the new house closer. Or you can schedule the two closings for the same day.

HOMES IN A COLD MARKET . . .

A low-demand, slow-paced real estate market is a buyers' market. The supply of houses (the number of listings for sale) exceeds, sometimes by a lot, the number of active buyers in the marketplace. Properties tend to linger on the market, sometimes for six to nine months or more. Some simply don't sell and their owners withdraw to try at another time. Actual selling prices tend to be considerably lower than asking prices.

In 2008 the market in most parts of the nation was a floating iceberg. Some streets had FOR SALE signs at almost every third house. Foreclosures were threatening more homeowners than ever before. Builders were lowering their prices on new construction or offering more and more "free" upgrades. Prospecting homebuyers came across repeated *"Price Reduction!"* banners in the real estate classified sections of newspapers and their numbers ran to pages on Realtor printout sheets.

Before You Put Your House Up for Sale

Buyers' markets are usually bad times for sellers, but not always. If a seller has a house with strong appeal, he or she may be able to sell that property even in a dead-in-the-water market. Now, the sale price may not be anywhere near something you'd like to shout about, but on the flip side, there well may be shoutworthy celebrations about the choices available for buying the next house and about the very real bargains available for the bidding.

In a cold market, it is essential that you get to know your local marketplace well. Gather information on time on the market, the difference between asking price and selling price, the number of properties similar to yours on the market (go to see as many as you can), how your type of property is selling in comparison to "average" and "median" sales of every kind of property. Are there any extenuating circumstances for your local area? A new highway project proposed? Community revitalization being supported by state funds?

Set your home in the framework of the local marketplace. What is its probable fair market value? What can you offer that will entice the few buyers who are out looking? Can you throw in some extras like appliances or even a lawn mower? Can you offer seller financing? Or a mortgage buy-down? (For more information on buy-downs, see Chapter 5.)

And then ask yourself: "why do I want to sell?" Think about it. Can you postpone selling until the market begins to swing toward a sellers' market again?

Or is it *damn the torpedoes, full speed ahead!?*

Sell First, Then Buy

Almost every real estate agent will tell you to sell before you buy in a slow market. Essentially the advice is given for the same financial-security reasons that exist in a sellers' market; however, all risks are

WORDS TO *GO!*

A *right of first refusal* is a clause in a purchase contract or a lease that allows a named person (usually an interested buyer, the tenant residing in the property, or the condominium or cooperative Home Owner's Association) to match an acceptable offer from another buyer and take the property.

intensified by the creeping pace of the buyers' market. The plus point to selling first in a buyers' market is the delightful array of houses available after you get that sale contract on yours. Consider the following:

- You have more houses to choose from and your choice can be made with little or no pressure from competing buyers.
- Sellers are willing to negotiate and often throw in extras.
- Builders will actually negotiate a bit and often offer multiple upgrades.
- Be certain that the purchase contract on your old house is secure (contingencies either met or are very likely to be met) before you commit to buy. In a slow market, it is not a good idea to allow the buyer of your house to include a clause making their purchase of your house dependent on the sale of their home. Even if you set your closing date off by six months, a house that doesn't sell can cause a domino effect voiding or causing renegotiation of many contracts.
- If you find a "perfect house" and you really want to buy it, but your house is not even listed yet, consider negotiating for a **right of first refusal** rather than signing a purchase contract. Then put your house on the market immediately. The right of first refusal will allow you to match an acceptable-to-the-seller offer made by another party at a later date and take the house at that price. When *and if* such an offer comes in, you will have to decide where you are

in your own home-selling program. Remember, when you execute the right of first refusal, you are entering into a contract to buy. Closing date can be a factor here, especially if the seller wants a quick closing. It really comes down to how much risk you want to take to buy that particular house.

Buy First, Then Sell

"Buy first, then sell" is risky business in a cold market. It is very easy to be caught owning two houses and carrying two mortgages. But if all goes as you would hope, you will take a long closing date on the house you are buying and you will sell your home during that waiting time. The following are some reasons to choose buying first in a slow market and some strategies to deal with your choice.

- Money is not important to you. You have found your dream home and you are going to buy it. If it does not matter exactly how much you get for the house you are selling, set the asking price a little below predicted fair market value and you most likely will sell it, even in a slow market.

- You choose to have a new home built for you and you want to take advantage of the lowered price and multiple upgrades being offered by the builder. The builder gives you a completion date in nine months. If you price your home accurately and make it appealing to prospective buyers, you should sell it within this timeframe. If you begin to get nervous about completion and the approaching closing date, lower your asking price.

- If you have closed on your new house and have not been able to sell your old house, you can try renting it until the real estate market takes a turn for the better. Do NOT rent with an **option to buy**. If you do, you will put all the advantages in the buyers' court. At the end of the lease and the option term, if the market is still down and there are a great many bargains being offered, your tenants can walk away from any commitment to your property. If, on the other hand, the market has turned and your property is now worth let's say $20,000 more than you were asking for it two years ago, the tenants can exercise their option to buy at the old price. You are out $20,000.

As an incentive to buy, some sellers set aside a portion of the rent toward a down payment if the tenant decides to exercise the option. This often works, but there is a better way.

- If prospective buyers want to buy your property but cannot do so because mortgage money is scarce and expensive, you can offer a **land contract**, also called an *agreement for deed*. This arrangement gives the buyer **equitable title**, but if the buyer does not make scheduled payments, foreclosure can be immediate and without red tape since the deed to the property never changes hands. The contract should set a date by which the buyer must obtain financing (usually at least three years to allow the market time to turn). The advantage of the land contract is that the house is essentially sold and the seller does not have to go through refurbishing and marketing again as after a rental period. Also all maintenance responsibility is on the buyers. Have a land contract drawn by an attorney and talk with your accountant about its tax consequences.

ABOUT REAL ESTATE COMMISSIONS

For well over half a century, 6 percent of selling price has been the customary and usual real estate commission on residential sales. It is *not*, however, mandated by law, not anywhere. The amount of commission to be paid for the services of a real estate professional is a matter of agreement between a broker and a seller (or sometimes between a broker and a buyer when a buyers' agent is employed). It can be anything (flat fee or any percentage of the selling price).

Sometimes when an agent will earn a commission from a house you bought through him or her, that agent will be willing to accept a somewhat lower commission on the listing of the home you must sell. But don't negotiate too hard over that commission on the listing contract because every real estate agent deciding which houses to show to prospective buyers will glance at the amount of commission available. Before you settle on the amount of commission to be paid, talk with your agent about local marketplace practices, about policies within the office (you may be able to list at a lower commission rate if you forgo advertising, for example), and about the term of the listing (if you list

WORDS TO *GO!*

An *option to buy* is an agreement that gives a person the right to buy a given piece of property at an agreed-upon price and terms on or before a specified date. If a prospective buyer holds an option, the property cannot be sold to anyone else during the option term. Sometimes an option to buy is included in a lease with a certain portion of the rent to be applied toward the purchase price if the tenant exercises the option.

Especially in the commercial and investment marketplaces, an option is more often purchased (sometimes at a flat fee, sometimes at a percentage of the purchase price) rather than included in a lease agreement. Sometimes the option fee is applied toward the purchase price, sometimes not.

A *land contract* or an *agreement for deed* is actually short-term seller financing. Under this agreement, the seller continues to hold legal title to the property while the buyer makes installment payments. Most land contracts require that the buyer refinance through a conventional source within a specified period of time.

Equitable title (sometimes called *equitable ownership*) is the legal possession by a person who does not hold legal title to the property, such as a buyer under a land contract. Technically, the term also applies to the trustor (buyer) under a deed of trust mortgage because legal title to the property is held by the trustee until the loan is paid in full.

for a longer term, the broker may be willing to take your listing at a lower rate). Above all else, the agreed-upon amount of commission *and* when it is to be paid should be recorded in writing in both the listing contract and the future purchase contract.

The negotiability of commission has stimulated the rise and spread of the discount brokerage industry. There are now flat fee brokers, 2 percent brokers, Internet brokers, by-owner brokers, and many others, each offering different limitations on service. In fact, virtually everything about brokerage services is negotiable. Even full-service

Realtors who belong to the National Association of Realtors will accept, share, and advertise listings at negotiated commission rates (usually between 5 and 7 percent).

Many discount brokers now want access to and cooperation with the shared listings of NAR members. In many states, they have taken the matter to court. There have been some decisions in favor of the discount brokers, but all issues are not yet resolved. If you decide to use a discount broker, either for buying or selling, be sure that you review with the agent exactly what the firm will do and will not do for you and how they will handle commission splits with full-service brokers.

There is one aspect of negotiated real estate commission that many buyers and sellers do not know about. Unless an offer is made at full asking price and without contingencies, brokerage commission is still negotiable. Most sellers honor their commitment and pay the percentage of the actual selling price that they agreed to pay in the listing contract. But sometimes when negotiations have been particularly hard, especially in a cold buyers' market, sellers feel that they simply cannot accept any less for their property. And sometimes buyers simply can't pay more and still get a mortgage. To make the deal, brokers can, and sometimes do, agree to cut the amount of their commission.

DON'T GO TO JAIL

When a real estate commission is agreed upon as a percentage of the sale price, all parties should establish, in writing in the listing contract and later in the purchase contract, that the amount due is to be paid from the proceeds of the sale *upon closing*. Anything else can make you liable for payment of commission, even if the buyer backs out.

Flat fee brokers often take all or part of the payment in advance. This fee is rarely refundable if the property does not sell.

If you get into tough negotiations and both seller and buyer are feeling financial pain, it's OK to spread the pain around a bit. If both the listing and selling brokers agree, it can be written into the purchase contract that the commission will be a named dollar amount that is less than the percentage amount agreed to in the listing contract. But remember, only the broker in charge of each office (both selling and listing) can make the decision to reduce the commission. Be sure that you not only put the new amount *in writing* on the purchase contract but also that every broker and every salesperson involved in the transaction signs every copy.

THE QUICK TURNAROUND FIXER-UPPER

The carefully chosen fixer-upper often sells itself in a hot market, especially if it is located in a homogeneous community where other houses are well maintained and desirable. After improving the curb appeal of your fixer-upper, you may need only a sign on the lawn, especially if the neighborhood has a number of real estate FOR SALE signs already on the front lawns and an agent or two is conducting an open house in the neighborhood almost every weekend.

The fact that you are selling a vacant house, however, can mean a few extra challenges. It is difficult for most people to picture themselves living their lifestyle in an empty room. Buyers invariably imagine their own furniture as larger than it is and they see empty rooms as smaller than they are. Be sure, therefore, that you include every room dimension on your information sheet.

If you are selling a fixer-upper in a cold market, you will have to work a little harder. Even though the property is not in prime condition, you will need to price competitively with other similar properties in the area. You will also have to play on a few heartstrings, in other words, make the place "look like home."

Beg, borrow, rent, or buy some furniture. It can be used furniture, of course. Salvation Army and Goodwill stores have a lot to offer. Put up some window treatments; even simple curtains will help.

The furniture you put in will help prospective buyers imagine their own furniture in the house. I'm talking minimums here, of course. For example, you can put a small table—even a folding card table will do—under the light fixture in the kitchen eating area. A few chairs around it will provide a place to sit and discuss pros and cons of any feature. Dining rooms do well with a table beneath the chandelier. That's a good place to leave the sales brochures and information sheets; plus, the table prevents wandering buyers from banging their foreheads. A couch or some chairs help buyers to get perspective in the living room. Those people who are interested in the property will invariably sit down for a few minutes and just "be" in the house.

Bedrooms don't really need furniture, but I have heard so many buyers say, "Oh, I don't think our bed will fit in here." (For some reason, imagined beds always take up more space than actual beds!) If you are indeed sure that a room is large enough to take a king, queen, or two twins, you can prove it by laying paper exactly the size of the beds in question on the floor. I suggest you use the white paper that movers use for wrapping (they'll sell it to you) and that you tape it down with painters' tape.

If you have used (but still in good condition) curtains, draperies, rods, and blinds in your home storage area or otherwise available and you have the time, put them up wherever appropriate. Window treatments alleviate the dead, echoing sound of an empty house.

And finally, add some decorative touches. A tall vase on the floor in the foyer is welcoming. Fill it with pussy willows or forsythia in spring, gladiolas in summer, reeds and dried arrangements in fall, and pine boughs in winter. Or use whatever is seasonal in your area, or even "silk flowers" if you prefer. You can place artificial floral arrangements on a mantle, on countertops, and on tabletops, but don't go overboard. Crowding is worse than emptiness.

Hang towels (not your best ones, of course) in the bathrooms. And install some plug-in room fresheners about the house. Be sure you buy the room fresheners all in one scent, however. It may jar prospective buyers into too much awareness if, for example, you choose cinnamon and spice for one room and lilies of the fields for another room.

WHY SELL A MONEY MAKER?

Here's a dilemma: you own a multifamily house in which you occupy a unit. The income from it pays the mortgage and leaves some pocket money each month. Your local marketplace is virtually frozen, but interest rates are relatively low. Should you sell the multifamily and use the money to get a good deal on a single-family house? Or should you refinance the multifamily and use the cash you take out of it as the down payment on the single family?

At first, the answer seems obvious: don't sell! If you don't sell, you will still own the multifamily, although after refinancing the cash flow may not be quite so positive. When the market turns, you then can sell if you want to and probably for a higher price.

All true, but as always there are a few other considerations.

• If you don't sell and you rent the unit that you had been occupying, you will lose your homeowners' tax benefit for the portion of the house that you occupied. That means your capital gains tax on the multifamily will be higher when you do sell it.

• The market value of multifamily houses responds more closely to the overall economic health of the area than to the pace of the single-family house marketplace. If there is a strong demand for rental housing in the area, a multifamily might indeed sell quickly and at a profitable price. You could then claim your homeowners' tax benefits.

• When deciding to sell or not to sell investment property, it is essential to look ahead at future value. Future value is determined mostly by what will be happening in the neighborhood. If new businesses are moving into town or a proposed road will make commuting easier in five years or so, it may be a good idea to keep the property. On the other hand, if more and more multifamily houses in the area are no longer owner-occupied and their maintenance is beginning to reflect the owners' absence, you may do better if you sell that property now. You can take the profit and use it as a down payment on a smaller (and easily salable) single-family house and another investment property that promises real appreciation.

• Remember that real estate is a local commodity. There is no guarantee that property in the neighborhood of your multifamily will increase in value, even if the marketplace nationally turns red hot.

CHANGING VEHICLES

The question of *when* to sell investment property brings up another question: what should you buy? Each type of investment property makes different demands on the owner. The advantage of staying with the same vehicle (fixer-uppers, rental property, or mixed-use property, for example) is experience.

If you've been a while in the investment corner of the marketplace, you've certainly made a mistake (or two) or some decisions that you regret, and you're quite sure that you won't do the same again. That knowledge and attitude is one of the best arguments for staying with a familiar investment vehicle. If you do, you'll be able to estimate property value more quickly and accurately, you'll know the problems inherent in this particular investment vehicle, and you'll have worked out your management plan.

On the other hand, not every type of real estate is a good investment at a given time in a given location. For example, the passage of time proved that condominiums were a poor short-term investment in the late 1980s. Owners who had to sell after only a few years of ownership often had to bring money to the closing. By contrast, those investors who could hold their condos into the mid-1990s and beyond sold their units for large profits. A long-term investor who owned a few multifamily houses in the 1980s could have sold them and used the profit to change vehicles into several condo units at very low prices. If he or she rented the units for five to seven years, especially with some positive cash flow, the profits from the condominiums would have been significantly larger than holding the multifamilies for the same period of time.

Mixed-use buildings are another investment that is very much dependent on the local economy and not the pace of the real estate marketplace. Perhaps some of you remember a classic movie from the early 1970s called *The Last Picture Show*. In that film, the viewer is witness to the problems of a group of people in a town that is becoming the twentieth-century version of a ghost town. Real estate values are going nowhere but down, no matter what state the national economy is in—unless, of course, industry or suburbia were to claim the nearby land and thus create future value.

Experience, therefore, may not be enough reason to stay in a particular investment vehicle if the potential appreciation of that vehicle is negative or less than other available vehicles. Be wary, however, when you decide to make a switch. You should ask yourself if you are the right type of investor for the new vehicle. In other words, how much time, skill, and money does the vehicle demand? And how much of each do you have?

MAPPING THE MARKETPLACE

Our game is just about over, and I hope no one has declared bankruptcy! Like playing the MONOPOLY game, playing in the real estate marketplace is a move-by-move process. It requires some knowledge of *what is* and *what might be*, some courage, and some luck.

The American real estate marketplace is gigantic, multifaceted and, in fact, rather demanding. Did you know that more than 250 colleges in the United States offer studies in real estate? And if you want to make real estate your career, almost 100 colleges and universities offer graduate degree programs. Where does this book fit in? It's a beginning, a road map through the more accessible playing fields.

The MONOPOLY Guide to Real Estate focuses on residential real estate because that is the safest and least demanding of the many possibilities for making money and securing future wealth in one of the nation's largest industries. It is also a marketplace where you will be playing against opponents (either buyers or sellers) who have skills, experience, and resources relatively equal to yours.

Equal or better knowledge and skills, that's how you win in MONOPOLY and in the real estate marketplace. You won't have much fun at MONOPOLY if you don't understand property value, building wealth, and negotiating. And you won't get very far into the *real* real estate marketplace. But if you do, ahhh, the victories and satisfactions that await you . . .

RULES AND STRATEGIES

- Value in the real estate marketplace is determined by a complex web composed of many factors.

- The future worth of a piece of real estate is largely determined by the economic aspects of what is happening around it.

- A sellers' market is high demand and low supply.

- A buyers' market is low demand and high supply.

- When buying and selling in either type of market, one must calculate the pros and cons of *buy first/then sell* or *sell first/then buy.*

- Remember that real estate commissions are negotiable.

- In deciding when to sell an investment property and how to re-invest the proceeds of the sale, you should consider local market conditions and economic health *plus* your personal goals, skills, financial resources, and available time

ACKNOWLEDGMENTS

My thanks to Realtor Peggy Baldwin, who read the manuscript for working updates.

My appreciation and admiration go to my agent, Jeanne Fredericks, for her perseverance, attention to detail, and faith.

Five stars to Meredith Hale for being a first-rate editor and a pleasure to work with.

Apologies and gratitude to my family—David, Kristle, Laura, Chris, Bill, Meredith, Caitlin, Tommy, Sarah, and Michael—for their understanding that I was "busy."

Three cheers for Kathy Kainer, my "sister in spirit," who listened, worried, and checked up on me.

And love, hugs, and kisses for my husband, Joe, who wanted to help, and kept out of my hair.

INDEX